Preface

NOTES FOR TEACHERS

I think the major questions the COBOL teacher has to ask himself are these:

1. Do I teach the Divisions in the order they are coded or in the order of their importance to the task of programming? The first method is straightforward, but the details of the Environment and Data Divisions at best can be meaningless to the learner until he has learned something of the Procedure Division, and at worst are boring. The alternative method can leave the student puzzled about the whole picture right until the end.

2. Do I cross all the t's and dot all the i's as I go along in lectures, or do I concentrate on broad essentials, to get the students writing a simple program quickly? The first can be tedious or can lead to the student losing the important concept in the mass of detail. The second is attractive but means that either the student ends the course without knowing the complications, or the teacher must go back and cover the same territory in finer detail.

3. Do I teach the COBOL dialect that applies to the computer I am using, or do I try to distinguish the particular from the general? The first is clearly a more practical approach in the short term, but the second may prove of more value to the student in the long term.

4. How do I keep the threads developing with a mixed ability group? If the teacher goes too quickly, he will lose the slower or less experienced students, or he will be building on misconceived foundations. If the teacher goes slowly, spending a lot of time anticipating misconceptions, he risks turning the quicker student off the subject altogether.

5. Should I organise the course so that program structure is introduced first, showing how these designs can be implemented in COBOL, or should I give a grounding in elementary COBOL and introduce structured programming on this foundation?

Each of these problems is a dilemma, and there is room for discussion of the answer. I give below my reasons for adopting the solutions as developed here, but I hope you will find sufficient flexibility in this text to put into effect the method you personally prefer (e.g. by covering the material in a different order).

The method of this book

The book is in three parts. Part 1 concentrates on the fundamentals of the language and takes the student to the point where he can write a modestly-sized COBOL program using sequential files. Part 2 assumes a competence in elementary COBOL and explains program design and other programming techniques which should be part of the professional programmer's repertoire. Part 3 extends the student's knowledge of the language by explaining some of the more advanced features of COBOL.

Each Part has Sections which can accompany a course of lectures. The teacher explains the material in the Section (which takes about one hour), concentrating on concepts and skipping as much detail as desired to this end. He then invites the students to study the text for that section.

The text consists of a few frames of fast-moving narrative followed by questions designed to be a real test of the student's understanding of both concept and detail. Quick learning or experienced students will be able to complete the section in approximately one hour. Many students will be able to complete the text without assistance. The teacher can concentrate his attention on those students who are unable to complete the text on their own.

To return to the five questions, this book answers them as follows:

1   After the introductory section (which can be omitted for experienced students) a brief look is taken at all four Divisions. Thereafter, Procedure Division and Data Division entries are introduced in the order which I think to be natural for a good understanding. The student is reminded of the relationships of the Divisions at several points. For the practical exercise at the end of Section F, the teacher gives the student Identification Division and Environment Division entries to copy down. These latter Divisions are treated in the last section, J, in Part 1, together with a substantial exercise based on a data validation program.

2   The teacher can concentrate on concepts in his talk. The student learns the detail through the text.

3   The text is machine independent and follows the American National Standard COBOL. Where the standard allows for interpretation by the compiler implementor, common variations are treated. Where I have found a contradiction between an implementation and the standard, I have mentioned the variation.

Only the common entries in the Environment Division have been dealt with. Similarly, to go into all the ins and outs of USAGE COMPUTATIONAL and its variations would be a major task in itself. The teacher will use his judgement at points such as these, knowing the machine the students will use.

4   Because all students will have worked the text for the previous Section, they are at a more equal level of development at the outset of a lecture than may be the case with other methods. Many common misconceptions are dealt with in the text. Furthermore, while the text is being worked, the teacher can concentrate on helping those most in need of assistance.

5   On the whole a more precise and useful explanation of structured programming can be given if the student is assumed to have an existing knowledge of programming and has experienced the

difficulties of problem solving with the control structures available in the language. Thus program design is deferred to Part 2. If the student is learning COBOL as a second language, though, there is a very good case to be made for starting with some of the topics in Part 2.

Keller plan teaching

If it is the teacher's aim that every student should master the skills of programming in COBOL, and he is prepared to deal with very different rates of progress towards such mastery, the system of 'personalised instruction' promoted by Professor F. S. Keller should be considered. Although this text is not intended to be fully self-instructional, a student who uses it for self-instruction can make good progress if tutorial help is available when needed.

A novice student can master Part 1 of the book in about 15 weeks with about three hours study and practical work per week. A Keller plan of 10 or 11 units, plus two to four programming assignments, can be mastered in this time by virtually 100% of undergraduate students if they have two opportunities for tutorial advice and unit tests per week. The number of assignments which should be expected is sensitive to the computer service. I usually set two assignments for a 'pass' and use additional assignments for grading, if this is required.

NOTES FOR STUDENTS

Have you got the right book?

This is not a teach-yourself text. It is intended to accompany a course of lectures.

On the other hand, if you already have an appreciation of computer programming, you may find this book a very fast way of becoming proficient in COBOL. If you already know a little COBOL, Parts 2 and 3 of the book may extend your horizons.

If you want a self-study text, I have written an introductory one called *COBOL Workbook*. This is a slim and easy volume, also published by Edward Arnold. Even if you are following a taught course, you may find this book useful since it gives a lot of exercise and rehearsal of the concepts covered in Part 1 here.

How to learn COBOL

When you learn a foreign language – French, for example – you can understand its concepts and structure by listening to a teacher or by reading an educational book about it. This will not help you much when you step off the plane at Orly. The only way you can become fluent in the language is by speaking it. The reinforcement of saying the words, making up your own phrases and sentences, is an essential ingredient of learning and remembering.

Learning COBOL is similar, except that COBOL exists only as a written language. Proficiency in COBOL is acquired by writing it.

This book contains many exercises which call for written answers; it is essential that you do write down the answers. Eager students are sometimes tempted to answer the questions 'mentally' in their impatience to make progress with the subject. Resist this temptation, or you may end up arriving at Orly having only read a book about French.

How to use this book

Each Section of the book (Section A, Section B etc.) contains a number of **frames** (frame A1, A2 etc.). At the end of each frame there are some questions. Read the frame and write down your answers to the questions.

If you are unable to answer a question, read the relevant parts of the frame again. If you get stuck, or if there is a point that is not clear, ask the tutor.

ACKNOWLEDGEMENTS

Repeated thanks must be extended to Roger Barnes, David Howe and Derek Ruffhead for their assistance with the first edition. Hardly a day has gone past since publication of the first edition without my being the unworthy recipient of some worthy idea offered in the classroom, the staff room or through the post. Even if I could remember all these sources, the list of acknowledgements would be too long to include. Appreciation is offered to the many students and staff of Leicester Polytechnic and the New South Wales Institute of Technology, who have helped, as well as to the Dutch translators of the first edition, H. J. Stomps and A. M. Korff, who, with assistance from their students, came up with a gold mine of corrections and suggestions. I am also particularly grateful to Bob Coats for the time and advice he has donated.

Acknowledgement is also due to those organisations who have contributed to the development of the COBOL language. I reproduce here a statement at their request:

"COBOL is an industry language and is not the property of any one company or group of companies, or of any organisation or group of organisations.

No warranty, expressed or implied, is made by any contributor or by the COBOL Committee as to the accuracy and functioning of the programming system and language. Moreover, no responsibility is assumed by any contributor, or by the committee, in connection therewith.

Procedures have been established for the maintenance of COBOL. Inquiries concerning the procedures for proposing changes should be directed to the Executive Committee of the Conference on Data Systems Languages.

The authors and copyright holders of the copyrighted material used herein: FLOW-MATIC (Trademark of Sperry Rand Corporation), Programming for the UNIVAC I and II, Data Automation Systems copyrighted 1958, 1959, by Sperry Rand Corporation; IBM Commercial Translator Form No. F 28-8013, copyrighted 1959 by IBM; FACT, DSI 27A5260-2760, copyrighted 1960 by Minneapolis-Honeywell have specifically authorised the use of this material in whole or in part, in the COBOL specifications. Such authorisation extends to the reproduction and use of COBOL specifications in programming manuals or similar publications."

Contents

Contents

Part 1
Fundamentals

A Background concepts— a review

A1 THE COMPUTER

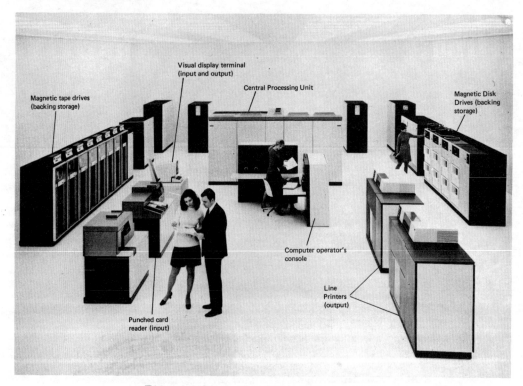

Fig. 1: General view of a computer
(photo courtesy of IBM (United Kingdom) Ltd)

A digital computer consists of a **central processing unit** (CPU) to which are attached, by wires, certain **peripheral devices**.

The CPU has three main parts: a **control unit**, which controls all the operations of the machine and executes the instructions contained in the program; an **arithmetic unit**, which does addition, multiplication etc.; and a **memory**, which holds the program while it is being executed, together with the data on which the program is currently working.

The control unit fetches an instruction from memory, executes it, fetches the next instruction, executes that, and so on.

Programs start off with some raw data (the **input**) and process it in some way to produce some new data (the **output**).

The machine slavishly executes the instructions given to it, and it is practically unknown for a computer to execute an instruction incorrectly. Therefore, if the output is wrong, there is almost certainly an error in the input data or a logic error in the instructions of the program.

The peripheral devices are separate machines which work under the control of the CPU. There are **input devices** (for getting data and programs into memory), **output devices** (for outputting from memory the results of the program) and **backing storage devices** (which are mainly used to store output data which will need to be re-input at a later stage for further processing).

Exercise

Now write down the answers to the following questions, from memory if possible. If you are unable to answer a question, try to get the answer from the frame. If there is any point which is not clear, ask the tutor (this procedure applies to all the frames which follow).

When you are satisfied with your answers, check them with the solutions at the end of the section and continue to frame A2.

1   What is the purpose of an input device?

2   What is the purpose of backing storage devices?

3   What are the two main causes of error in computer output?

4   Where is the computer program held while it is being executed?

5   Can data which has been output also be used as input?

A2   THE VISUAL DISPLAY UNIT

One of the most common input devices is the keyboard attached to a visual display unit (VDU), also commonly called a terminal – see Fig. 2 overleaf.

The screen of a typical VDU can display 20 lines with 80 characters on each line. The position of a character in a line is often referred to by its **column number**. Thus the first character in a line is in column 1; the twentieth character in a line would be in column 20.

Each successive character keyed on the keyboard is usually displayed on the screen. The characters keyed are often held in a **buffer**, internally in the VDU, until the RETURN key is depressed. When this happens all the characters in the line concerned are transmitted to the central processing unit. Thus the basic unit being dealt with by the operator is the line of characters; the operator prepares a line and, when it is prepared, depresses the RETURN button to release the line to the computer.

If the terminal is **unbuffered**, each individual character is sent to the computer as soon as the key is depressed. Unbuffered terminals are quite common in business departments, but terminals attached to computers used for programmer training courses are more often the buffered sort.

Fig. 2 also illustrates another input device sometimes used with unbuffered terminals – the **light pen**. This device detects the light coming from the screen and transmits to the CPU the co-ordinates of the point on the screen at which it is aimed.

The VDU can also be used as an output device. A message prepared in the memory of the computer is sent to the VDU to be displayed on the screen. Usually only one line is sent at a time but, on a 20-line VDU, the previous 19 lines remain visible unless a command is given to clear the screen. The display is lost when the VDU is switched off. When a permanent message is required, it may be preferable to print 'hard copy' as explained in the next frame.

Fig. 2: A visual display unit with keyboard
(photo courtesy of IBM (United Kingdom) Ltd)

It is up to the programmer to decide whereabouts on the line any particular item of data is to be keyed. The columns allocated for keying a particular group of characters are called a **field**. Thus the line is divided into fields, each of which contains one or more characters. Sometimes it is desirable to imagine that a field is divided into two or more smaller fields; in this case the larger field is called a **group** field. Fields which are not subdivided are called **elementary** fields.

Exercise

1   How many columns does the typical VDU have? How many characters can be entered on one line? How many characters can be displayed on the whole screen?

2   If a line contained a name (13 characters), an address (40

characters) and an account number (6 digits), how many columns would be used? How many elementary fields are there in the line?

3   The 'account number' field in a line contains a one-digit area code field, a one-digit customer-type field and a four-digit serial-number field. How large is the group field?

A3   THE LINE PRINTER

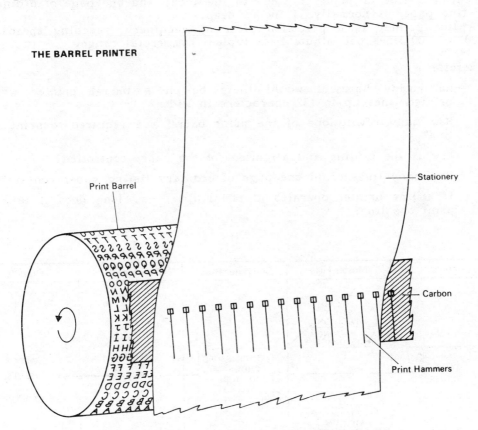

THE BARREL PRINTER

Print Barrel

Stationery

Carbon

Print Hammers

Fig. 3: The barrel printer

The most common means of outputting data for human beings to read is the line printer. A typical line printer is the **barrel** printer, but there are many varieties, e.g. chain printers, matrix printers, daisywheel printers, ink-jet printers and laser printers.

In the case of the barrel printer, there is a metal barrel with all the characters engraved around its circumference – a row of A's, a row of B's, and so on. Next to the barrel is some carbon ribbon, stationery and a row of print hammers, one hammer corresponding to each possible position in the line of print. The paper and carbon are sandwiched between the hammers and the barrel. The barrel rotates at high speed.

A whole line of print is set up in memory, ready for printing out. As each row of characters appears opposite the hammers, if that character is needed in a particular position in the line then the corresponding hammer will strike, pressing the paper onto the character, with the ribbon in between. In this way, all the A's in the line are printed simultaneously, then all the B's, the C's, and so on until the whole line is built up.

The paper itself is continuous fanfeed stationery. It is kept aligned and is fed through the printer by sprockets which engage in sprocket holes on both sides of the paper. There are usually 10 characters to the inch in a line of print; 6 lines to the inch; and one page of ordinary listing paper is normally 11 inches deep.

A line printer is a precision piece of machinery, reaching speeds of 300 to 2000 lines per minute in a typical commercial range.

Exercise

1 How many hammers would there be on a barrel printer which printed lines up to 132 characters in width?

2 How many revolutions of the print barrel are required to print one line?

3 How is the feeding and alignment of the paper controlled?

4 How many lines could one page of ordinary listing paper contain?

5 If a line printer operates at 600 l.p.m., how long does it take to print one line?

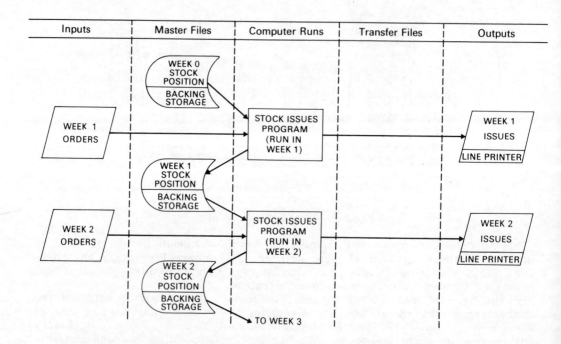

Fig. 4: Updating a file on backing storage

A4   BACKING STORAGE DEVICES

Not all the results of running a program need be printed out. For example, suppose a program is to prepare a list of the issues from stores for a warehouse, using the orders that have been placed during the week as the input. It will be desirable to have available details of all the current stocks in hand, in a form that can be read by the computer. The issues made will reduce the amount of those stocks, resulting in an **updated** stock position, for each type of stock held. It is not necessary to print out these updated stocks; they can be written out on a backing storage device, and the **file** of information so created can be re-input at the next week's updating run (see Fig. 4).

Two popular types of backing storage are **magnetic tapes** and **magnetic disks.**

Information is recorded on reels of magnetic tape by a **tape deck.** This may be thought of as working in the same way as a home cassette tape recorder, such as is used with personal computers, except that with business computers it works much faster and uses longer reels of tape (2400 feet is a common size). Since data can be recorded on the tape at 1600 or more characters per inch, several millions of characters of data can be recorded on a single reel of tape. This may be much more data than can be held in the memory of the CPU, so programs are written to process one **record** of data at a time, write that out, process another record, write that out, and so on.

Record is the name given to any convenient group of related fields. Thus, the data on one line of a VDU could make a record; the data in a line of print could make a record. Examples of records in a magnetic tape file could be as follows.

Stock position file: each record in the file would contain

    1   A stock item number
    2   A description of the type of stock
    3   The amount of stock in hand
        etc., etc.,

Payroll master file: each record in the file would contain

    1   Employee number
    2   Employee name
    3   Rate of pay
    4   Deductions from pay
    5   Pay to date
    6   Tax to date
        etc., etc.,

I put 'etc., etc.' because in practice the records in such files would have more fields than the ones listed, but the nature of those extra fields would depend on the exact use to which the files were put.

Information is recorded on magnetic tape in **blocks** of data. Recording can take place only when the tape is moving at the designed tape speed.

Since the tape must stop after each block is written out, a gap is left after each block, to allow for deceleration, as in Fig. 5 overleaf.

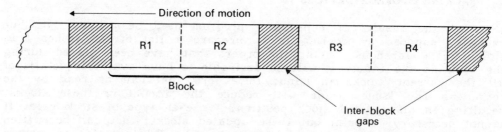

Fig. 5: *Format of blocks and records on magnetic tape*

This gap is in practice about half an inch long. It will be seen that if blocks are short - say, 80 characters - a reel of tape will contain a large quantity of inter-block gaps and very little data between them. For this reason, and to reduce the frequency of stopping at inter-block gaps, it is usual to write tape blocks as large as practicable; the limiting factor may be the amount of spare space available in memory for forming the block prior to writing it out.

The length of the record the program is dealing with may be much less than the desired block length. Thus, it is usually necessary to group two or more records together to get a useful block length (as with R1, R2 in Fig. 5 above). Fortunately, in COBOL, facilities exist for handling automatically the blocking of records.

In order to completely specify a file for a COBOL program, it is necessary to define four levels:

FILE – its name and the medium on which it is recorded
BLOCK – the number of records in a block
RECORD – the fields that make up the record
FIELD – the characters that make up the field.

The first record on a reel of tape is a special one; the **header** label. This identifies the information held in the file. There is also a **trailer** label marking the end of the file.

Essentially the same considerations apply to files on magnetic disks except that the latter also permit direct access to a nominated record. In Fig. 5, for example, to read record 4 on regular magnetic tape, the computer would have to search along past records 1, 2 and 3. But on magnetic disk, record 4 could be retrieved directly. How this is done is explained in Section T.

A modern commercial tape drive could read characters equivalent in number to the total characters in this book in a time somewhere between 10 seconds and two minutes, depending of course on the speed of the tape movement and the time it takes to stop and start again in the inter-block gaps, as well as on the number of characters chosen to be in a block.

Exercise

1   Name four types of peripheral device. Classify them as input, output or backing storage devices.

2   What is the purpose of a header label?

3   How are data blocks separated on magnetic tape?

4   What usually limits the size of a block on magnetic tape?

5   What are the four levels of file definition required by a COBOL program?

6   Will a payroll program contain the name of each employee in the organisation? If not, where will the names be held?

A5   THE PROGRAM SPECIFICATION

Before a COBOL program is written, a detailed specification must be drawn up showing exactly what is to be done by the program. This is in three main parts:

1   Input: a description of the file and record layouts for the input data.

2   Output: a description of the file and record layouts of the output data.

3   Processing: a description of the processes the program must follow to get the output from the input.

The processing section of the specification may be translated into a **flowchart** by the programmer. This is a diagram showing the logical sequence of events in the program; for example

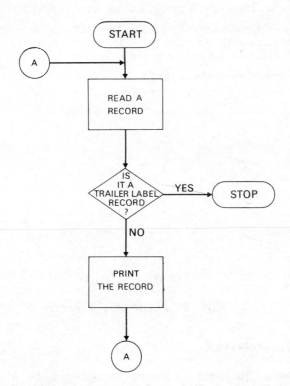

Fig. 6: Flowchart of a program to list a tape file

This program would print out on the line printer all the records in a tape file. The symbols used are as follows.

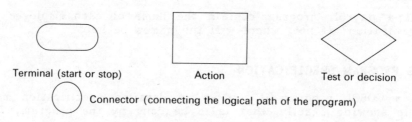

Terminal (start or stop)   Action   Test or decision

Connector (connecting the logical path of the program)

Fig. 7: Flowchart symbols

The flowchart is a fundamental way of describing any process and is widely used in many branches of engineering. However, it is now recognised that flowcharting is an error-prone method of working when dealing with large computer programs. A better method is introduced in Part 2 of this book. In the meantime, the use of flowcharts should be confined to simple cases.

Exercise

1   Name the three parts of a program specification.

2   How can the logic of a program be represented diagrammatically?

3   Redraw the flowchart, to count the number of records and print out the count as well as the records. The count is to be printed only after all records have been read.

4   What do these symbols mean?

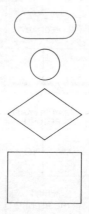

Fig. 8: Frame A5, exercise 4

A6   THE COBOL COMPILER

COBOL (COmmon Business Oriented Language) is a computer language developed in the United States of America in 1959. The body responsible for maintaining and further developing the language is the Conference on Data Systems Languages (CODASYL), a voluntary organisation which includes representatives of users and manufacturers of computers. The

USA Standards Institute, in 1966, proposed a standard version of the language based on the CODASYL recommendations as they stood in 1965. This standard version was ratified in 1968 and came to be called American National Standard COBOL (ANS COBOL) or, sometimes, COBOL '68. In 1974, a much extended and revised version of the language was adopted for ANS COBOL and this is now widely available. This text is based on this version, COBOL '74, although reference is also made to numerous extensions and enhancements to the language which have been proposed up to 1982. These extensions are not widely available.

Because it is a language resembling English, and because it is not limited to the facilities of a particular computer, COBOL is called a **high-level** language. A **low-level** language resembles the language used internally by the particular machine it is associated with. High-level languages are sometimes called **problem-oriented**, whereas low-level languages are **machine-oriented**.

The programmer writes his program on coding sheets. These statements are usually transferred to a file on magnetic disk by being keyed in at a terminal. Sometimes they are transferred onto punched cards by means of a keypunch. The statements written by the programmer are called the **source** program.

The source program needs to be translated into the language used internally by the computer. This language is called the **machine code** and the program, after it has been translated into machine code, is called the **object** program. The translation process is itself done by a computer program: the COBOL compiler.

Thus, the COBOL compiler reads the source program into the computer from a disk file or from punched cards and translates this into an object program in machine code. This object program is usually written onto backing storage; it can then be loaded into the machine and executed. The process can be illustrated as follows.

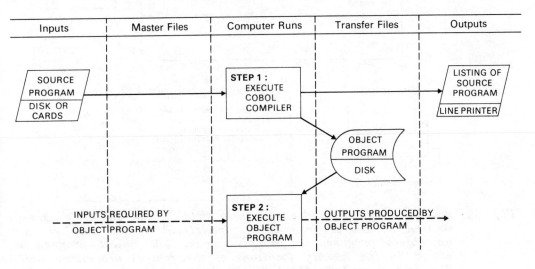

Fig. 9: The compilation process

Exercise

1 What is a compiler?

2 What is the name given to the statements the programmer writes? The –––––– program.

3 What is the name given to the program after it has been translated into machine code?

4 What does C O B O L stand for?

5 In Fig. 10, pretend you are the control unit following the instruction fetch cycle. What data is output when instruction 7 is executed?

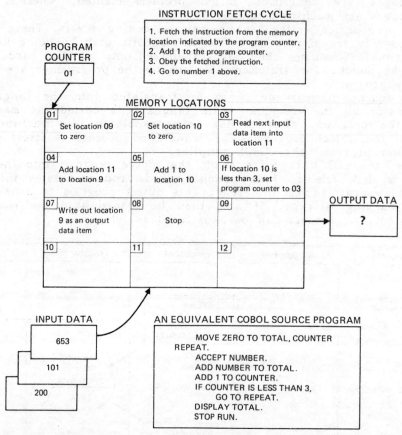

INSTRUCTION FETCH CYCLE

1. Fetch the instruction from the memory location indicated by the program counter.
2. Add 1 to the program counter.
3. Obey the fetched instruction.
4. Go to number 1 above.

PROGRAM COUNTER

01

MEMORY LOCATIONS

01 Set location 09 to zero	02 Set location 10 to zero	03 Read next input data item into location 11
04 Add location 11 to location 9	05 Add 1 to location 10	06 If location 10 is less than 3, set program counter to 03
07 Write out location 9 as an output data item	08 Stop	09
10	11	12

OUTPUT DATA

?

INPUT DATA

653
101
200

AN EQUIVALENT COBOL SOURCE PROGRAM

MOVE ZERO TO TOTAL, COUNTER
REPEAT.
    ACCEPT NUMBER.
    ADD NUMBER TO TOTAL.
    ADD 1 TO COUNTER.
    IF COUNTER IS LESS THAN 3,
        GO TO REPEAT.
    DISPLAY TOTAL.
    STOP RUN.

Fig. 10: How a computer works, in more detail. The source program, written by the programmer, is translated by the compiler into an object program, in machine code. The object program is stored in the memory locations of the central processing unit. The control unit in the CPU has built-in logic which slavishly executes the instruction fetch cycle.

ANSWERS - SECTION A

Frame A1

1   To read data and programs into the memory of the computer.
2   To store intermediate results which will be read back into the computer at a later time.
3   Error in data; error in program.
4   In memory.
5   Yes. Results output to a backing storage device may be input at a later time.

Frame A2

1   80; 80; 1600.
2   59; 3. Note that this answer assumes there is no space between the fields.
3   The group field, 'account number', has 6 digits.

Frame A3

1   132.
2   One (maximum).
3   By sprockets engaging in sprocket holes in the paper.
4   66 (11 x 6); but the top and bottom lines are often not printed on, leaving only 64.
5   One-tenth of a second.

Frame A4

1   VDU (keyboard - input; screen - output).
     Line printer - output.
     magnetic tape deck, magnetic disk drive - backing storage.
2   To identify the information held in the file.
3   By an inter-block gap.
4   The amount of spare space (i.e. space not taken up by the program or other data) available in memory for preparing the block before writing it out. (On computers with a large memory, though, the limit may be dictated by characteristics of the backing storage hardware.)
5   File; Block; Record; Field.
6   No. The employees' names (along with other data such as their rate of pay and tax allowances) would be held in a file - possibly on magnetic tape, one record per employee.

Frame A5

1   A description of the input, output, processing.
2   By a program flowchart (sometimes called a block diagram or computer procedure flowchart).
3   See Fig. 11 overleaf (this assumes that the counter starts at zero).

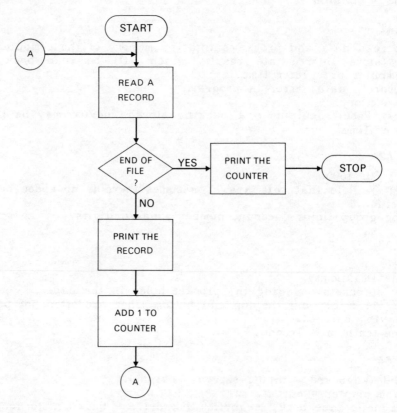

Fig. 11: Answer to Exercise 3

4   Terminal; connector; decision or test; action.

Frame A6

1   A computer program that translates instructions given in a high
     level language into the machine's internal instructions.
2   Source program.
3   Object program.
4   COmmon Business Oriented Language.
5   954.

B COBOL essentials

B1 COBOL SYNTAX

COBOL statements are written in sentences. A statement is a phrase that starts with a COBOL verb. A sentence is terminated by a full stop, and may contain one or more statements. Thus,

> SUBTRACT TAX FROM PAY.

is a sentence with one statement, while

> SUBTRACT TAX FROM PAY
> ADD BONUS TO PAY.

is a sentence with two statements. (In this example, TAX, PAY and BONUS might be the names of three fields in a record whose data had been read into memory. The statements would instruct the machine to subtract the contents of the TAX field from the contents of the PAY field and add the contents of the BONUS field to the contents of the PAY field.)

Sentences may be grouped together in paragraphs. A paragraph may contain one or more sentences. (In special circumstances it might be desirable to have a paragraph which contains no sentences – this will be dealt with much later.)

Sentences and paragraphs may also be grouped together into sections. The COBOL compiler expects certain paragraphs and sections to appear in every COBOL program. It recognises these by the special paragraph or section names given to them. The programmer may decide to make up other paragraphs or sections, in which case he also devises a name to call each one by.

The sentences, paragraphs and sections are also grouped into divisions. There are only four divisions and they must all be present in a complete COBOL program. They are:

> IDENTIFICATION DIVISION.
> ENVIRONMENT DIVISION.
> DATA DIVISION.
> PROCEDURE DIVISION.

and they appear in that order.

Each division has a separate purpose, as follows.

IDENTIFICATION DIVISION. Shows the name of the programmer, the name and purpose of the program, where and when it was written. These are largely comments and will be ignored by the compiler, except to check that they are syntactically correct.

ENVIRONMENT DIVISION. Shows the type of computer which is to accept the source and object programs, and other details of the computer configuration.

DATA DIVISION. Describes all the data and files used by the program. The nature of each file is described in detail, as well as the structure of the records contained in the file. The compiler uses this information to assign a place in memory to hold the blocks of data when they are read in (or before being written out). Data which is not part of a file is assigned to **working storage.**

PROCEDURE DIVISION. This is where the programmer writes statements telling the compiler what procedures are to be performed on the data.

Exercise

1   How does the compiler know where one sentence ends and another starts?

2   'That is data processing', shortened to 'i.e. D.P.', is a mnemonic sometimes used by programmers to remember something important about COBOL programs. What?

3   Examine the coding entered on the example coding form in Fig. 12. (The 77 appearing in this program will be explained later. It just tells the compiler what type of data is being described in the Working-Storage Section.) What do you think would be the result of executing this program? Make a guess, but try to phrase your answer carefully.

4   (a) How many characters of memory do you think the compiler would assign to hold the data in the program of Fig. 12?
    (b) Can you tell how many characters of memory will be used up for the procedures?

5   You may not mention the name of a peripheral device in the Data Division. In which division do you think you tell the compiler the names of the devices which are to be used for reading or writing files?

6   Does the compiler itself execute the procedures written in the Procedure Division?

B2   CODING RULES

COBOL programs are written in block capitals on a coding sheet (see Fig. 12). This sheet is divided into 72 columns and usually 20 or so lines. The terminal operator keys in the data from each line, copying exactly from the coding sheet. The first six columns may be used to number the lines in sequence; but when keying at a terminal it is more usual to arrange for the computer to number the lines automatically. It is usual to number in tens or hundreds to make subsequent insertion easier. The last eight columns of the line (column 73 onwards) are ignored by the compiler except to print them out on your program listing. When a program is to be keyed onto punched cards, it is usual to insert a brief title of the program in these columns; otherwise they are left blank.

Some of the words used in a COBOL program have a special meaning to the compiler. These are called **keywords** or **reserved words.** DIVISION, DATA, SUBTRACT and TO are reserved words you have already met. There are about 300 reserved words, and the programmer may use these only in the strict context allowed by the rules of the COBOL language.

COBOL CODING FORM

PROBLEM _____

CODER _____

DEPT. _____

PAGE ___ OF ___ PAGES

DATE _____

IDENTIFICATION 73 [ ] 80

PAGE	SERIAL	CONT	A	B	
ØØ	Ø1Ø1Ø		IDENTIFICATION DIVISION.		
	Ø2Ø		PROGRAM-ID. SHOWDATE.		
	Ø3Ø	**		THIS COULD BE A COMPLETE COBOL PROGRAM.	
	Ø4Ø	**			
	Ø5Ø		ENVIRONMENT DIVISION.		
	Ø6Ø		CONFIGURATION SECTION.		
	Ø7Ø		SOURCE-COMPUTER. computer-name.		
	Ø8Ø		OBJECT-COMPUTER. computer-name.		
	Ø9Ø				
	1ØØ		DATA DIVISION.		
	11Ø		WORKING-STORAGE SECTION.		
	12Ø		77 TODAYS-DATE; SIZE IS 6.		
	13Ø		PROCEDURE DIVISION.		
	14Ø		PARA-1.		
	15Ø		DISPLAY TODAYS-DATE.		
	16Ø		STOP RUN.		
	17Ø				

Fig. 12: COBOL coding form

The programmer may also make up words for naming paragraphs, sections or data. Examples of **programmer-defined words** are TAX, PAY, BONUS, TODAYS-DATE. There are also some other uses of programmer-defined words – these will be dealt with much later.

There are two margins on the coding sheet. Margin A starts at column 8 and Margin B at column 12. COBOL sentences are written anywhere to the right of Margin B (but not beyond column 72, of course).

Division, section and paragraph names are written at Margin A. This margin is also used in the Data Division for file and record descriptions – this will be covered in Section E. Paragraph names must be followed by a space and the words DIVISION and SECTION respectively, and a full stop.

It has been proposed to do away with the two margins in COBOL, so that sentences and paragraphs, etc., can be coded anywhere. But even if your compiler does not demand the margins, it is recommended that you use them to achieve a neat layout to your program. (If you are not using line numbers, you could of course have the margins at columns 1 and 5.)

There must be at least one space between words written in a sentence. There is no maximum limit. It is a good habit to write only one statement on each line, but this is not a limitation imposed by COBOL rules.

The compiler assumes a space between column 72 on one line and Margin B on the next line, i.e. you can write a word ending in column 72 with the next word on the next line starting at Margin B. You can join column 72 to Margin B, for a word broken over the line, by putting a dash ('-') in the continuation column, column 7, of the next line. (The dash goes at the beginning of the line if using a compiler that does not recognise margins. It has been proposed to amend this rule so that the dash goes at the end of the line, as in normal English punctuation, but this is not yet standard.) Continuations are best avoided, if possible. It is preferable to omit the word that would be broken and start it on the next line.

Exercise

1   How can the compiler tell where a division, section or paragraph ends?

2   How can the compiler distinguish between a paragraph name and the first (or only) word in a sentence?

3   In the program illustrated in Fig. 12, how many sections are there? How many paragraphs? How many sentences in the Procedure Division?

4   Suppose you were writing a COBOL program and you mis-spelled ENVIRONMENT DIVISION as (a) ENVIRONMENTDIVISION or (b) ENVIROMENT DIVISION. Would the compiler accept (a) or (b) or both or neither?

5   Students new to COBOL sometimes get hold of a list of the reserved words and try to write a program in ENGLISH, using those words as they think fit. Why is this approach doomed to failure?

B3 NAME FORMATION AND PUNCTUATION

Programmer-defined names for data can be made up from any of the alphabetic characters A to Z, the numbers 0 to 9 and the dash ('-'), providing there is at least one alphabetic character and the dash is not first or last. Thus, ABC-2 and 1-XYZ would be legal names. They would not, though, be **good** names, because they are meaningless. A good programmer will make up names that describe the data, e.g.

        PAYROLL-NUMBER
        PARTNUMBER
        TAX-CODE
        BONUS.

Use of good names makes the program longer to write, but this is a small price to pay for clarity. Names may not exceed 30 characters.

The same rules also apply to programmer-defined names for paragraphs, except that paragraph names may, in addition, be all numeric. However, it is a good habit to avoid the latter, since paragraph names should also be meaningful. Programmers sometimes write P1., P2., P3., and so on for consecutive paragraph names. This system certainly helps to locate the paragraph on the listing, but a good name will also describe the procedures in the paragraph, e.g.

        P1-ACCEPT-DATE.
        P2-WRITE-REPORT-HEADINGS.
        P3-WRITE-SUB-HEADINGS.

The full stop terminates a sentence. Although commas and semi-colons may be used to improve the readability of COBOL, there are rather precise rules surrounding this. The programmer is better advised to omit them and achieve readability through the use of extra spaces or new lines. Full stops (and other punctuation if used) should always be followed by at least one space. (It is proposed that the precise rules about punctuation should be relaxed.)

Exercise

1 What is wrong with this sentence?

        ADD INTEREST,PAY-IN TO CAPITAL.

2 Which of the following names for data are illegal?

    (a) 7464 (b) A (c) P76 (d) – (e) –1 (f) 2–2 (g) A–1
    (h) B-B-B-B-B (i) 2-A (j) FRED (k) QUEENELIZABETHTHESECOND
    (l) WORKING STORAGE

3 On a coding sheet, write a paragraph which will perform the following: add BONUS to PAY, subtract SAYE from PAY, subtract PAYE from PAY. Write it first as three sentences, then as one sentence. Make up a paragraph name and start with line number 002200.

4 Is the following sentence legal?

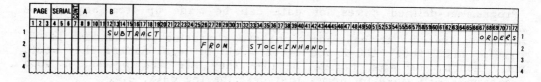

Fig. 13: Exercise 4

B4   LITERALS AND FIGURATIVE CONSTANTS

Data used in files or working storage are described and given names in the Data Division. Such items are often called **variables**, because the value of the data in these fields changes either as new records are read or through being manipulated by the procedures.

If a program was going to number all the pages of a report as it was produced on the line printer, the page number would be a variable. At the end of each page, 1 would be added to the page number. The 1 added is a **constant**; its value remains unchanged throughout the program. When you refer to a constant by its value rather than by a name, this is called a **literal**. Thus, 1 is a **numeric literal**. A numeric literal may be formed by any string of numbers, with a decimal point inserted if needed, and preceded by a + or − sign. For example,

        1.0
        +12
        123.45
        −7
        −7.24612

The decimal point may not be the last character. If no sign is given, + is assumed. Numeric literals may not exceed 18 digits.

Constants which are not to be used for arithmetic may be declared by **non-numeric literals**. Anything enclosed in quotation marks is a non-numeric literal, e.g.

        "FRED SMITH"
        "START OF JOB"
        "LOAD NEXT TAPE REEL"
        "SALES REPORT"
        " "

Note that a space counts as a character. A non-numeric literal may be up to 120 characters long.

It may happen that a non-numeric literal needs to be broken over more than one line of a coding sheet. In this case, the literal is written right up to column 72, a dash is entered in column 7 of the next line, quotation marks are entered anywhere to the right of Margin B and the literal is continued in the next column. Terminating quotation marks are entered as before, see Fig. 14.

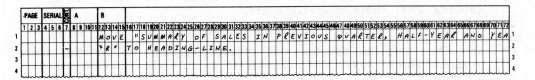

PAGE	SERIAL	CONT	A	B																							
1			MOVE	"SUMMARY OF SALES IN PREVIOUS QUARTER, HALF-YEAR AND YEA																							1
2		-	"R" TO HEADING-LINE.																								2
3																												3
4																												4

Fig. 14: Continuation of a non-numeric literal

If a non-numeric literal ends exactly in column 72, apart from the terminating quotation marks, it is continued as above and the final quotation marks are entered in column 13. It will be seen later, however, that through suitable organisation of working storage the need to continue literals over a line can be avoided.

The distinction between numeric and non-numeric data can be important in COBOL, since the compiler may treat these types of data differently.

Certain constants can be referred to by using reserved words. These are known as **figurative constants** and can be used in place of literals. The compiler assigns the appropriate value to the constant as signified by the reserved word, i.e.

ZERO, ZEROS, ZEROES   zeros
SPACE, SPACES   spaces
QUOTE, QUOTES   quotation marks
HIGH-VALUE, HIGH-VALUES   the highest value possible
LOW-VALUE, LOW-VALUES   the lowest possible - often zero

Whether the plural or singular version is used does not affect the value assumed by the compiler. The reason for this will be clear when the MOVE verb is considered, later.

Exercise

1   Which ones are not valid numeric literals?

(a) +1.0 (b) -7.7687796 (c) 1,123,746 (d) .7 (e) $93.12
(f) 3.14157

2   Which ones are not valid non-numeric literals?

(a) "FRD SMITH" (b) "127.6" (c) "ADD A TO B" (d) "ZEROES"
(e) "END OF JOB

3   Why, do you think, may not the decimal point be the last character in a numeric literal?

4   Why did the designers of the language allow for the figurative constant quote?

ANSWERS - SECTION B

Frame B1

1   The full stop shows where one sentence ends and another starts.
2   It shows the initial letters of the four divisions, in the correct order.
3   Whatever data was contained in the characters of working storage

called TODAYS-DATE would be displayed (probably on the operator's console display, but that is incidental). We have no way of knowing what those characters are.

4   (a) 8 characters; (b) No.
5   ENVIRONMENT DIVISION.
6   No. The compiler creates the object program. It is the object program which drives the computer to execute the Procedure Division statements. If you do not understand this point, read frame A6 again.

Frame B2

1   Division   - when a new division name is met
     Section   - when a new section name is met
     Paragraph   - when a new paragraph name is met
     or, in each case, when the physical end of the program is met.
2   The paragraph name starts at Margin A; sentences start to the right of Margin B. (Alternative answer if the compiler does not recognise margins: sentences always start with a COBOL verb.)
3   Two sections (Configuration, Working-Storage). Four paragraphs (Program-Id, Source-Computer, Object-Computer, Para-1). Two sentences.
4   Neither.
5   The reserved words may be used only in the strict context allowed by, and with the limited meanings defined in, the rules of COBOL. Their use in English may be quite different.

Frame B3

1   No space after comma. Better to omit comma.
2   (a), (d), (e), (f), (1). The last has an embedded space.
3   (i)
002200 CALCULATE-NET-PAY.
002210   ADD BONUS TO PAY.
002220   SUBTRACT SAYE FROM PAY.
002230   SUBTRACT PAYE FROM PAY.
     (ii)
002210   ADD BONUS TO PAY
002220   SUBTRACT SAYE FROM PAY
002230   SUBTRACT PAYE FROM PAYE.
4   Yes, but weird.

Frame B4

1   (c), (e).
2   (e).
3   The compiler could not easily distinguish between a full stop ending a sentence and a decimal point.
4   """" might be taken to mean start a non-numeric literal, end a non-numeric literal, start another non-numeric literal. Actually, COBOL does allow a construction rather like this, by treating two adjacent quotation marks as a single occurrence of a quotation mark in a non-numeric literal, e.g. "AB""CD" would declare a non-numeric literal AB"CD.

C The arithmetic verbs

C1 THE PROCEDURE DIVISION – ADD AND SUBTRACT

Although the Procedure Division is coded last in a COBOL program, it is helpful to learn some of its features before looking at the other divisions.

We have already seen the verbs ADD and SUBTRACT used in examples. The ADD statement takes one of two forms:

1 ADD $\left\{ \begin{matrix} \text{identifier-1} \\ \text{literal-1} \end{matrix} \right\}$ $\left\{ \begin{matrix} \text{identifier-2} \\ \text{literal-2} \end{matrix} \right\}$ ... TO identifier-m $\left[\text{ROUNDED} \right]$

$\left[\text{ON SIZE ERROR imperative-statement} \right]$

2 ADD $\left\{ \begin{matrix} \text{identifier-1} \\ \text{literal-1} \end{matrix} \right\}$ $\left\{ \begin{matrix} \text{identifier-2} \\ \text{literal-2} \end{matrix} \right\}$ $\left[\begin{matrix} \text{identifier-3} \\ \text{literal-3} \end{matrix} \right]$ ...

GIVING identifier-m $\left[\text{ROUNDED} \right]$ $\left[\text{ON SIZE ERROR imperative-statement} \right]$

In this formal description, underlined words in capitals are keywords. Other words in capitals are optional words which can be omitted without changing the meaning. Square brackets indicate that the word or phrase is optional, but if included will usually change the meaning. When items are stacked one above the other, a choice must be made from one of the items in the stack. The **ellipsis**, ..., shows that the preceding bracketed item can be repeated as often as required. Curly brackets (**braces**) are used to enclose a compulsory item or stack of items. 'Identifier' is the name of a field; 'imperative-statement' means one or more imperative statements.

This method of description is universally used in technical manuals about COBOL, so it is worthwhile to understand it; but some licence has been taken in this text, to avoid complicating the issues too much, to simplify these descriptions in the expectation that the student's common sense will take him down the right path. The complete formats are given in Appendix D.

Legal ADD statements would be:

```
ADD A TO B.
ADD A TO B ROUNDED.
ADD 12.7 B GIVING C ON SIZE ERROR DISPLAY "ERR100".
ADD A B C GIVING D ROUNDED.
ADD 1272.437 TO B ROUNDED ON SIZE ERROR STOP RUN.
```

Note that the word TO may not be included when the GIVING option is used.

The result of the addition is in the right-most operand. The other operands are left unchanged. That is:

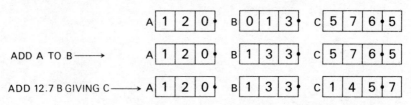

Fig. 15: The effect of an ADD operation

In Fig. 15, it is assumed that A and B have been defined in the Data Division as fields with three integer places and no decimal places, while C has three integer places and one decimal place.

Suppose instead that C had been defined in the Data Division as a field with no decimal places. After execution of the last instruction, C would contain 145 only; the result would be truncated by dropping the final .7. This is not as accurate a result as 146 would have been. 146 is the **rounded** result. Thus, if the example had been ADD 12.7 B GIVING C ROUNDED, and C were defined as a whole number, the answer would have been rounded to the nearest whole number before being put in C, i.e. rounded to 146. A half would be rounded up. The same logic applies whenever the operand receiving the answer has insufficient decimal places to hold the entire result. ROUNDED causes rounding of the least significant digit.

A **size error** occurs when the result field has insufficient space to hold the whole-number (integer) part of the answer. In the statement ADD 1272.437 TO B ROUNDED ON SIZE ERROR STOP RUN, suppose B had been defined as having three places before and after the decimal point, and that it had an initial value of −272.000. After execution of the instruction, it should hold +1000.437, but because there are only three integer places in B, the left-most digit will not fit, leaving B containing only 000.437. If ON SIZE ERROR is specified, this condition will be detected and the imperative statement (STOP RUN in the example) will be executed.

The programmer should use the SIZE ERROR clause whenever there is a chance, however small, of losing the most significant digit of the result.

Exercise

1

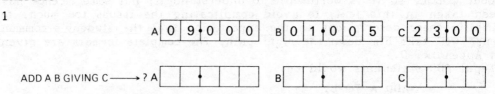

Fig. 16: Exercise 1 - complete the drawing

2   Look up in Appendix D the formats of the first two versions of the SUBTRACT statement. Which of these statements are legal?

(i)   SUBTRACT A B

(ii) SUBTRACT A B C FROM D

(iii) SUBTRACT B FROM ZERO GIVING FRED ROUNDED

3 The right-most operand in an ADD or SUBTRACT statement may not be a literal. Why not?

4 On a coding sheet, write down the statements to do: A = B+C-D+E-F+G. All the operands have two decimal places and two integral places, and may be positive or negative.

5 Is this statement legal? ADD A AND B TO C.

6 Is this statement legal? ADD A TO B GIVING C.

7 Remembering that A and B are variables that may take any value in the range allowed by their number of digits, why is the ADD statement in Fig. 16 unsatisfactory?

C2 MULTIPLY AND DIVIDE

The multiply statement, at its simplest, takes the form

$$\underline{\text{MULTIPLY}} \left\{ \begin{array}{l} \text{identifier-1} \\ \text{literal-1} \end{array} \right\} \underline{\text{BY}} \ \text{identifier-2}$$

There are GIVING, ROUNDED and SIZE ERROR options as with ADD and SUBTRACT. In every case, the result of the multiplication is placed in the right-most operand, the other operands being left unchanged.

The divide instruction is similar:

$$\underline{\text{DIVIDE}} \left\{ \begin{array}{l} \text{identifier-1} \\ \text{literal-1} \end{array} \right\} \underline{\text{INTO}} \ \text{identifier-2}$$

Again, there are GIVING, ROUNDED and SIZE ERROR options and the result is in the right-most operand. Some old compilers allow you to say DIVIDE A BY B, in which case the left operand contains the result. This use is not standard and contradicts the general rule for ADD, SUBTRACT, MULTIPLY and DIVIDE that the answer is in the right-most operand. However, DIVIDE A BY B GIVING C, being equivalent to DIVIDE B INTO A GIVING C, does not go against this rule, and is allowed in ANS COBOL.

On most large compilers, you can directly obtain the remainder of a division, e.g. DIVIDE 3.1416 INTO CIRCLE GIVING DIAMETER ROUNDED REMAINDER REM-1 ON SIZE ERROR etc. Here the remainder will be put in the field called REM-1 (the remainder being defined as what you would get by subtracting from the dividend (CIRCLE) the product of the unrounded result and the divisor (DIAMETER before rounding x 3.1416)).

Exercise

1 In Fig.17 what would be the contents of A, B, C and D after the following instruction? (Consider each case independently.)

(i) MULTIPLY A BY B

(ii) MULTIPLY A BY B ROUNDED

(iii) DIVIDE B INTO A GIVING C REMAINDER D
(iv) DIVIDE A INTO B GIVING C
(v) DIVIDE A INTO B GIVING C REMAINDER D

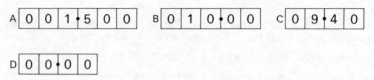

Fig. 17: Exercise 1

2   What is wrong with this statement?

   MULTIPLY RADIUS BY 3.1416.

3   What is the difference in effect of these two statements? Or is there no difference?

   DIVIDE A INTO B GIVING C
   DIVIDE B BY A GIVING C

4   What would happen when these statements are executed?

   (i) SUBTRACT A FROM A
        DIVIDE A INTO B GIVING C ON SIZE ERROR STOP RUN.
   (ii) SUBTRACT A FROM A
        DIVIDE A INTO B
        ADD 1 TO A
        DISPLAY A.

5   Your compiler does not have the REMAINDER option. You wish to calculate AVERAGE = SIGMA1/N. There is another item, SIGMA2, which has been defined with the same number of digits as SIGMA1; both are integers. Write statements which will place the remainder of the division in SIGMA2. (This is done by taking advantage of the fact that truncation will occur when the ROUNDED option is omitted.)

C3 COMPUTE

The COMPUTE verb is not available on some small compilers. It takes the form:

$$\underline{\text{COMPUTE}} \text{ identifier-1 } \left[\underline{\text{ROUNDED}}\right] = \left\{ \begin{array}{l} \text{identifier-2} \\ \text{literal-1} \\ \text{arithmetic-expression} \end{array} \right\}$$

$$\left[\text{ON } \underline{\text{SIZE}} \text{ ERROR imperative-statement}\right]$$

The expression to the right of the = sign is evaluated and the answer placed in identifier-1. The expression is a string of literals or identifiers with arithmetic operators placed between them. These operators are:

   +   addition

- subtraction
/ division
* multiplication
** exponentiation (raising to a power).

For example, a legal expression would be

COMPUTE ALPHA ROUNDED = BETA - BETA / N * N.

To human beings, this statement would be ambiguous (do you do the subtraction first, or the division? i.e. (beta - beta)/n.n is not the same as beta - (beta/n.n)...nor is beta/(n.n) the same as (beta/n).n).
The compiler works to a strict hierarchy when evaluating the operators, as follows:

First   **
Second   * and /
Third   + and -

Within the hierarchy, evaluation takes place from left to right.
If you do not wish this hierarchy to apply, you may use brackets to contain the portion of the expression you wish to be evaluated first. The use of brackets is recommended whenever the expression is complicated, even when they are not strictly necessary, because you are less likely to make a mistake and your statement will be easier for someone else to understand. A space should be left on either side of an arithmetic operator.
There may be a trap for the unwary in the use of the COMPUTE verb, caused by a size error condition occurring in the calculation of some intermediate part of the expression. For example, if the sequence of calculations includes the division of a very large number by a very small fraction, a size error may occur even though the result field may be large enough to hold the answer when the rest of the calculations are done. The SIZE ERROR option will detect this condition; if it is included with every use of COMPUTE there will be no risk of undetected size errors.

Exercise

1   Is this statement legal?

COMPUTE A = B ROUNDED.

2   What is unsatisfactory about this statement?

COMPUTE AVERAGE = (A + B + C) / N * 2.

3   The area of a circle is $3.1416r^2$ and you have declared suitable items CIRCAREA and RADIUS. Calculate CIRCAREA, firstly without the COMPUTE verb, secondly with it.

4   Taxable income is made up of ANNSAL and BONUS, less super-annuation and allowances. Superannuation has not been declared as a field in the Data Division, but it is always 5% of ANNSAL. TAX is 40% of taxable income. Calculate TAX with a single COMPUTE statement.

5   Many compilers relax the rule about having a space on either side of arithmetic operators, but still require a space on either side of a minus sign when it is used as an arithmetic operator. Why?

ANSWERS - SECTION C

Frame C1

1   C contains 10.00; A and B unchanged.
2   (ii), (iii). Note that a figurative constant is a legal alternative to a literal - see frame B4.
3   Because the field receiving the answer should be put at the right.
4   ADD B C E G GIVING A
    ON SIZE ERROR
        DISPLAY "RESULT TOO LARGE"
        STOP RUN.
    SUBTRACT D F FROM A
    ON SIZE ERROR
        DISPLAY "RESULT TOO LARGE"
        STOP RUN.
5   No. (Some old compilers do allow this construction, but ANS COBOL confines the use of the word AND to that of a a logical connector between conditions. This topic is treated in Section I.)
6   No.
7   The sum of A and B at maximum could be 199.998. Either the SIZE ERROR clause should be used, or C should be declared with three integer places. It is probably also the case that the lack of rounding is unsatisfactory.

Frame C2

1   (i) B = 015.00; A, C and D unchanged.
    (ii) as (i).
    (iii) C = 00.15; A, B and D unchanged.
    (iv) C = 06.66; A, B and D unchanged.
    (v) C = 06.67; A and B unchanged. D = 10.00 - (6.66 x 1.5) = 0.01.
2   Attempt to store answer in literal.
3   No difference.
4   (i) Machine would stop.
    (ii) Indeterminate, depends on machine. Most modern computers abandon the program when a zero division, not trapped by a SIZE ERROR clause, occurs.
5   DIVIDE N INTO SIGMA1 GIVING AVERAGE
        ON SIZE ERROR take suitable action.
    MULTIPLY AVERAGE BY N GIVING SIGMA2.
    SUBTRACT SIGMA2 FROM SIGMA1 GIVING SIGMA2.

    If a rounded result is required in AVERAGE, this could now be achieved by:

    ADD 0.5 TO AVERAGE
    ON SIZE ERROR take suitable action.

Frame C3

1   No, only results can be rounded.
2   SIZE ERROR clause should be used. Probably AVERAGE should be rounded.
3   (i) MULTIPLY RADIUS BY RADIUS GIVING CIRCAREA ROUNDED

ON SIZE ERROR imperative statement.
MULTIPLY 3.1416 BY CIRCAREA ROUNDED
ON SIZE ERROR imperative statement.
(ii) COMPUTE CIRCAREA ROUNDED = 3.1416 * RADIUS ** 2
ON SIZE ERROR imperative statement.

4 COMPUTE TAX ROUNDED = (ANNSAL + BONUS – ALLOWANCES – (ANNSAL
* 0.5)) * 0.4
ON SIZE ERROR imperative statement.

Or, a somewhat more compact version,

COMPUTE TAX ROUNDED = (ANNSAL * 0.95 + BONUS
– ALLOWANCES) * 0.4
ON SIZE ERROR imperative statement.

5 If this rule were not made, the compiler could not distinguish
between a single identifier with an embedded hyphen and two
identifiers, one of which is to be subtracted from the other.

D   Transfer of control

D1   GO TO; SIMPLE CONDITIONAL STATEMENT

The GO TO statement is followed by a paragraph name. The computer normally executes statements in the sequence they are coded; when a GO TO is encountered, execution continues at the first sentence in the paragraph specified.

Thus, to transfer control to a paragraph you have called READ-NEXT-CARD, you would simply code GO TO READ-NEXT-CARD.

The GO TO is often made subject to a **condition**. A condition is specified by starting a sentence with the word IF, and the simplest condition is 'equality' e.g.

```
IF RECORD-TYPE = 1
    GO TO CALCULATE-1.
GO TO CALCULATE-OTHERS.
```

If the condition is true (i.e. RECORD-TYPE contains 1), then control will be transferred to the paragraph called CALCULATE-1. If the condition is not true, the statements in the conditional sentence are ignored and execution continues at the next sentence. In this example, the next sentence will cause control to be passed unconditionally to CALCULATE-OTHERS.

Any sentence can be made conditional by starting it with an IF statement. Any condition can be negated by the word NOT; e.g.

```
IF RECORD-TYPE NOT = 1
    GO TO CALCULATE-OTHERS.
GO TO CALCULATE-1.
```

A special case of the GO TO, used rarely in practice, looks like this:

```
GO TO PROCESS-1 PROCESS-2 DEPENDING ON INPUT-DATA.
```

If the field referred to by the identifier INPUT-DATA contained 1, control would pass to the paragraph called PROCESS-1; if INPUT-DATA contained 2, control would pass to PROCESS-2. Any number (say, **n**) paragraph names may be specified, but you must make sure that the identifier field contains an integer in the range 1 to **n**. If it does not, no transfer of control takes place.

Some small compilers do not offer the DEPENDING ON option.

Exercise

1   Part of a program appears as follows.

```
    COMPUTE B = 0.
LOOP.
    ADD A TO A.
```

```
      ADD 1 TO B.
      IF B = 2
          GO TO NEXT.
      GO TO LOOP.
NEXT.
```

The initial value of A was 3. Assuming that no size errors occur, what value will A have when control reaches the paragraph called NEXT?

2   Write a statement to divide A by B. If a zero division occurs, transfer control to a paragraph called ZERO-DIV.

3   The value of ITEM can be 12, 24 or 36. If it is 12, you wish processing to continue at P12; if 24, at P24 and if 36 at P36. Code this logic (a) using DEPENDING ON and (b) without using DEPENDING ON.

4   Write Procedure Division statements which will multiply an item called MULTIPLIER by an item called MULTIPLICAND. Both numbers are positive integers, and the answer is to be in an item called RESULT. Only one problem – you are to do it without using the MULTIPLY, DIVIDE or COMPUTE verbs.

D2   ALTER

This verb is mentioned here only for the sake of completeness. It is proposed to delete it from future standard COBOL.

The ALTER verb is used to change the destination specified in a GO TO statement. For example, you may have a paragraph

```
      FLIP-FLOP.
          GO TO FLIP.
```

At a later stage in the program, you could write

ALTER FLIP-FLOP TO PROCEED TO FLOP.

After execution of the ALTER statement, if control returns to the paragraph called FLIP-FLOP, the GO TO in it will be executed as if it said GO TO FLOP.

This verb is somewhat redundant, since there is always another way of achieving the desired result. I recommend you avoid this verb like the plague, because it makes it extremely difficult to follow the path of the program. (As a matter of interest, you should avoid GO TO for the same reason; however, I am not advocating that quite yet – this is discussed in Sections K and L.)

Sometimes it is possible to make a program a little smaller or faster by using ALTER, but the cost of the confusion that results is a dear one.

Exercise

1   Why should you avoid the ALTER verb like the plague?

2   All right, why does it make following the path of the program difficult?

D3   CONCEPTS OF PERFORM

The PERFORM verb is one of the most useful ones in the COBOL language. A thorough understanding of both the concepts and practical use of the verb is essential.

The simplest form of the verb is

PERFORM paragraph-name-1 $\left[\underline{\text{THRU}} \text{ paragraph-name-2}\right]$

Suppose the statement PERFORM CALC-AVERAGE was executed. Control would be transferred to the first sentence in the paragraph called CALC-AVERAGE, just as if a GO TO CALC-AVERAGE had been executed. However, unlike a GO TO, when the last full stop in CALC-AVERAGE is reached, control **returns** to the statement immediately after the PERFORM statement. Another example:

```
        PERFORM CHECKTOTAL.
        ADD 1 TO CHECKED-QUANTITY.
```

This would cause the paragraph called CHECKTOTAL to be executed, the program then continuing with the sentence ADD 1 TO CHECKED-QUANTITY.

It may be that the statements you wish to perform cannot conveniently be contained in one paragraph. In this case, you use the THRU option, naming the first and last paragraphs of the sequence of paragraphs you wish to be executed. For example

```
        PERFORM CHECKTOTAL THRU ENDCHECK
```

would cause all the sentences to be executed from the first sentence in CHECKTOTAL to the last sentence in ENDCHECK. In this example, PERFORM CHECKTOTAL THRU ENDCHECK would be said to be coded **in-line**; the coding in the paragraphs CHECKTOTAL THRU ENDCHECK is said to be **out-of-line**. Thus, the PERFORM statement causes the specified out-of-line coding to be executed, with control returning to the next statement in-line.

The most valuable use of the PERFORM verb is in breaking down a large program into smaller parts which are easier to write. Suppose you wanted to write a program to accept the day and month from the operator, turn this into a number of days, and display the result. You could code the entire in-line logic of the program as follows:

```
        PROCEDURE DIVISION.
        P1. PERFORM ACCEPT-DATE.
            PERFORM CALCULATE-DAYS.
            PERFORM TYPE-RESULT.
            STOP RUN.
```

(Note that standard COBOL requires a paragraph name before the first sentence in the Procedure Division, even if it is not referred to elsewhere - hence, P1. It is proposed to drop this requirement.)

Now that you have designed the **macro-logic** of your program, you can devote your entire attention to coding the **micro-logic** of each out-of-line paragraph. For example, you might continue:

```
        ACCEPT-DATE.
            DISPLAY "ENTER 2-DIGIT LUNAR MONTH".
            ACCEPT MONTH.
            DISPLAY "THANK YOU, ENTER 2-DIGIT DAY".
```

```
        ACCEPT DAY.
    CALCULATE-DAYS.
        SUBTRACT 1 FROM MONTH.
        MULTIPLY MONTH BY 28 GIVING TOT-DAYS.
        ADD DAY TO TOT-DAYS.
    TYPE-RESULT.
        DISPLAY "THANK YOU, THE DAY NUMBER IS "  TOT-DAYS.
```

Of course, the sequence in which these out-of-line paragraphs are coded is not important to the logic, although it helps clarity if they are coded with some consistent relationship, e.g. in the order they are first mentioned in the in-line coding.

(This example assumes that the operator will correctly enter digits only. In practice such an assumption would not be made; the program would be expanded to check that no non-digit character had been entered.)

Exercise

1   It is a rule of COBOL that you must not write, within a range of paragraphs which are performed from some other part of the program, a GO TO which has a destination outside that range, where the subsequent control does not return to the last paragraph in the range. (But if you were to do this, it so happens that most compilers would not signal that you had made an error.) Why would such a practice be undesirable, anyway, from the point of view of someone trying to understand your program?

D4 NESTED PERFORMS

Suppose that it was desired to amend the example program in frame D3 to work with calendar months instead of lunar months. The logic will clearly be more involved, if the number of days equivalent to the months is to be calculated. We could solve this problem, and still preserve our original straightforward logic, by breaking out the instructions needed to find the number of days equivalent to the month number into a separate paragraph called, say, FIND-DAYS-IMPLIED-BY-MONTH. This paragraph could be performed from an appropriate point in the program, e.g.

```
1     PROCEDURE DIVISION.
2     P1. PERFORM ACCEPT-DATE.
3         PERFORM CALCULATE-DAYS.
4         PERFORM TYPE-RESULT.
5         STOP RUN.
6     ACCEPT-DATE.
7         DISPLAY "ENTER 2-DIGIT MONTH".
8         ACCEPT MONTH.
9         DISPLAY "THANK YOU, ENTER 2-DIGIT DAY".
10        ACCEPT DAY.
11    CALCULATE-DAYS.
12        PERFORM FIND-DAYS-IMPLIED-BY-MONTH.
13        ADD DAYS TO TOT-DAYS.
14    TYPE-RESULT.
15        DISPLAY "THANK YOU, THE DAY NUMBER IS "  TOT-DAYS.
16    FIND-DAYS-IMPLIED-BY-MONTH.
```

```
17          IF MONTH = 1
18              COMPUTE TOT-DAYS = 0.
19          IF MONTH = 2
20              COMPUTE TOT-DAYS = 31.
            (etc., for the rest of the months)
```

Let us take stock of what we have done. The statement at line 3 causes control to be transferred to line 11. The statement at line 12 causes control to be transferred to line 16. When execution of this last paragraph is complete, control will return to line 13; when that has been executed, control will return to line 4.

When an out-of-line paragraph itself contains a PERFORM statement, that PERFORM is said to be **nested**. This is the case with the PERFORM in line 12. The paragraphs executed by a nested perform must be coded either wholly inside or wholly outside the range of paragraphs referenced by the in-line PERFORM (in the example, they are wholly outside). Nesting may take place as often as required, including nesting within nesting.

Exercise

1   Pretend you are the computer executing the example program in this frame. List out the paragraph-names as you encounter them (this is called 'tracing' the program). Indent the list when you are executing a nested PERFORM.

2   On a coding sheet, write an amended version of the program in this frame to accept the day, calendar month and year from the operator, calculate the day-number and display the result. The year is accepted as four digits, and, if it is a leap year, February will have 29 days. Assume the year is a leap-year if it has zero remainder when divided by 4. (Suggestion: assume February has 28 days and add 1 if the year is a leap-year and the month is February. Put the logic for the leap-year in a separate out-of-line paragraph.)
Have a quick peek at the answer if you are really stuck for ideas. Pay attention to the accuracy of your coding.

3   What is wrong with the following coding?

```
PROCEDURE DIVISION.
PARAGRAPH-1.
    PERFORM PARA-2 THRU PARA-5.
PARA-2.
    (etc.)
PARA-3.
    (etc.)
PARA-4.
    PERFORM PARA-5 THRU PARA-6.
PARA-5.
    (etc.)
PARA-6.
```

D5   EXIT

The EXIT verb may be used in conjunction with PERFORM...THRU... when it is desired to make an early return from performed paragraphs,

i.e. omitting one or more paragraphs from the end of the subroutine.
Suppose part of a program appears as follows:

```
          PERFORM P1 THRU P4.
          -
          -
P1.
          -
P2.
          -
P3.
          -
P4.
          -
```

Now suppose that in P2 some condition may arise which dictates that P3
and P4 should not be executed. The problem is – how to avoid these
paragraphs without breaking the rule about GOing TO a destination
which is outside the range of the performed paragraphs?

The EXIT verb exists for this case. It is put in an extra paragraph at
the end of the subroutine, so that a GO TO that paragraph can be made
if an early exit is needed. EXIT is the only word in the paragraph.

Our problem, therefore, can be solved as follows:

```
          PERFORM P1 THRU P5.
          -
P1.
          -
P2.
          IF condition
               GO TO P5.
P3.
          -
P4.
          -
P5.
          EXIT.
```

There is no exercise for this frame.

ANSWERS - SECTION D

Frame D1

1   12
2   DIVIDE B INTO A ROUNDED, ON SIZE ERROR GO TO ZERO–DIV.
3   (a) DIVIDE 12 INTO ITEM.
         GO TO P12 P24 P36 DEPENDING ON ITEM.
    (b) IF ITEM = 12
            GO TO P12.
         IF ITEM = 24
            GO TO P24.
         GO TO P36.
    (Note that this answer assumes that the value of ITEM was firmly
    established to be in the range 12, 24 or 36; if there was any
    doubt, the last sentence would be coded IF ITEM = 36 GO TO P36.
    and followed with statements to handle the error.)

4   (You could COMPUTE RESULT = ZERO if there was any doubt that its initial value was zero.)

```
ADD-UP.
    IF MULTIPLIER NOT = ZERO
        SUBTRACT 1 FROM MULTIPLIER
        ADD MULTIPLICAND TO RESULT
        GO TO ADD-UP.
```

Would your answer have catered for the case where one of the operands was zero?

Frame D2

1   Because it makes it difficult to follow the program path.
2   What you see written on the coding sheet or listing is not necessarily what the computer will do.

Frame D3

1   When you encounter a PERFORM statement, you expect control to return to the next statement in-line. This will not be the case if a GO TO has been made to a destination outside the range of the performed paragraphs, unless a further GO TO is issued which gets control back in the range. As will be seen later, the student is advised, as a matter of good practice, never to use a GO TO which takes control outside the range of performed paragraphs.

Frame D4

1   P1

```
        ACCEPT-DATE
        CALCULATE-DAYS
            FIND-DAYS-IMPLIED-BY-MONTH
        TYPE-RESULT
```

2   PROCEDURE DIVISION.

```
        PERFORM ACC-DATE.
        PERFORM CALC-DAYS.
        PERFORM TYPE-RESULT.
        STOP RUN.
    ACC-DATE.
        DISPLAY "ENTER 2-DIGIT DAY".
        ACCEPT DAY.
        DISPLAY "ENTER 2-DIGIT MONTH".
        ACCEPT MONTH.
        DISPLAY "ENTER 4-DIGIT YEAR".
        ACCEPT YEAR.
    CALC-DAYS.
        PERFORM FIND-MONTH-DAYS.
        ADD DAY TO TOT-DAYS.
    TYPE-RESULT.
        DISPLAY "THE DAY NUMBER IS " TOT-DAYS.
    FIND-MONTH-DAYS.
        IF MONTH = 1
            COMPUTE TOT-DAYS = 0.
        IF MONTH = 2
            COMPUTE TOT-DAYS = 31.
        IF MONTH = 3
```

```
          COMPUTE TOT-DAYS = 59
          PERFORM CHECKLEAP.
     IF MONTH = 4
          COMPUTE TOT-DAYS = 90
          PERFORM CHECKLEAP
     and so on.
CHECKLEAP.
     DIVIDE 4 INTO YEAR GIVING YEAR REMAINDER anyname.
     IF anyname = ZERO
          ADD 1 TO TOT-DAYS.
```

(Take this opportunity to check your coding accuracy:

Did you start paragraph names in column 8 if your compiler is not free-format?
Did you code only one character per box, using capitals?
Did you start sentences to the right of column 12?
Did you put full stops after each paragraph name?
Did you put full stops at the end of each paragraph and at the end of each IF sentence?
Did you observe local conventions for the letter O and zero?
Did you leave a space after full stops and around the = sign?)

3   The nested PERFORM in PARA-4 executes paragraphs not wholly inside, nor wholly outside, the range of paragraphs executed by the PERFORM in PARAGRAPH-1.

Many students find the concept of PERFORM, particularly the nested PERFORM, difficult to grasp. Do not worry if this applies to you; time is needed for this concept to cement itself. Opportunities for further practice with PERFORM will be given later; in the meantime this analogy may assist understanding.

A PERFORM statement may be likened to a round trip bus tour, in the sense that you always end up back where you started. The paragraphs being performed are like the places you stop at on the tour.

Suppose, at one of these stopping places, you get off the bus and go on another round trip tour, rejoining your original bus when you get back. You will have been on a 'nested' tour, analogous to a nested PERFORM.

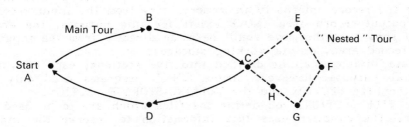

Fig. 18: Nested bus tour

To extend the analogy to cover the rules for nesting, the places you visit on the second tour must be different from those you visit on the first tour (as in Fig. 18), or they must form a subset of the places you visit on the first tour. The second tour must not take you to any places which you visit on the first tour if it is also going to some new places.

E The Data Division

E1 INTRODUCTION

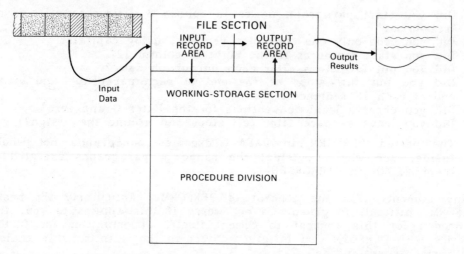

FILE SECTION

INPUT RECORD AREA → OUTPUT RECORD AREA

Output Results

Input Data

WORKING-STORAGE SECTION

PROCEDURE DIVISION

Fig. 19: Contents of memory at execution of a program

Fig. 19 illustrates the concepts underlying a COBOL program. A record in an input file can be read into an area of memory, under the control of the procedures of the program (a verb READ exists for this purpose). A record for an output file can be written from an output record area (WRITE exists for this purpose). It will be appreciated that in order even to write out the same record that was input, it will be necessary to move the record internally in memory, i.e. from the input record area to the output record area (MOVE exists for this purpose; the arrows in Fig. 19 show that the move could be made directly from the input to the output record area, or via working storage).

The Data Division can be divided into five sections, each of which has a special purpose. However, simple COBOL programs need only two of these, the FILE SECTION and the WORKING–STORAGE SECTION.

In the FILE SECTION, you define the files which are to be used by the program. The compiler uses this information to reserve the input and output record areas in memory. For example, suppose you had a deck of cards with a number keypunched in the first two columns of the card, and you wished to find the total of all the numbers. Each card would be a record in the file, and the first two columns would be the field or data element you are interested in. When you define this card file in the FILE SECTION, the compiler will allocate an input record area to hold the data from the card when it is read in.

The total you wish to accumulate, as the cards are read in, is no part of the file. It is an element of data which does not belong to a file. Such elements of data are defined in the WORKING–STORAGE SECTION.

In the Data Division, therefore, you define the records and fields or data elements which are to be used by the program, and give a name to each record and data element. The compiler uses this information to map out the locations of the data in memory. Then, when you refer to the data by name in the Procedure Division, the compiler can link the two names and translate your procedure statements into machine code which will operate on the correct locations.

Exercise

1   Refer to Fig. 10, page 12. What data names must have been declared in the Data Division of the COBOL program in that figure?

2   The compiler will give you an error message, called a fatal diagnostic, if it cannot translate your program into machine code through some error on your part. If you referred to a data element in the Procedure Division, but had failed to name it in the Data Division, do you think the compiler would give your program a fatal diagnostic?

3   If you named an element of data in the Data Division, but did not refer to it at all in the Procedure Division, would the compiler give a fatal diagnostic?

4   A program is to read in a magnetic disk file and, amongst other things, count how many records there are on it.
(a) In which Section would you define the magnetic tape records?
(b) What other field would you need, and where would you define it?

E2   THE FILE SECTION

You tell the compiler that you are starting the File Section by coding the section name immediately after the division name, i.e.

        DATA DIVISION.
        FILE SECTION.

Each file which is to be used by the program is then defined by two types of entry, a **File Definition** (FD entry) and one or more **Record Descriptions** (01 entry).

File definitions can be quite complex, and for a complete description you should consult the computer manufacturer's technical manual. The important features to learn now are given in this abbreviated form:

FD filename [BLOCK CONTAINS integer RECORDS]

        LABEL RECORDS ARE { STANDARD / OMITTED }

        [VALUE OF IDENTIFICATION IS literal]

The letters FD, which signify a File Definition, are coded at Margin A on compilers that expect margins; the rest of the entry is made to the right of Margin B. The filename is made up by you, in accordance with the rules for name formation (frame B3). The optional BLOCK CONTAINS clause can be used to specify, for magnetic tape and disk files, the number of records in a block (frame A4).

If LABEL RECORDS ARE STANDARD is specified, the file must be labelled as defined by the computer manufacturer; for example, by having header and trailer labels (frame A4). If labels are standard, a VALUE OF IDENTIFICATION (the word IDENTIFICATION is not standard – other words used for the same purpose are FILE-ID or just ID) may be specified. If it is specified, the literal mentioned is the name recorded on the header label as the file identification.

If there is more than one type of record in a file, each type of record is described in detail in a separate record description entry following the relevant file definition.

Example: A program reads records from two files, one a card file, the other a magnetic tape file. The card file has no label records, and has two different types of data record, one to be called DEBITS and the other to be called CREDITS. The tape file has standard labels with the identification "MASTERFILE" recorded on the header label. The records on the tape are blocked in threes. This file has only one type of record, to be called TAPE-REC.

```
DATA DIVISION.
FILE SECTION.
FD  CARDFILE      LABEL RECORDS OMITTED.
(here follows the record description entry for DEBITS)
(here follows the record description entry for CREDITS)
FD TAPEFILE       BLOCK CONTAINS 3 RECORDS
                  LABEL RECORDS STANDARD
                  VALUE OF IDENTIFICATION "MASTERFILE".
(here follows the record description of TAPE-REC)
```

The LABEL clause is presently compulsory in standard COBOL, but it is proposed to make it optional. On most modern computers, the identification of the file (as well as other characteristics such as blocksize) can be established at the time of program execution by means of commands to the operating system (these commands are not part of COBOL and are non-standard). When this procedure is followed, the file definition need contain only FD filename.

Exercise

1   A magnetic disk file, which has PARTMASTER recorded on a standard label, has records to be called PARTREC blocked in 100's. Write the file definition, calling the file INPUTMASTER.

2   A file to be called PRINTFILE is to be output on the line printer. The records are to be called LINE-OF-PRINT. Write the file definition (no labels).

E3   RECORD DESCRIPTION ENTRY

A record description entry is essentially a sequence of statements of the form:

level-number data-name $\left[\underline{\text{PICTURE}} \text{ IS picture-string}\right]$.

A level number of 01 (Margin A) shows that you are about to give a name to the whole record. Level numbers of 02 to 49 are used to describe the fields which are contained within the record. Thus level 02 denotes a field within a record. A level 02 field can be split up into sub-fields by giving each sub-field a level number of 03, and so on. (The leading zero in a single-digit level number is optional, but most programmers put it in.)

The PICTURE clause is used to describe the number and type of characters in the field. PICTURE XXX would mean three characters of any type (alphanumeric); PICTURE 9999 would mean four characters of numeric data; PICTURE A would mean one character of alphabetic data (but PICTURE X would include alphabetic characters, so A is not commonly used); PICTURE XX99 would mean two alphanumeric characters followed by two numeric characters, and so on. To avoid writing down long strings of characters for large items, a multiplier can be placed in brackets — the PICTURE will be interpreted as if the character before the multiplier had been repeated the number of times specified by the multiplier. For example, instead of writing PICTURE XXXXXXXXXX you could write PICTURE X(10); instead of PICTURE 999999, PICTURE 9(6); for PICTURE XXXXX9999, PICTURE X(5)9(4). The word PICTURE may be abbreviated to PIC.

If a deck of punched cards contained a number in the first two columns, the rest being blank, the card record could be described as follows:

```
01   DATA-CARD.
     02   NUMBER-IN    PIC 99.
     02   NOTUSED      PIC X(78).
```

The compiler would glean from this that DATA-CARD was the name of a record; that NUMBER-IN was the name of the first two characters in the record, and that the type of data in those characters is numeric; that NOTUSED is the name of the next 78 characters of the record, and the type of data is alphanumeric. Instead of giving a programmer-defined name to a field which is not referred to in the Procedure Division, as with NOTUSED here, it may be given a reserved word name, FILLER.

A complete example of both file and record descriptions can now be given.

```
DATA DIVISION.
FILE SECTION.
FD CARDFILE      LABEL RECORDS OMITTED.
01   DATA-CARD.
     02   NUMBER-IN    PIC 99.
     02   FILLER       PIC X(78).
```

Notice that DATA-CARD itself is not given a PICTURE. The compiler will calculate the length of DATA-CARD from the fields contained within it; the type of data of a group item is assumed to be alphanumeric (irrespective of the definitions made of the elementary items contained in the group). Thus any group field is deemed to be as long as the sum of the elementary items it contains and to be alphanumeric; and it is not given a PICTURE.

Exercise

1   A file called REPORT-FILE is to be written to the line printer. The lines of print have five fields: a 6-digit account number, a

3-character filler field, an alphanumeric 9-character name, a 3-character filler field and a 26-character address. Write all the Data Division entries needed to describe this file. What length will the compiler attribute to the record?

2　Write the record description entries to describe this record layout:

Record-name	DEBIT-RECORD						
level 02	ACCOUNT-NUMBER			DATE			INVOICE-NO	AMOUNT
level 03	AREA-CODE	SERIAL	CHECK-DIGIT	DAY	MONTH	YEAR		
type of data	X	9999999	X	99	99	99	99999999	99999999

Fig. 20: Exercise 2

3　A record description entry appears as follows:

```
01   PART-RECORD.
     02   PART-NUMBER.
          03   CHARACTERISTICS-CODE.
               04   MATERIAL    PIC X.
               04   SHAPE       PIC X.
          03   DIMENSIONS.
               04   LENGTH          PIC 99.
               04   X-SECTION-AREA  PIC 9999.
          03   SERIAL          PIC 9999.
     02   DESCRIPTION         PIC X(10).
```

Draw a diagram similar to the one in Fig. 20 above, to illustrate this record layout.

ANSWERS – SECTION E

Frame E1

1　TOTAL, COUNT, NUMBER.
2　Yes.
3　No.
4　(a) In the File Section.
　　(b) A count field, in the Working-Storage Section.

Frame E2

1　FD　INPUT-MASTER　　　BLOCK CONTAINS 100 RECORDS
　　　　　　　　　　　　　　LABEL RECORDS STANDARD
　　　　　　　　　　　　　　VALUE OF IDENTIFICATION "PARTMASTER".
(here follows the record description of PARTREC)
2　FD　PRINTFILE　　　　LABEL RECORDS OMITTED.
(here follows the record description of LINE-OF-PRINT)

Did you spell the word OMITTED correctly? Did you put a full stop at the end of the file definition, and nowhere else?

Frame E3

1   DATA DIVISION.
    FILE SECTION.
    FD   REPORT-FILE   LABEL RECORDS OMITTED.
    01   PRINTLINE.
        02   ACCOUNT-NO PIC 9(6).
        02   FILLER   PIC XXX.
        02   NAME   PIC X(9).
        02   FILLER   PIC XXX.
        02   ADDRESSE   PIC X(26).

(ADDRESS is a reserved word. For the time being, you can get over this type of problem by mis-spelling, e.g. ADDRESSE; a better method is explained in Section M.)
    The length of the record is 47 characters.

2   01   DEBIT-RECORD.
        02   ACCOUNT-NUMBER.
            03   AREA-CODE   PIC X.
            03   SERIAL   PIC 9(7).
            03   CHECK-DIGIT PIC X.
        02   DATE-IN.
            03   DAYE   PIC 99.
            03   MONTH   PIC 99.
            03   YEAR   PIC 99.
        02   INVOICE-NO   PIC 9(X).
        02   AMOUNT   PIC 9(8).

It is not essential to indent higher level numbers, as I have here, but it is usually done, to aid clarity.

3   See Fig. 21.

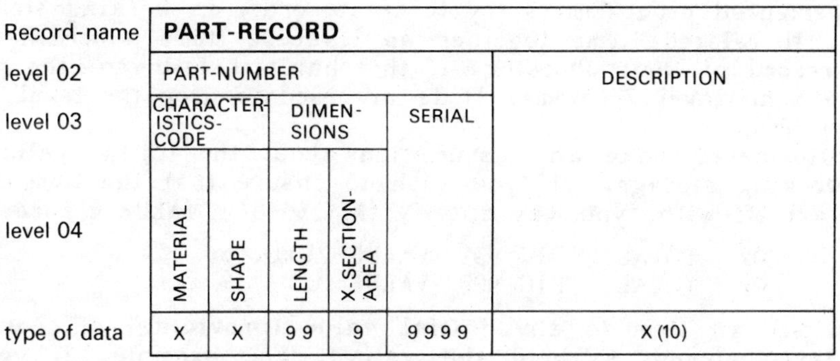

Record-name	PART-RECORD						
level 02	PART-NUMBER					DESCRIPTION	
level 03	CHARACTER-ISTICS-CODE		DIMEN-SIONS		SERIAL		
level 04	MATERIAL	SHAPE	LENGTH	X-SECTION-AREA			
type of data	X	X	9 9	9	9 9 9 9	X (10)	

Fig. 21: Answer to Exercise 3

F Further Data Division entries

F1 THE WORKING-STORAGE SECTION

Elements of data which do not form part of a file may be named in the Working-Storage Section. Standard COBOL at present provides a special level-number, 77, to indicate a data item that does not form part of a record. If you wished to accumulate a total in three digits, you might write:

```
WORKING-STORAGE SECTION.
77   TOTAL    PIC 999.
```

From the point of view of the logic of the program, a level 77 item can always be replaced by a level 01 item. Thus the above example could be written

```
01   TOTAL    PIC 999.
```

However, the implication of an 01 level is that it is to be broken down into further subordinate items, or it is to be input or output as a record on a peripheral device. The level 77 item cannot be subdivided nor used as a record. Some computer manufacturers have taken advantage of this different expectation to arrange for level 77 items to be stored in memory in a more economical or efficient fashion than level 01 items.

Most experienced programmers try to create order in working storage by grouping all related items together as level 02 items subordinate to a level 01 record of their choosing. If this habit is followed, the program will contain no level 77 items. It is proposed to drop the level 77 from standard COBOL.

You should never make any assumption about the initial value of an item in working storage. If you wish to ensure that the item contains zero to start off with, you may specify this with a VALUE clause, e.g.

```
02   TOTAL    PIC 999  VALUE ZERO. or
02   TOTAL    PIC 999  VALUE 0.
```

You can set an item to any initial value (providing, of course, the item is large enough to hold the value). For example, if you were intending to number the pages of a report produced on the line printer, you might wish to start your page counter with a value of 1:

```
01   PAGE-COUNTER    PIC 99 VALUE 1.
```

A non-numeric literal can be used to initialise a non-numeric item, e.g.

```
01   PAGE-HEADING PIC X(31) VALUE "SALES REPORT FOR THE
-            "LAST TWELVE MONTHS".
```

With an alphanumeric item, if the non-numeric literal specified in the

VALUE clause is shorter than the item, the literal is left–justified in the item and the remaining right–hand positions are filled with spaces.
The VALUE clause may NOT be used in the File Section.
Level 77 and level 01 items can be coded in any order in working storage. It is often useful to build up a record (i.e. fill it with data) in the Working–Storage Section and then move it to a record in the File Section for writing out. This is especially useful if any of the fields in the record contain constants, since you may not give an item an initial value in the File Section. Suppose you wished to define a line of print like this:

(salesman no.) : (name) : (sales this month) : (sales to date)

The colons and the spaces are constants, the other items are variables. The record could be mapped out in working storage as follows:

```
01   LINE-OF-PRINT.
     02   SALESMAN-NO        PIC 9(4).
     02   FILLER             PIC X(5)      VALUE " : ".
     02   SALESMAN-NAME      PIC X(20).
     02   FILLER             PIC X(5)      VALUE " : ".
     02   SALES-THIS-MONTH   PIC 9(5).
     02   FILLER             PIC X(5)      VALUE " : ".
     02   SALES-TO-DATE      PIC 9(6).
```

The word FILLER may be used as many times as may be needed, but only on elementary items. Since the word FILLER indicates only that the data item is not going to be referred to in the Procedure Division, CODASYL has proposed that this word be optional; if no data-name appears for an elementary item, it will be assumed to be a filler.

Exercise

1   What is wrong with this coding?

```
FILE SECTION.
FD   CARDIN   LABEL RECORDS OMITTED.
01   CARDREC PIC X(80)    VALUE SPACES.
```

2   Write Working-Storage Section entries which will allow you to print out the heading "PAYROLL ANALYSIS" preceded by 10 spaces, followed on the next line by a double underscore under the heading (use the = sign), i.e.

```
PAYROLL ANALYSIS
================
```

3   The date is to be printed out to the right of the words PAYROLL ANALYSIS in question 2, after a gap of 20 spaces. This will take the form dd/mm/yy where dd mm and yy are the two-digit day, month and year which will be inserted by Procedure Division statements. The oblique strokes, however, are constants to be defined in the heading.
    Amend your answer to question 2 to define this record (the date is not to be underscored).

F2   THE PICTURE CLAUSE – NUMERIC PICTURES

We have seen the picture clause used to define simple numeric, alphabetic and alphanumeric items. We are now going to complete our knowledge of numeric pictures and look at a special case of alphanumeric pictures – the edited item.

Numeric pictures, in addition to the picture character 9, can also contain the characters S, V and P.

S shows that the number may take a negative value, i.e. it may be signed. S must be the first character in the picture, when it appears, and it does NOT add to the length of the item unless the optional phrase SIGN LEADING SEPARATE is added. For example,

    02   TAX-AMOUNT   PIC S999.

describes a three–digit numeric field which may be positive or negative, whereas

    02   TAX-AMOUNT   PIC S999 SIGN LEADING SEPARATE.

describes a three–digit numeric field preceded by a one–character field containing a + or – sign.

V shows the position of a decimal point, and it does NOT add to the length of the item. The decimal point is **assumed** by the compiler to be in the position specified by the V; an actual decimal point must not appear in the data. So

    02   TAX-AMOUNT   PIC S999V999.

shows a signed, five–digit field whose decimal point is assumed to be between the third and fourth characters, while

    02   DISCOUNT   PIC V99.

shows a two–digit positive field with an assumed decimal point at the beginning.

P is a scaling factor rarely used in practice. It is used to locate an assumed decimal point at some notional position to the left or right of the item, e.g.

    01   MILLISECONDS   PIC VPPP999.

describes a three–digit numeric field which is to be treated in arithmetic as if it had .000 preceding it.

    01   ROUND-MILLIONS   PIC 999P(6).

is a three–digit numeric item which is to be treated in arithmetic as if it had six zeros following it. P does NOT add to the length of the item.

On most computers, it is possible to influence the way numeric data is held inside the machine by specifying USAGE COMPUTATIONAL after a numeric picture clause. For example, 03 NUMERIC-ITEM PIC 9(6)V999 USAGE COMPUTATIONAL would, on most machines, cause NUMERIC-ITEM to be held internally as a binary, as opposed to a decimal, number. This can theoretically make a program execute more quickly if it does a lot of arithmetic, and it can result in less memory being needed to hold large numbers. The actual number of characters allocated to a picture with USAGE COMPUTATIONAL varies from machine to machine. For further information on USAGE, and the related clause SYNCHRONIZED, consult the manufacturer's technical manual; a knowledge of these variations is not required for this text.

USAGE COMPUTATIONAL (which may be abbreviated to COMP) may not be declared when SIGN LEADING SEPARATE has been declared. These clauses are contradictory since COMP tells the compiler to expect a non-character representation of the number, including the sign, whereas SIGN LEADING SEPARATE tells it to make a character representation of the sign. Either clause may be used at group level (e.g. level 01), in which case all subordinate items will be treated as USAGE COMPUTATIONAL or SIGN LEADING SEPARATE.

Exercise

1   01   AUDIT-RECORD SIGN LEADING SEPARATE.
        02   TOTAL-DEBITS   PIC S9(8)V99.
        02   TOTAL-CREDITS   PIC S9(8)V99.
        02   NO-OF-DEBITS   PIC S9(6).
        02   NO-OF-CREDITS   PIC S9(6).

How long is the group record?

2   What is wrong with this coding?

01   INVOICE COMP.
        02   GROSS   PIC 9(8)V99.
        02   DISCOUNT-RATE   PIC V99.
        02   DISCOUNT-AMOUNT   PIC 9(8)V99.
        :
COMPUTE DISCOUNT-AMOUNT ROUNDED = GROSS * DISCOUNT-RATE * -1.

3   What is wrong with this coding?

01   SUMMARY   COMP.
        02   INSTOCK   PIC 9(8).
        02   BACKORDERS   PIC 9(8).
        02   FREE   PIC 9(8).
        02   NEXT-DELIVERY-DATE PIC X(6).

F3   THE PICTURE CLAUSE - EDITED ITEMS

Additional editing characters can be put in a picture string, which will modify the data when it is inserted into the field concerned.
Insertion characters (, (comma) B (blank) 0 (zero) and / (stroke or solidus) insert the character(s) specified into the field, e.g. the item

01   AMOUNT   PIC 99,999.

would always have a comma in the third character position. If you moved data of 01276 into AMOUNT, it would then contain 01,276. Note that the insertion character DOES increase the length of the item; AMOUNT is a six-character field. Furthermore, it is NOT a numeric field. The presence of the special character means that this field cannot be used in an arithmetic operation (although it may contain the result when the GIVING option is used). This rule applies to all edited items.
Other examples: moving data with a value of 311255 to an item DATE-EDITED PIC 99B99B99 would give the eight-character item called DATE-EDITED the value 31 12 55. (The underscore here represents a space.) Moving data of 1234 to an item ROUND-THOUSANDS PIC 9,999,000 would give this nine-character field a value of 1,234,000.
Four insertion characters (+ (plus) − (minus) $ (dollar) and £ (pound)) may be placed at the left-hand side of a picture string. $ and £ work just like the characters already described. The + sign will be changed to a − sign if the data moved to the item is negative. The

- sign will be changed to a **space** if the data is positive or zero. Thus, if there is an item RESULT PIC -999,999 and you moved a negative amount of 100000 to it, it will contain -100,000. Moving a positive amount of 100000 to it will give a result of _100,000. The plus and minus sign may also be placed at the right-hand end of a picture string, where they are interpreted with the same effect.

The two characters CR or DB may also be placed at the right-hand end of a picture string. They cause the letters CR or DB respectively to be printed out if the data sent to the item is negative; otherwise, two spaces are printed out.

A special insertion character is the decimal point (.). If an item's picture string includes a decimal point, the assumed decimal point in the data is lined up with the actual decimal point in the item. If data with a value of 47v45 (four digits, the v showing the position of the assumed decimal point) was sent to an item ANSWER PIC 99.99, then ANSWER would contain the five characters 47.45. If the receiving field is larger than the data item sent to it, zeros will be placed in the unused positions, e.g. sending 47v45 to LONG-ANSWER PIC 999.999 would give the latter item a value of 047.450.

Suppressing and floating characters are used to replace the leading zeros in the data by some other character. As soon as a significant digit is encountered in the data, all suppressing and floating characters work as if they were the character 9.

The simplest case is the character Z, which replaces leading zeros in the data by spaces. If data of 001008v89 was sent to a field with PICTURE ZZZ,ZZ9.99 the result would be __1,008.89. If data of 0v0 was sent to the same field, the result would be _____0.00 (note that the insertion character, comma, is treated like a Z in this case).

The cheque protect character * (star or asterisk) works in the same way. Sending data of 0017v45 to a field with PIC *****.99 would give a result of ***17.45.

The characters plus, minus, dollar and pound may also be repeated to **float** the corresponding symbol down to the left of the first significant digit in the data. For example, sending data of 0012v34 to a field PIC $$$$9.99 will give a result of __$12.34. When the floating symbols are used, an extra symbol should be placed at the left of the picture string to allow for the case where the data sent has no leading zeros.

If you want a field to contain only spaces when a zero amount is sent to it, you can specify BLANK WHEN ZERO after the picture clause, or give it a picture of all Z's. Even if an otherwise all-Z item contains commas and a decimal point, it will print out blank when a zero amount is sent to it. For example, consider a receiving item PIC Z,ZZZ.ZZ; if data of v50 is sent to it, it will print _____.50; if sent data of v05 it prints _____.05; if sent data of zero, it prints eight spaces.

Editing works only when data is moved internally in the memory of the computer, e.g. as a result of an arithmetic operation with a GIVING clause, or as a result of a MOVE (see frame G4). Data read in from an input device into a field with an edit picture will not be edited.

Exercise

1   The data in a field described by the PICTURE in the left-hand column is to be moved to a field with the picture given in the right-hand column. Write down the resulting contents of the receiving field. Use an underscore to show the presence of a space.

	Sending PICTURE	Data	Receiving PICTURE	Result
(a)	AAA9	TSR2	AAAB9	
(b)	9(5)	00176	ZZ,ZZ9.99	
(c)	99v9	231	£££.99	
(d)	9	0	£££.99	
(e)	S999v99	12645(+ve)	++++9.9999	
(f)	999	100	9PP	
(g)	9	2	$$$$$9.99	

2   The following cases were not specifically covered in the text. Write down your guess of what happens.

	Sending PICTURE	Data	Receiving PICTURE	Result
(a)	9999V99	123456	ZZ9.99	
(b)	999V999	234567	£ZZ9.99	
(c)	99V99	3456	£ZZ9.99	
(d)	S99V99	3456(–ve)	–ZZ9.99	
(e)	999	100	9PPP	
(f)	V99	01	VPP9	

3   Examine this picture string: PIC $,$$$,$$9.99. Can you see why it does not make sense (and will be illegal on some compilers)?

F4   PRACTICAL EXERCISE PART 1

This is the first part of a practical exercise which will be completed when the verbs OPEN, CLOSE, READ, WRITE and MOVE have been considered in the next section.

A file of records has standard labels with the identification NUMBERS. Each record has four 4-digit numbers recorded in the first 16 columns, each having one decimal place. The records are 80-characters long but the other characters are not used by the program.

A program is to be written which will read each record, calculate the average of the numbers on the record and print out the result, together with the original numbers. The records are to be counted, and the record number printed out along with the input numbers and the average. One small complication; the fourth number is always negative although it is not recorded as negative, i.e. it must be subtracted from the other numbers before the average is found.

The layout of the printed report is as follows:

```
RECORD-NO    NO 1  NO 2  NO 3  NO 4  AVERAGE
=========    ====  ====  ====  ====  =======
```

The record number (maximum 999 records) is to be printed in positions 4 to 6. The four numbers are to be printed in positions 14 to 17, 20 to 23, 26 to 30, 33 to 36 respectively. The fourth number is to be followed by a minus sign in every case. The average is to be printed in positions 39 to 45, followed by a minus sign if it is negative. The average is taken to two decimal places.

1   Copy out Identification Division and Environment Division entries from information given to you by your tutor.

2   Write a complete Data Division for this program.

3   You will write the Procedure Division, and run the program, when the next section has been covered.

An outline flowchart of the program is given below.

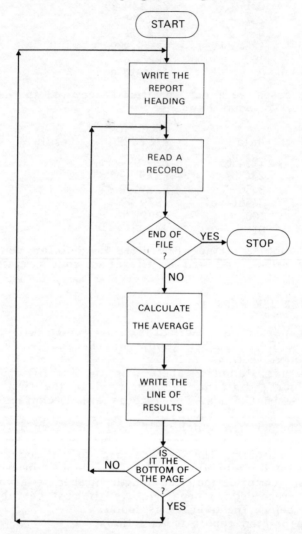

Fig. 22: Outline flowchart for practical exercise

Try to make sure that the column headings are lined up with the printed data and edit the fields sensibly. To test page overflow, assume that there are only 5 lines per page.

ANSWERS – SECTION F

Frame F1

1   The value clause may not be used in the File Section.
2   WORKING–STORAGE SECTION.

```
01    HEDDING.
      02   FILLER   PIC X(10)      VALUE SPACES.
      02   FILLER   PIC X(16)      VALUE "PAYROLL ANALYSIS".
01    UNDERSCORE.
      02   FILLER   PIC X(10)      VALUE SPACES.
      02   FILLER   PIC X(16)      VALUE "================".
```

A shorter but less plain solution would be along the lines
01 HEDDING PIC X(26) VALUE "   PAYROLL ANALYSIS", etc. The
plain solution may seem a little long-winded, but on the whole it is
less error-prone and more easy to amend.

3   WORKING-STORAGE SECTION.

```
01    HEDDING.
      02   FILLER   PIC X(10)      VALUE SPACES.
      02   FILLER   PIC X(36)      VALUE "PAYROLL ANALYSIS".
      02   DAYE     PIC 99.
      02   FILLER   PIC X          VALUE "/".
      02   MONTH    PIC 99.
      02   FILLER   PIC X          VALUE "/".
      02   YEAR     PIC 99.
```

UNDERSCORE would be as before. Many other variations are legal.
For the sake of example, this answer has taken a short cut to the
extra 20 spaces by taking advantage of the rule about non-numeric
literals being right space-filled when assigned to a long data item.
A plain solution which spells out the number of spaces is arguably
more professional. A shorter solution would use the editing facilities
explained in frame F3 to insert the oblique strokes, e.g.
HEADING-DATE PIC 99/99/99.

Frame F2

1   36 characters.
2   Negative result – DISCOUNT-AMOUNT should have a PICTURE starting
     with S.
3   Alphanumeric item (NEXT-DELIVERY-DATE) cannot be declared as
     USAGE COMPUTATIONAL.

Frame F3

1   (a) TSR 2
     (b)   176.00
     (c) £23.10
     (d)   £.00
     (e)   +126.4500
     (f) T
     (g)   2.00
2   (a) 234.56
     (b) £234.56
     (c) £ 34.56
     (d) – 34.56
     (e) 0
     (f) 0
3   The first comma apparently caters for the case where the value is
     1 million or more. But data of such value moved to this picture
     would result in no $ sign being printed at all. There should be at
     least two $ signs before the comma.

G File handling and moving data in memory

G1 OPEN AND CLOSE

Before you can read a record from a file, or write a record to a file, the file must be **open**, either for input or for output as appropriate. The OPEN verb is:

$$\text{OPEN} \quad \left\{ \begin{array}{ll} \underline{\text{INPUT}} & \text{file-name-1} \ [\text{file-name-2}] \ \ldots \\ \underline{\text{OUTPUT}} & \text{file-name-3} \ [\text{file-name-4}] \ \ldots \end{array} \right\} \ \ldots$$

Thus, if you wanted a program to read cards and use them to update a master file on magnetic disk, you might code at the beginning of your program:

```
OPEN INPUT CARD-FILE OLDMASTER
     OUTPUT NEWMASTER PRINTFILE.
```

The file names used are the same ones as you made up in the FD statement. Opening causes a file with standard labels to have the header label checked (input) or written out (output). In the case of a disk file, the label will probably not be stored at the head of the file, but in a special directory area of the disk.

After you have processed all the records on the file, the file must be closed. At the logical end of your program, you could code:

```
CLOSE OLDMASTER CARDFILE NEWMASTER PRINTFILE.
```

Closing causes trailer labels to be written out on output tape files, but the exact meaning of CLOSE with files on other types of device tends to vary slightly from one brand of computer to another. Similarly, for the exact meaning of the variants CLOSE...WITH NO REWIND and CLOSE...WITH LOCK, consult the manufacturer's reference manual. With at least one compiler, if you do not close an output file WITH LOCK, it is assumed that the file you created in the program was only required temporarily, and the file is deleted when the program terminates.

Sometimes it is desired to add records to the end of a file that has already been created. With most machines you can do this on both magnetic disk and tape files by declaring OPEN EXTEND file-name.

Exercise

1   Once you have opened a file, you may not issue a further OPEN instruction unless the file is first closed. Why is this?

2   What is the difference between the logical end of a program and the physical end?

G2   READ AND WRITE

The READ statement causes the next record in the file specified to be read into memory, in the area described by the record description entry you made for that file.

READ file-name RECORD AT END imperative-statement

For example, if you had called a file TRANS-IN and you wished to get the next record, you could code READ TRANS-IN RECORD AT END PERFORM CLOSE-FILES. The AT END is true only if the trailer label (or other indication of the end of the file) is encountered when the computer tries to read a record. In this way, you can detect the end of the file and, in the example, the paragraph called CLOSE-FILES would be performed.

When the input file is read on a device such as a card reader or visual display unit and has no trailer label, the operating system usually expects some special message in the input, to signal end of file. The nature of this message varies from one type of computer to another; examples are a card containing the characters /* in columns 1-2, or a VDU line containing the characters ?END. When this data is encountered in the input as a result of a READ, the AT END condition becomes true.

You may read an input record straight into another record in working storage by using the INTO option, e.g.

        READ TRANS-IN RECORD INTO WORK-TRANS
        AT END
            PERFORM CLOSE-OFF.

Writing a record is similar, except that this time you must specify the **record** name that you wish to be written. For example:

        WRITE DISK-REC-1

would cause the record you had defined as DISK-REC-1 in the File Section to be written out to the file to which it belongs. For the record which belongs to a printer file, WRITE LINE-OF-PRINT would cause the record to be output on the printer. In most cases the printer would move the paper forward one line, either before or after writing the line, depending on the particular computer. Most computers advance the paper and then print the line, but some do not advance the paper at all, so that this form of WRITE instruction would result in one line being over-printed on another.

You may write a record straight out of working storage by using the FROM option, e.g.

        WRITE LINE-OF-PRINT FROM WORK-HEADING.

Exercise

1   Write the statement to read the next record from the file you have called INPUT-TAPE. The record is called INPUT-REC at the 01 level. If the trailer record is encountered, you are to perform a paragraph called CLOSE-OFF and stop the run.

2   You have a file called PRINT-FILE which has been defined as having records called PRINTLINE-1 and PRINTLINE-2. Write the statements which will cause PRINTLINE-1 and PRINTLINE-2 to be written on successive lines (assume your computer does not

overprint).

3   A file may contain more than one type of record, i.e. two or more record description entries may follow the file definition entry. Knowing this, can you explain why you READ file names but WRITE record names?

G3   WRITING RECORDS TO THE LINE PRINTER

Additional facilities are given for controlling the line spacing when writing records to the line printer, the format being:

$$\underline{\text{WRITE}} \text{ record-name } \left\{ \begin{matrix} \text{AFTER} \\ \underline{\text{BEFORE}} \end{matrix} \right\} \text{ ADVANCING } \left\{ \begin{matrix} \text{identifier LINES} \\ \text{integer LINES} \\ \underline{\text{PAGE}} \end{matrix} \right\}$$

Different computer manufacturers have adopted either BEFORE or AFTER as standard for their machines, although most offer both. All offer the 'integer LINES' option, whereby the actual number of lines to be advanced is specified, e.g.

WRITE PRINTLINE BEFORE ADVANCING 10 LINES

would cause a gap of nine lines to be left between successive lines printed by the instruction.
When the 'identifier' option is used, e.g.

WRITE PRINTLINE AFTER SPACING

the paper will advance the number of lines indicated by the integer data element (probably in working storage) that you have called SPACING.
The PAGE option gives the straightforward statement WRITE PRINTLINE BEFORE ADVANCING PAGE.
It is a common requirement in programming to count the number of lines as they are printed and to take some special action when the foot of the page is reached. This can be achieved automatically by deploying the LINAGE phrase in the FD entry of the file concerned, to specify how many lines precede the foot of the page, and an AT END-OF-PAGE clause in the WRITE statements of the file concerned to trigger off the desired action. For example,

```
FD   PRINTFILE LABEL RECORDS STANDARD LINAGE 50 LINES.
01   PRINTREC    PIC X(132).
  :
     WRITE PRINTREC AFTER ADVANCING 2 LINES
     AT END-OF-PAGE
         PERFORM WRITE-FOOTING-LINES
         PERFORM WRITE-PAGE-HEADINGS.
```

The statements following END-OF-PAGE will be executed if, after the WRITE is done, the line count on the page is equal to or greater than the linage (50 in this example). Use of WRITE with the PAGE keyword (in the paragraph called WRITE-PAGE-HEADINGS, in this example) resets the line counter.

Exercise

1   Write the statements which will write a record called DETAIL-LINE
     before advancing two lines, unless the item called LINECOUNT
     contains the value 60, in which case DETAIL-LINE is to be printed
     before advancing to the head of the next page. The program is to
     continue at a paragraph called READ-NEXT-RECORD. (This is the
     style one has to adopt if the LINAGE clause is not available.)

2   Amend your answer to question 1 so that a paragraph called
     WRITE-REPORT-HEADINGS is performed if a throw to the head of the
     form is made.

G4   MOVE

The MOVE verb is used to move data about within memory. Consider the
following program:

```
DATA DIVISION.
FILE SECTION.
FD   DISKIN   LABEL RECORDS OMITTED.
01   DISKREC PIC X(80).
FD   PRINTOUT      LABEL RECORDS OMITTED.
01   ALINE     PIC X(80).
PROCEDURE DIVISION.
P1.
     OPEN INPUT DISKIN OUTPUT PRINTOUT.
READ-A-RECORD.
     READ DISKIN
     AT END
          GO TO CLOSE-FILES.
     MOVE DISKREC TO ALINE.
     WRITE ALINE BEFORE ADVANCING 2 LINES.
     GO TO READ-A-RECORD.
CLOSE-FILES.
     CLOSE DISKIN PRINTOUT.
     STOP RUN.
```

This program will simply list the disk records out on the line printer,
unedited. The MOVE verb is used to move the data in the input record
area to the output record area.
  If it was desired to edit the output, it would be necessary to define
each field in the input and the output, e.g.

```
01   DISKREC.
     02   FIRST-AMOUNT        PIC 9(4)V99.
     02   SECOND-AMOUNT       PIC 9(4)V99.
     02   FILLER              PIC X(68).
```

and

```
01   ALINE.
     02   AMT-1               PIC ZZZ9.99.
     02   FILLER              PIC XX.
     02   AMT-2               PIC ZZZ9.99
     02   FILLER              PIC X(64).
```

The Procedure Division could then be amended to state:

```
                OPEN INPUT DISKIN OUTPUT PRINTOUT.
                MOVE SPACES TO ALINE.
           READ-A-RECORD.
                READ CARD-IN AT END GO TO CLOSE-FILES.
                MOVE FIRST-AMOUNT TO AMT-1.
                MOVE SECOND-AMOUNT TO AMT-2.
                WRITE ALINE BEFORE ADVANCING 2 LINES.
                GO TO READ-A-RECORD.
```

The first MOVE fills the whole of ALINE with spaces (remember, you cannot give an initial VALUE in the File Section). The second and third MOVEs transfer the individual fields and ensure that they get edited in the output record.

The following rules apply to common MOVEs:

Alphanumeric item to alphanumeric item.   The data in the sending field is left-justified in the receiving field. If the receiving field is too large, it is right-filled with spaces. A group field (e.g. a record) counts as an alphanumeric field.

Numeric item to numeric item.   The data in the sending field is aligned on the assumed decimal point in the receiving field. If the receiving field is too large, leading or trailing zeros are inserted as required.

Numeric item to numeric edited item.   The assumed decimal point in the sending field is aligned to the actual decimal point in the receiving field, and the rules for editing are followed (frame F3).

It is also legal, but rarely required, to send an integer numeric item to an alphanumeric item. In this case, the sending field is left-justified in the receiving field; if the receiving field is too large, it is right-filled with spaces. Similarly, an alphanumeric item may be sent to a numeric item; the alphanumeric item is assumed to contain an integer, and the rules for numeric/numeric moves are followed. It is up to the programmer to ensure that the sending field contains an integer.

If the receiving field is too small, with any type of move, the result will be truncated.

Exercise

1   02   ALPHA-1 PIC X   VALUE "1".
     02   ALPHA-2 PIC X(4).

What will be the content of ALPHA-2 after MOVE ALPHA-1 TO ALPHA-2?

2   02   NUM-1   PIC 9V9   VALUE 2.3.
     02   NUM-2   PIC 99V99   VALUE 0.

What will be the content of NUM-2 after MOVE NUM-1 TO NUM-2?

3   02   NUM-1   PIC 99   VALUE 23.
     02   ALPHA-2 PIC X(4).

What will ALPHA-2 contain after MOVE NUM-1 TO ALPHA-2?

G5   MOVE WITH LITERALS

The sending field in a MOVE may be a literal; the ordinary rules for MOVE still apply. A numeric literal counts as a numeric sending field, while a non-numeric literal counts as an alphanumeric sending field.

When the sending field is a figurative constant, the whole of the receiving field is filled up with the constant specified. It makes no difference whether the singular or plural version of the figurative constant is used.

Thus, MOVE SPACE TO PRINTLINE has the same effect as MOVE SPACES TO PRINTLINE. The whole of PRINTLINE will be filled with spaces.

A similar effect can be achieved with any literal by specifying ALL literal. Suppose you have an item AFIELD PIC X(10). After MOVE "*" TO AFIELD, AFIELD would contain one asterisk followed by ten spaces. But after MOVE ALL "*" TO AFIELD, the whole of AFIELD would be filled with asterisks. The keyword ALL may also be used in a VALUE clause, e.g. 02 AFIELD PIC X(10) VALUE ALL "*" would have the same effect of filling AFIELD with asterisks.

If the sending field in a MOVE ALL is more than one character long, the string of characters is repeated until the receiving field is full. After MOVE ALL "ABC" TO AFIELD, AFIELD would contain ABCABCABCA.

Exercise

1   MOVE ALL HIGH-VALUES TO AFIELD would be a legal statement in COBOL, but it contains a redundancy. Why?

G6   PRACTICAL EXERCISE PART 2

You are now in a position to complete the practical exercise started in frame F3.

Make up test data to test your program after you have a successful compilation. Include a record with all zeros, a record with all nines, a record in which the first number is 0001 and the others all zero and a record in which the first three numbers are zero, the fourth being 1.

To test your page overflow routine, instead of constructing a really large number of test cases you could set the number of lines to, say, 5 per page.

ANSWERS - SECTION G

Frame G1

1   The header label has already been read in and checked, or written out. A further OPEN statement is logically inconsistent.
2   Physical end = last statement coded.
     Logical end = last statement executed.

Frame G2

1   READ INPUT-TAPE AT END PERFORM CLOSE-OFF STOP RUN.
2   WRITE PRINTLINE-1.
     WRITE PRINTLINE-2.
3   A file may contain several different types of record. A READ statement causes the next record on the file to be input into memory, whatever type it is. When the READ is executed, the type of record that is **next** on the file is not known, so it is impossible to specify a record-name that is to be read. Therefore, READ goes with the file-name.

The several record descriptions for the file are each taken to define the same record area. It is up to the program to discover, by inspecting identifying data in the record, what type of record it is dealing with.

Conversely, when a WRITE statement is executed, the machine must be told which of the different record types which may belong to the file is to be written out. So WRITE goes with the record-name.

Frame G3

```
1    IF LINECOUNT = 60
         WRITE DETAIL-LINE BEFORE PAGE
         GO TO READ-NEXT-RECORD.
     WRITE DETAIL-LINE BEFORE 2
     GO TO READ-NEXT-RECORD.
2    IF LINECOUNT = 60
         WRITE DETAIL-LINE BEFORE PAGE
         PERFORM WRITE-REPORT-HEADINGS
         GO TO READ-NEXT-RECORD.
     WRITE DETAIL-LINE BEFORE 2.
     GO TO READ-NEXT-RECORD.
```

Frame G4

```
1    1___
2    0230
3    23__
```

Frame G5

1   The ALL is redundant. MOVE HIGH-VALUES TO AFIELD would have the same effect. Figurative constants imply MOVE ALL.

H Qualification, redefinition, subscripts

H1 QUALIFICATION

The names you make up for the records used by your program must all be different. However, it is legal to use the same names for data items in different records, e.g.

```
01    DISKIN.
      02    AMOUNT-1     PIC 9(4)V99.
      02    AMOUNT-2     PIC 9(4)V99.
      02    FILLER       PIC X(68).
01    PRINTOUT.
      02    AMOUNT-1     PIC ZZZ9.99.
      02    FILLER       PIC XX.
      02    AMOUNT-2     PIC ZZZ9.99.
      02    FILLER       PIC XX.
      02    TOTAL        PIC Z(4)9.99.
```

A statement in the Procedure Division such as MOVE AMOUNT-1 TO AMOUNT-1 will be ambiguous and it is therefore necessary to **qualify** references to these fields in the Procedure Division, e.g.

```
MOVE AMOUNT-1 OF DISKIN TO AMOUNT-1 OF PRINTOUT.
MOVE AMOUNT-2 IN DISKIN TO AMOUNT-2 IN PRINTOUT.
ADD  AMOUNT-1  OF  DISKIN  TO  AMOUNT-2  IN  CARDIN
GIVING TOTAL.
```

The keywords OF and IN are synonyms, and relate the field to the group item in which it is found.

Since the use of duplicate names can result in much longer statements to manipulate the data, most programmers choose to avoid them.

In the 1974 COBOL standard, there is a CORRESPONDING option of MOVE, ADD and SUBTRACT which allowed for abbreviated instructions. For example, instead of the first two MOVEs above we could have written:

```
MOVE CORRESPONDING DISKIN TO PRINTOUT.
```

The compiler would examine each field in DISKIN to see if there was a field with the same name in PRINTOUT; if so, the move of that field would take place. The fields to be moved must have the same level numbers and the same group field names (if any). Fillers are ignored.

Although at face value it looks as though CORRESPONDING could save a lot of coding, in practice it does not work out this way very often, since the extra work of name qualification usually exceeds the saving from the use of CORRESPONDING. There is also much less need for the use of duplicate names when the Report Writer facilities described in Section S are available, and when files are updated in place rather than by copying them forward (Section T). It is now proposed to delete the CORRESPONDING option.

H2   REDEFINITION

A file contains records as follows:

Characters	1–6	account number
	7–25	name
	26–85	address
	86–165	shipping address
	166–169	quantity-ordered
	170–171	currency code (01 = sterling £p,
		02 = US $, etc.)
	172–178	amount (3 places of decimals if sterling,
		2 if dollars, none if lira, etc.)

The record layouts are identical except that the number of places of decimals in the amount field will vary with the currency code. One way over this problem would be to define three different records for the file, but this would be tedious considering most of the layout is identical. A better solution would be to define the amount field in three different ways, i.e.

```
01   INVOICE-REC.
     02   ACC-NO           PIC X(5).
     02   NAME             PIC X(19).
     02   ADDR             PIC X(60).
     02   SHIP-ADDR        PIC X(80).
     02   QUANTITY         PIC 9999.
     02   CURRENCY         PIC 99.
     02   AMT-STERL        PIC 9(4)V999.
     02   AMT-DOLL REDEFINES AMT-STERL PIC 9(5)V99.
     02   AMT-LIRA REDEFINES AMT-STERL PIC 9(7).
```

In the Procedure Division, if you refer to AMT-STERL, the field will be assumed to have three decimal places; if to AMT-DOLL, two decimal places and if to AMT-LIRA, no decimal places. REDEFINES, therefore, is used to give an alternative name and description to a given field. The redefining item must have the same field length as the redefined item. The redefining item describes the same memory locations as the redefined item.

Group items may also be redefined. For example, suppose ACC-NO above contained a two digit country code, a one digit credit code and a three digit serial number for overseas customers, while home customers have a five digit serial number following a special prefix "H". You could describe these variations:

```
     02   ACC-NO-FOREIGN.
          03   COUNTRY     PIC 99.
          03   CRED-CODE   PIC 9.
          03   SER-F       PIC 999.
     02   ACC-NO-HOME REDEFINES ACC-NO-FOREIGN.
          03   PREFIX      PIC X.
          03   SER-H       PIC 9(5).
```

Note that the two groups are the same length (six characters); they are alternative ways of describing the same six characters of memory. REDEFINES may not be used at the 01 level in the File Section (it is redundant here, anyway, since records belonging to the same file are assumed to be redefining one another in the input or output record area).

Exercise

1   When using REDEFINES in the Working-Storage Section, you may use the VALUE clause with the item being redefined, but you may not use the VALUE clause with the redefining item. Why is this?

2   A six digit date field on a visual display line is to be defined at the 02 level. The subfields within the date may be either English (DDMMYY), American (MMDDYY) or Julian (YYDDD). If the date is in Julian format, the sixth digit is not used. Write the Data Division entries which describe the date field and its subfields.

H3   OCCURS N TIMES

This clause may be used to describe a group of adjacent fields which have the same picture. Suppose a record contained 12 four-digit numbers, each with two decimal places. This could be described:

```
01   PAYMENTS-DUE.
02   AMOUNT OCCURS 12 TIMES PIC 99V99.
```

This saves you from having to name each field. Now, to refer to a particular field, you must place a **subscript** in brackets after the name of the field. For example, AMOUNT(1) would refer to the first field in the record; AMOUNT(2) the second, and so on.

A group field may also be made to occur several times, e.g.

```
01   PAYMENTS-DUE.
02   PAYMENT-GROUP OCCURS 12 TIMES.
03   MONTH        PIC 99.
03   AMOUNT       PIC 99V99.
```

This would describe 12 group data items, each containing a two-digit month and a four-digit amount. You could access the first group with PAYMENT-GROUP(1); the first data item in the first group with MONTH(1); the second data item in the first group with AMOUNT(1), and so on.

You do not have to put a literal as the subscript. It may be a variable with an integral value in the correct range (i.e. in the range 1 to 12 in this example). This is a very powerful feature. Suppose in the example above we wished to total all the amounts. We could write ADD AMOUNT(1), AMOUNT(2), AMOUNT(3), etc., but this would be very tedious. By defining two items in working storage:

```
02   SUB     PIC 99 COMP.
02   TOTAL   PIC 9(4)V99 COMP.
```

we could add up all the amounts with Procedure Division statements as follows:

```
        MOVE 1 TO SUB.
    SUM-AMTS.
        ADD AMOUNT(SUB) TO TOTAL
        ON SIZE ERROR
            (take necessary action).
        ADD 1 TO SUB.
        IF SUB LESS THAN 13
            GO TO SUM-AMTS.
```

It is usually especially important to declare data items that are used as subscripts with an efficient USAGE. On most computers, this is COMP or COMP SYNC RIGHT.

It is not legal to use a VALUE clause with an item or group that OCCURS. If you wish to insert a value, this can be achieved by redefinition, e.g.

```
01  TABLE.
    02  TABLE-CONTENT.
        03  FILLER  PIC XXX  VALUE "JAN".
        03  FILLER  PIC XXX  VALUE "FEB".
        03  FILLER  PIC XXX  VALUE "MAR".
        03  FILLER  PIC XXX  VALUE "APR".
        03  FILLER  PIC XXX  VALUE "MAY".
        03  FILLER  PIC XXX  VALUE "JUN".
        03  FILLER  PIC XXX  VALUE "JUL".
        03  FILLER  PIC XXX  VALUE "AUG".
        03  FILLER  PIC XXX  VALUE "SEP".
        03  FILLER  PIC XXX  VALUE "OCT".
        03  FILLER  PIC XXX  VALUE "NOV".
        03  FILLER  PIC XXX  VALUE "DEC".
    02  TABLE-2 REDEFINES TABLE-CONTENT.
        03  ALPHA-MONTH OCCURS 12 TIMES PIC XXX.
```

ALPHA-MONTH(1) will therefore contain the characters JAN, ALPHA-MONTH(2) will contain FEB, and so on. I set out all these fillers for clarity in exposing the concept. When dealing with non-numeric values (or with unsigned numeric values with display usage), the same effect can be achieved with less writing by declaring a value for a group item. For example,

```
01  TABLE VALUE "JANFEBMARAPRMAYJUNJULAUGSEPOCTNOVDEC".
    02  ALPHA-MONTH OCCURS 12 TIMES PIC XXX.
```

There is some argument that the plain but long approach is the more professional one, since the program is more easily amended; but perhaps this is not so important with a very stable set of data like the names of the months. If the table content may require updating, it is preferable to record the table data in a file, and read this data into the table at the start of the program.

When a value is declared for a group item, there must not be any contradictory declaration (e.g. another value) for any subordinate item of the group.

OCCURS may not be used at the 01 level.

Exercise

1 The File Section of a program contains an input record in VDUFILE and an output record in PRINTFILE as follows:

```
01  LINE-IN.
    02  DATE-IN.
        03  DAY-IN      PIC 99.
        03  MONTH-IN    PIC 99.
        03  YEAR-IN     PIC 99.
01  LINE-OUT.
    02  FILLER.         PIC X(100).
    02  DAY-OUT         PIC Z9BB.
```

```
02    MONTH-OUT          PIC XXXBB.
02    YEAR-OUT           PIC 99.
```

Write the Working-Storage Section and Procedure Division entries which will read in one line and output the date on the line printer. MONTH-OUT is to be the three-character equivalent of MONTH-IN, and can be found by using MONTH as the subscript of an item in a table.

ANSWERS – SECTION H

Frame H2

1   If a value were put on the redefining item as well as the redefined item, you would be asking the compiler to put two different values into the same area of memory – impossible.

2
```
02    E-DATE.
      03    E-DAY        PIC 99.
      03    E-MON        PIC 99.
      03    E-YEAR       PIC 99.
02    US-DATE REDEFINES E-DATE.
      03    US-MON       PIC 99.
      03    US-DAY       PIC 99.
      03    US-YEAR      PIC 99.
02    J-DATE REDEFINES E-DATE.
      03    J-YEAR       PIC 99.
      03    J-DAY        PIC 99.
      03    FILLER       PIC 99.
```

Frame H3

1
```
WORKING-STORAGE SECTION.
01    TABLE VALUE "JANFEBMARAPRMAYJUNJULAUGSEPOCTNOVDEC".
      02    ALPHA-MONTH OCCURS 12 TIMES PIC XXX.
PROCEDURE DIVISION.
P1.
      OPEN INPUT VDUFILE OUTPUT PRINTFILE.
      READ VDUFILE
      AT END
            DISPLAY "NO LINES IN VDU FILE - JOB ABORTED"
            GO TO CLOSE-ETC.
      MOVE SPACES TO LINE-OUT.
      MOVE DAY-IN TO DAY-OUT.
      MOVE ALPHA-MONTH(MONTH-IN) TO MONTH-OUT
      MOVE YEAR-IN TO YEAR-OUT.
      WRITE LINE-OUT.
CLOSE-ETC.
      CLOSE VDUFILE PRINTFILE.
      STOP RUN.
```

▮ Further Procedure Division entries

I1   CONDITIONAL EXPRESSIONS

These are of the form:

$$\underline{\text{IF}} \quad \left\{\begin{array}{l}\text{simple-condition}\\\text{compound-condition}\end{array}\right\} \quad \left\{\begin{array}{l}\text{statement-1}\\\underline{\text{NEXT}}\ \underline{\text{SENTENCE}}\end{array}\right\} \quad \left[\underline{\text{ELSE}}\ \text{statement-2}\right]$$

We have already seen this used where the simple-condition is one of the equality of two items (frame D1), e.g.

        IF RECORD-TYPE = 1
            PERFORM CALCULATE-1.

The ELSE variation allows you to make a statement which will be executed only if the condition is not true, e.g.

        IF RECORD-TYPE = 1
            PERFORM CALCULATE-1
        ELSE
            PERFORM CALCULATE-OTHERS.

Other simple conditions which can be specified are summarised below.

$$\left\{\begin{array}{l}\text{identifier-1}\\\text{literal-1}\end{array}\right\} \quad \text{IS} \quad \left[\underline{\text{NOT}}\right] \left\{\begin{array}{l}\underline{\text{GREATER}}\ \text{THAN}\\\underline{\text{LESS}}\ \text{THAN}\\\underline{\text{EQUAL}}\ \text{TO}\\=\\>\\<\end{array}\right\} \quad \left\{\begin{array}{l}\text{identifier-2}\\\text{literal-2}\end{array}\right\}$$

Where both fields being compared are numeric items, an algebraic comparison is made (+ve > 0 < −ve). In other cases, the fields are compared character by character from left to right, the shorter field being treated as if it had spaces to the right. Although all computers treat Z as greater than A and 9 greater than 0, practice varies when a letter is compared with a number or where special characters are involved. In ASCII (American Standard Code for Information Interchange, which is also the ISO 7-bit code and the British Standard Data Code), digits are less than upper case letters, which are less than lower case letters. In EBCDIC (Extended Binary Coded Decimal Interchange Characters), digits are greater than uppercase letters, which are greater than lower case letters.

The mathematical symbols > and < may be used in place of GREATER THAN and LESS THAN.

Items can also be tested for type:

$$identifier\ IS\ \left[\underline{NOT}\right]\ \left\{\begin{array}{l}\underline{POSITIVE}\\ \underline{NEGATIVE}\\ \underline{ZERO}\\ \underline{NUMERIC}\\ \underline{ALPHABETIC}\end{array}\right\}$$

The picture of the item should be consistent with the test being made; in particular, a NUMERIC test cannot be made on an item which has an alphabetic picture, nor an ALPHABETIC test on an item with a numeric picture.

Exercise

1   An account number has six characters. The first is always the letter A, the next character can be anything and the last four characters should be a number in the range 0001 to 5000 inclusive. Write Data Division entries to describe this field, and Procedure Division statements which will check that the data in it conforms with these rules. Perform ERROR-P if the data is incorrect.

12   COMPOUND CONDITIONS

Simple conditions can be joined by the words AND or OR to make a compound condition. For example, you could code:

```
IF FIRST-CH = "A" AND LAST-FOUR GREATER THAN 0
      NEXT SENTENCE
ELSE
      PERFORM ERROR-P.
```

Both simple conditions must be true if PERFORM ERROR-P is to be avoided; so it follows that ERROR-P will be performed if either condition is false. If OR is used, the conditional statement will be executed if either condition is true; the logic of the previous example could also be expressed

```
IF FIRST-CH NOT = "A" OR LAST-FOUR LESS THAN 1
      PERFORM ERROR-P.
```

When both AND and OR are used in a compound condition, the result is a sentence which would be ambiguous in ordinary English. Although COBOL solves this by evaluating AND's first, the student is advised always to make his meaning clear by the use of brackets, e.g.

```
IF FIRST-CH NOT = "A" OR
(LAST-FOUR NOT GREATER THAN ZERO AND
LAST-FOUR NOT LESS THAN 5001)
      PERFORM ERROR-P.
```

The truth of an expression in brackets is always evaluated first. If you consider closely the bracketed expression in the preceding example, you will see that it is in error (always false). Remember that NOT GREATER THAN is the same as 'less than or equal to' and NOT LESS THAN is the same as 'greater than or equal to'. It is very easy for novice and experienced programmer alike to allow compound conditions to become tortuous and twisted exercises in logic. It is nearly always possible to simplify complicated conditions by eliminating NOTs and/or by writing the conditions in separate sentences. Sometimes this will involve inverting the branching logic by using the NEXT SENTENCE option. The preceding example should be re-written (correctly) as

```
IF FIRST-CH NOT = "A" OR
LAST-FOUR LESS THAN 1 OR
LAST-FOUR GREATER THAN 5000
    PERFORM ERROR-P.
```

Some experienced programmers take the view that, for simplicity, ANDs and ORs should not appear in the same compound condition. Some also suggest that compound conditions be avoided altogether.

Exercise

1   What is the logical contradiction in the condition in brackets above?

2   Write Procedure Division statements which express the following logic:

(a) If CUST-CODE is in the range A to D, DISCOUNT is to be 0.10. For other values of CUST-CODE, DISCOUNT is to be zero.
(b) If TRANS-DATE is not numeric or TRANS-MONTH is not in the range 1 to 12, the program is to perform REPORT-ERROR. In any case, it is to continue at the next sentence.

13   NESTED IF STATEMENTS

It is quite legal to embed an IF statement within another IF statement. This should be avoided since it can lead to unnecessary program complexity, unless it results from a thorough and well-documented analysis of the logic, as described in Part 2.
There are two main variations, the first being

```
IF A = B IF C = D PERFORM P1 ELSE PERFORM P2 ELSE PERFORM P3.
```

This means: perform P1 if both A = B and C = D; perform P2 if A = B but C $\neq$ D; perform P3 if A $\neq$ B. The rule is that the innermost ELSE is matched to the innermost IF, the next ELSE to the next earlier IF and so on, working outwards. If you cannot resist using nested IF's, you can help yourself and other readers of your program by indenting each IF statement and coding its corresponding ELSE statement underneath, i.e.

```
IF A = B
    IF C = D
        PERFORM P1
    ELSE
        PERFORM P2
ELSE
    PERFORM P3.
```

The other variation is as follows.

```
IF E = F PERFORM P4 ELSE IF G = H PERFORM P5 ELSE PERFORM P6.
```

This means: if E = F perform P4; if E $\neq$ F but G = H, perform P5; if E $\neq$ F and G $\neq$ H, perform P6. It should be coded

```
            IF E = F
                PERFORM P4
            ELSE
                IF G = H
                    PERFORM P5
                ELSE
                    PERFORM P6.
```

14   VARIATIONS OF THE PERFORM VERB

(a)   PERFORM.... $\left\{ \begin{array}{l} \text{identifier} \\ \text{integer} \end{array} \right\}$ TIMES

This will cause the specified paragraph(s) to be performed the number of times indicated. For example, to find the total of a number of fields described by an OCCURS clause

```
            02   AMT-1 OCCURS 100 TIMES    PIC 9(4)V99.
            02   ANSWER                    PIC 9(6)V99.
            02   SUB                       PIC 999 COMP.
```

we could code:

```
            MOVE ZERO TO ANSWER.
            MOVE 1 TO SUB.
            PERFORM ADD-UP 100 TIMES.
            PERFORM PRINT-ANSWER.
            STOP RUN.
        ADD-UP.
            ADD AMT-1(SUB) TO ANSWER.
            ADD 1 TO SUB.
```

(b)   PERFORM...UNTIL condition

This will cause the specified paragraphs to be performed until the condition is true. The condition may be simple or compound. The paragraph is **not** performed when the condition is true. To repeat and extend the last example:

```
            02   ANSWER                PIC 9(5)V99.
            :
            MOVE ZERO TO ANSWER.
            MOVE 1 TO SUB.
            PERFORM ADD-UP UNTIL SUB = 101 OR ERR-FLAG = "T".
            PERFORM PRINT-ANSWER.
            STOP RUN.
        ADD-UP.
            ADD AMT-1(SUB) TO ANSWER
            ON SIZE ERROR
                MOVE "T" TO ERR-FLAG
                MOVE ZEROS TO ANSWER.
            ADD 1 TO SUB.
```

The condition is tested before performing the paragraph, so if the condition is true at the outset, the paragraph will not be performed even once.

(c)   PERFORM...VARYING...FROM...BY...UNTIL condition

This is a handy form of the PERFORM verb which allows you to set up the initial and incremental values for performing the out-of-line paragraph. In the preceding example, we could omit setting the initial value of SUB and code:

```
        PERFORM ADD-UP VARYING SUB FROM 1 BY 1
        UNTIL SUB = 101 OR ERR-FLAG = "T".
        PERFORM PRINT-ANSWER.
        STOP RUN.
    ADD-UP.
        ADD AMT-1(SUB) TO ANSWER
        ON SIZE ERROR
            MOVE "T" TO ERR-FLAG
            MOVE ZEROS TO ANSWER.
```

Exercise

1   In the Ruritanian tax system, employees are given a code in the range A to G which shows the amount of allowances to be deducted from taxable income according to the following table:

Tax code	Deduction
A	0
B	100
C	200
D	350
E	550
F	800
G	1100

In working storage, these two tables are defined as follows.

```
01    TABLES.
      02    TABLE-OF-CODES          VALUE "ABCDEFG".
            03    TAX-CODE OCCURS 7 TIMES PIC X.
      02    TABLE-OF-DEDUCTIONS   VALUE "0000010002000350055008001100".
            03    DEDUCTION OCCURS 7 TIMES PIC 9(4).
      02    SUB         PIC 9 COMP.
```

An employee record has been read by the program. It contains a PICTURE X field called EMP-TAX-CODE which has been checked to be in the range A to G. Write statements which will subtract the appropriate DEDUCTION from TAXABLE-PAY. The program is to continue at CALC-NET-PAY.

2   Items are defined in working storage as follows.

```
01    CHECKING-ITEMS COMP.
      02    TEMP        PIC 999.
      02    WEIGHT      PIC 9.
      02    SUB         PIC 9.
      02    SUM         PIC 999.
01    ACC-NO.
      02    DIGIT OCCURS 6 TIMES PIC 9.
      02    CHECK-DIGIT PIC 9.
```

Each DIGIT is to be multiplied by a weight, giving a weighted digit. The weight is 7 for the first (left) digit, 6 for the second and so on down to 2 for the last. The sum of the weighted digits is to be divided by 10 and the remainder of this division, subtracted from 10, is to be put in CHECK-DIGIT. Code this.

ANSWERS - SECTION I

Frame 11

```
1   01   ACC-NO.
         02   FIRST-CH      PIC X.
         02   SEC-CH        PIC X.
         02   LAST-FOUR     PIC 9(4).
    PROCEDURE DIVISION.
         :
         IF FIRST-CH NOT = "A"
             PERFORM ERROR-P.
         IF LAST-FOUR NOT NUMERIC
             PERFORM ERROR-P.
         IF LAST-FOUR LESS THAN 1
             PERFORM ERROR-P.
         IF LAST-FOUR GREATER THAN 5000
             PERFORM ERROR-P.
```

If you wish that ERROR-P is done only once even if there is more than one type of error in ACC-NO, this can be achieved with a compound condition – see next frame – or by a GO TO after each PERFORM, to branch round the remaining tests.

Would your answer have detected the invalidity of account number AX10A1?

Frame 12

1   No number can be less than or equal to zero **and** greater than or equal to 5001.

2   (a)   IF CUST-CODE LESS THAN "A" OR CUST-CODE GREATER THAN "D"
                  MOVE ZERO TO DISCOUNT
              ELSE
                  MOVE .1 TO DISCOUNT.
    (b)   IF TRANS-DATE NOT NUMERIC OR
              TRANS-MONTH LESS THAN 1 OR
              TRANS-MONTH GREATER THAN 12
                  PERFORM REPORT-ERROR.

Frame 14

1   Many possible answers. A simple one:

```
         MOVE 1 TO SUB.
         PERFORM INCREMENT-SUB UNTIL EMP-TAX-CODE = TAX-CODE(SUB).
         SUBTRACT DEDUCTION(SUB) FROM TAXABLE-PAY.
         GO TO CALC-NET-PAY.
    INCREMENT-SUB.
         ADD 1 TO SUB.
```

2   Again many variations possible. Sample:

```
            MOVE 0 TO SUM.
            PERFORM CALC-AND-ADD VARYING SUB FROM 1 BY 1
            UNTIL SUB = 7.
            DIVIDE 10 INTO SUM GIVING SUM REMAINDER CHECK-DIGIT.
            SUBTRACT CHECK-DIGIT FROM 10 GIVING CHECK-DIGIT.
        :
    CALC-AND-ADD.
            SUBTRACT SUB FROM 8 GIVING WEIGHT.
            MULTIPLY WEIGHT BY DIGIT(SUB) GIVING TEMP.
            ADD TEMP TO SUM.
```

J Identification and Environment Divisions

J1 THE IDENTIFICATION DIVISION

This consists of a number of paragraphs of the form

    IDENTIFICATION DIVISION.
    PROGRAM-ID. program-name.
    [AUTHOR. comment.]
    [INSTALLATION. comment.]
    [DATE-WRITTEN. comment.]
    [DATE-COMPILED.]
    [SECURITY. comment.]

Only PROGRAM-ID is compulsory; the program-name inserted must conform to the rules for the particular computer concerned.

The remaining entries are not used by the compiler, except that it will insert the date of compilation in the DATE-COMPILED paragraph. This is of questionable value on modern computers since most compilers will automatically date the listing, anyway. This helps you to identify which is the latest listing of a program you are developing.

The other paragraphs are self-explanatory. Any comment can be written anywhere in the text area provided an asterisk is placed in column 7 of each line (free format compilers - at the beginning of the line). This makes the provision of special paragraphs for comments somewhat redundant, and it is now proposed to drop these entries from the standard. Nevertheless, it will still be a good practice to use these paragraphs as a checklist of comments which should be made at the outset of the program.

It can be particularly useful to give a summary of the objectives at the end of the Identification Division, e.g. in plain English:

```
*SUMMARY
*       INPUT    -CUSTOMER MASTER FILE BROUGHT FORWARD
*                -VALIDATED UPDATE RECORDS
*       OUTPUT   -CUSTOMER MASTER FILE CARRIED FORWARD
*                -ERROR REPORT OF AMENDING OR DELETING
*                 UPDATE RECORDS FOR WHICH THERE IS NO
*                 CORRESPONDING MASTER RECORD, AND OF
*                 INSERTING UPDATE RECORDS WHERE A MASTER
*                 RECORD ALREADY EXISTS
*       PROCESSING
*                -ACCORDING TO THE UPDATE CODE FIELD AS
*                 FOLLOWS
```

```
    *              A (AMEND): THE NON-BLANK FIELDS OF THE
    *              UPDATE RECORD ARE MOVED INTO THE APPROPRIATE
    *              FIELDS OF THE MASTER
    *              D (DELETE): THE MASTER RECORD IS NOT
    *              WRITTEN FORWARD
    *              I (INSERT): THE UPDATE RECORD IS WRITTEN
    *              FORWARD ONTO THE NEW MASTER
```

Exercise

1   Write the Identification Division for a program which reads any file
     of 80-character records, sorts them into ascending order on the first
     six characters, and lists them on the line printer. The installation
     is Central Computer Services and there is no security consideration
     for the program.

J2   THE ENVIRONMENT DIVISION

This division contains two sections, the Configuration Section and the
Input-Output Section. The entries used in these sections at a particular
installation may depend to some extent on the exact nature of the
equipment used at that installation.
The Configuration Section has three paragraphs, which are basically:

```
    CONFIGURATION SECTION.
    SOURCE-COMPUTER. computer-name.
    OBJECT-COMPUTER. computer-name.
   [SPECIAL-NAMES. entry.]
```

Against source and object computer are put the names of the computer
used for compilation and the computer to be used for execution
respectively. These are usually the same machine. The object computer
paragraph can be extended with some compilers to state many other
characteristics of the machine. Although these two paragraphs are
compulsory in standard COBOL, it is proposed to make them optional.
The optional Special-Names paragraph can be used to detect the status
of certain switches on the computer; to name a code set so that files
can be read or written in a code other than the one native to the
computer; to declare a substitute for the standard $ currency sign (this
is not necessary when the $ sign is replaced in the printer's character
set); or to declare that continental Europe conventions for decimal point
and comma are to be followed.
Most installations have a set of standard entries for this section,
which can simply be copied out for each program.
The Input-Output Section has two paragraphs, a simple definition of
which is:

```
    INPUT-OUTPUT SECTION.
    FILE-CONTROL.    {SELECT file-name ASSIGN TO device-name
                     [RESERVE integer AREAS] } ...

   [I-O-CONTROL.     SAME   RECORD   AREA   FOR   file-name-1
```

file-name-2⌉

The File-Control paragraph is used to link the file you have defined in a FD statement in the File Section to a particular peripheral device. The device-name used varies with the machine. Suppose you are using a machine that allows device-names of VDU and PRINTER; you could code

```
FILE-CONTROL.
     SELECT VDU-FILE ASSIGN TO VDU.
     SELECT REPORT-FILE ASSIGN TO PRINTER.
```

On some machines the device is not explicitly named, but instead the file is assigned to a symbolic name. This symbolic name is then linked to a physical device by means of commands issued to the operating system of the computer.

Each file has a certain amount of memory allocated to it which is used to hold the block of data currently being processed. This memory is called a buffer. Normally only one buffer is allocated to the file concerned. If RESERVE 2 AREAS is specified, two buffers are allotted to the file, a block being read into the second buffer while the first is being processed. This can speed up execution of the program in certain cases, although in other cases it might slow things down. The computer manufacturer's reference manual should be consulted for precise details of the effect of this clause on the computer you are using.

There is no exercise for this frame. Now study the specification of the example program and code it from your own flowchart.

J3   EXAMPLE PROGRAM SPECIFICATION

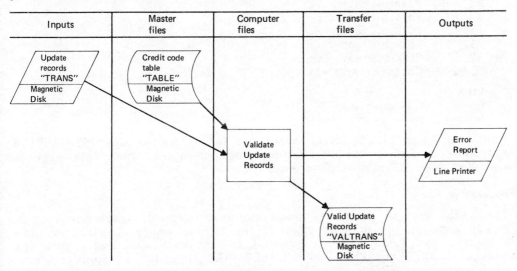

Fig. 23: Example program - computer run diagram

Inputs

TRANS has records as follows.

| 1 | Update code, 1 alphabetic. |
| 2–6 | Customer number, 5 digits. |

7	Credit code, 1 alphabetic.
8–16	Debit balance, 8 digits including 2 decimals, separate leading sign.
17–46	Customer name, 30 characters.
47–136	Customer address, 3 lines of 30 characters.

TABLE has records as follows.

1	Credit code, 1 alphabetic.
2–8	Credit limit, 7 digits.

Outputs

VALTRANS has the same record layout as TRANS.

ERROR REPORT has a layout consisting of a succession of groups of lines as follows.

Line 1

2	Update code
4–8	Customer number
10	Credit code
11	Left bracket
12–20	Credit limit, zero suppressed, comma inserted
21	Right bracket
23–32	Debit balance, unedited
34–63	Customer name
65–94	Customer address line 1
96–	Message "INPUT ERROR"

Line 2

2	Possible asterisk
4	Possible asterisk
10	Possible asterisk
23	Possible asterisk
34	Possible asterisk
65–94	Customer address line 2

Line 3

65–94	Customer address line 3

followed by a blank line.

The first page of the error report is to be headed up "TRANSACTION VALIDATION – ERROR REPORT" followed by one blank line. This page is to appear even if there are no errors.

Processing

The TABLE file is to be read and stored in memory. There are 1 to 26 records meant to be on this file. If the file is empty, or if more than 26 records are found, the program is to terminate abnormally with the message "TABLE FILE EMPTY" or "TABLE FILE INVALID" as appropriate.

Each record on TRANS is to be validated and the valid records written onto VALTRANS. If any field on TRANS is invalid, the record is invalid and is to be written on the error report as a group of lines. Line 2 of the group is to contain an asterisk under each field in error. The validation checks are as follows.

Update code must be "I", "A" or "D" (meaning Insert, Amend or Delete).

Customer number must be 5 digits.

Credit code must be equal to a credit code in the TABLE file.

Debit balance must be all spaces, or a sign followed by eight digits.

Debit balance must be blank or +zero if update code is "A".

Customer name must not be blank.

Contrary to the rules above, when the update code is "D" all fields other than customer number must be blank. When the update code is "A", any field other than customer number may be blank.

When details of an invalid record are being printed, if credit–code is valid and non–blank, the corresponding credit limit is to be printed out. Otherwise, the credit limit field is left blank on the report.

After the last invalid record reported, or at the outset of the report if there are no invalid records, is to appear the message:

VALID RECORDS: INSERTS ZZZ9 AMENDMENTS ZZZ9 DELETIONS ZZZ9
TOTAL VALIDS ZZZ9 TOTAL DEBIT BALANCE OF VALIDS –Z,ZZZ,ZZ9.99
INVALID RECORDS: INSERTS ZZZ9 AMENDMENTS ZZZ9 DELETIONS ZZZ9
TOTAL INVALIDS ZZZZ9

Neither this message nor an error group is to be split over a page – start a new page if necessary to ensure this.

You would be wise to reinforce your knowledge of Sections A to J by further practical exercise before proceeding to Part 2. A selection of practical exercises is included in Appendix B. The first five exercises can be completed using only the facilities learned so far.

J4 PROGRAM DEBUGGING

It will be most remarkable if any of the programs you write for practical exercise work properly first time, so you will be facing the task of program debugging, i.e. diagnosing program faults and fixing them. The following notes (based on research by J. Chan) may help you methodically to diagnose execution–time errors.

1   Study result listing (if any). Get a clear view of the symptom, i.e. precisely what is the difference between what you have got and what you hoped for.

2   Study the operating system messages for possible clues, e.g. abnormal termination, warning messages, excessive processor or input–output time.

3   Check input data file(s) for format, blocking factor and contents to see if they match the declared format in the program and have the content you intended.

4   Make a list of hypotheses as to what might be wrong with the program. A hypothesis is any explanation of the error which is capable of being proved or disproved.

5   For each hypothesis, starting with the likeliest ones or the ones easiest to test, check the part(s) of the program (or its data or operating instructions, etc.) relevant to the hypothesis made.

6   When testing hypotheses, the following approaches may be made.

(a) Forward Approach. Based on the hypothesis made, make a

step-by-step forward trace of a specific routine or branch where the
fault is suspected. Tracing here means pretending you are the
computer following the instructions.
(b) Backward Approach. Based on the hypothesis made, make a
step-by-step backward trace of statements in the specific subroutine
or branch of the program, starting at the place which is thought to
give rise to the error.

7   When a fault is located, check that it explains the symptom.

Remember, if the bug is not where you are looking, you must look
somewhere else.

To do a trace, write down the paragraph names as you execute them,
together with the values of variables of interest. When a paragraph is
PERFORMed, indent the subroutine paragraph-names until the subroutine
is concluded.   To illustrate with the following complicated example
(please do not write programs like this!):

```
P1.   MOVE ZERO TO COUNT.
      PERFORM P2 THRU P5.
P2.   PERFORM P3.
P3.   ADD 1 TO COUNT.
      IF COUNT = 5 MOVE ZERO TO COUNT.
P4.   ADD 3 TO COUNT.
P5.   DISPLAY COUNT.
P6.   ...what is the value of COUNT?
```

The trace is as follows.

```
P1    COUNT=0
P2
          P3   COUNT=1
      P3   COUNT=2
      P4   COUNT=5
      P5
P2
          P3   COUNT=6
      P3   COUNT=7
      P4   COUNT=10
      P5
      P6   COUNT=10
```

ANSWERS – SECTION J

Frame J1

```
1     IDENTIFICATION DIVISION.
      PROGRAM-ID. ISITOK.
      *
      *AUTHOR. yourname.
      *INSTALLATION. CENTRAL COMPUTER SERVICES.
      *DATE-WRITTEN. today's date.
      *
      *SUMMARY
      *    INPUT    -ANY FILE OF 80-CHARACTER RECORDS
      *    OUTPUT   -LISTING OF SEQUENCED FILE
```

```
*    PROCESSING
*            -THE FILE IS INPUT, SORTED INTO ORDER ON
*            CHARS.1 TO 6 (ASCENDING), AND PRINTED.
```

Part 2
Programming Techniques

K Structured programming constructs

K1 WRITING LARGE PROGRAMS

In Part 1 of this text, I concentrated on the rules of the COBOL language and how these are applied in writing small programs. The next two sections have nothing to do with the 'rules' of COBOL, but are concerned with recommended practices which will allow the programmer to write large programs well.

If the student has not discovered this already, he will soon appreciate that learning and applying the rules of COBOL is the easy part of programming. The difference between good and bad programmers has little to do with how well they know the intricacies of the language, but has more to do with how they design, document and test their programs, and how well they understand the assignments they are given.

This distinction often has little meaning to the student. This is because the programming problems he is set as exercises are usually short; perhaps only 30 or 40 COBOL statements and rarely more than 100. The problems of designing, documenting and testing such programs are quite small. The whole program listing will probably fit onto two pages of listing paper, the paragraphs and data used in the program can be readily located and there are probably only a few different paths of the program to be tested.

By contrast, COBOL programs written for applications in the real world are often rather large. A medium sized program may be measured in hundreds of statements, while a large one may contain thousands of statements. With programs of this size, the problems of design, documentation and testing are of a different order of magnitude. Indeed, as will be seen shortly, a major approach to dealing with these problems is to break the program down into smaller units which are of manageable size.

These smaller units may themselves be programs which have been separately compiled and tested, and then linked together as described in Section U, or they may be portions of a single compilation. The latter style will be assumed for the time being, but with experience and good facilities for program linkage, the former may be preferable.

The methods proposed in this Part are by no means universally adopted or understood. Many commercial programming departments develop their own methods and internal rules (programming standards). However, the methods and standards proposed in this book represent a workable and practical approach to writing large programs which will fit the student to adapt readily to other standards he may encounter.

The next section, Section L, is probably the most difficult in the book. This section, which prepares for Section L, is not simple either. Hopefully the organisation of the material will hasten your understanding of the topics, but you should realise that many programmers have taken years to fully learn them. You should not expect to master these sections without considerable effort. If you do take the pains these sections call for, I am sure that in the long run you will consider this to have been worthwhile.

The examples used in this section are those of frame J3 and the Population Explosion problem of Appendix B (the first exercise). It will help greatly if you have implemented these as part of your study of Part 1; failing this, you are advised to study the specifications and consider your method of solution before proceeding.

Exercise

1 Place these programming objectives in the order you think they are most important in a commercial programming department.

  (a) Minimising execution time and memory requirements.
  (b) Minimising the amount of pencils and coding sheets used.
  (c) Getting the results correct.
  (d) Minimising the total effort spent on developing and testing the program to productive status.
  (e) Minimising the total time spent on coding the program.
  (f) Enabling someone else to understand your program so that he can
      1   help you with a problem of logic,
      2   take over if you leave or are absent,
      3   amend the program after it is in production, to cater for an undiscovered fault or new requirements.

K2 DESIGN FOR TESTING

Since the most important objective in programming is to get the results correct, the program should be designed so that testing and proving it can be achieved without too much effort. As it happens, programs that are designed with testing in mind can also take less time to develop to productive status and can be more maintainable, thereby satisfying other important programming objectives.

A remarkable trait shared by many programmers is their optimism. They write their programs as if they were going to be right first time. In practice, it is a very rare event that a program of any size is written correctly at first attempt. I have seen experienced programmers code a large program in a matter of days and then spend weeks or even months trying to eliminate all the errors of logic. If they had spent a little more time on program design, their programs would have gone forward for compilation a day or so later, but this delay would have been compensated for many times over by reduction of the time needed for fault-finding and testing.

This also serves to encourage you to adopt a defensive attitude to programming. With such an attitude, programs are written in the expectation (which will almost certainly prove correct) that they will not work first time, and that much time and effort may be spent on finding errors.

As an example of how such an attitude can assist, consider the following. Possibly the most common error in programming, and certainly one of the hardest to find, occurs when intermediate data being used or manipulated by the program is incorrect or has been accidentally corrupted. Such errors are hard to spot because the data is 'invisible' when you have only the listing and the wrong results in front of you.

What usually happens is that at certain key points in a program, an assumption is made about the value of an intermediate result, e.g. a flag, a total or a subscript. These crucial assumptions are usually recognised by the programmer and are often asserted in a comment, e.g.

```
        * THE SUBSCRIPT NOW POINTS TO THE LAST CHARACTER OF
        * CUSTOMER NAME
or
        * THE FLAG IS ALWAYS SET TO ZERO ON FIRST ENTRY TO THIS
        * ROUTINE
```

This is very proper. However, as things stand, the only way of testing the truth of these assumptions is by mentally tracing through all the detailed logic of the program. This can be a demanding task to do without a slip, especially if one is being misled by one's own comment statements. Much better would be to incorporate DISPLAY statements (or debug line statements – see frame Q2) in the program at points such as these, when the program is first coded, to print out the important variables so that the assertions are tested. In other words, expect the worst. After a test execution, if all is well, the DISPLAY statements can be removed (or the debug line statements turned off).

Exercise

1   When DISPLAY is being used in the manner suggested, would you make the display device the computer operator's console or the line printer? What steps could you take to avoid a mountain of print–out resulting from the tests?

K3   CONTROL STRUCTURES

The problem of writing the Procedure Division of a COBOL program is one of defining the basic operations to be undertaken (ADD, MOVE, etc.) and the branches and repetitions which will ensure that these operations are undertaken in the desired sequence. Once the syntax and semantics of the programming language have been mastered, the difficulty in programming is mainly in exercising the branching and repeating control over basic operations. The philosophy behind structured programming is to limit control structures to three standard types which are believed to be less error prone than others. The three structures are illustrated in Fig. 24.

To be sure, an even better practice is to do away with control structures altogether by using high level verbs or very high level languages, in which the programmer just declares what he wants and does not have to worry about the mechanics of achieving it. STRING and UNSTRING (Section G) are examples of high level verbs. Other examples are given in Part 3. The COBOL Report Writer (Section S) has features typical of declarative languages. High level facilities should be used wherever possible. However, these facilities are not always available and often do not quite match the problem.

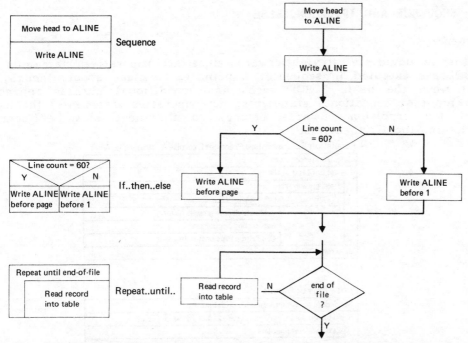

Fig. 24: The three control structures of structured programming. On the left are the structure diagrams, on the right the equivalent flowchart symbols.

Any program can be written using only the three control structures of Fig. 24. If we can resolve the problem using only these control structures, and we know how to give effect to the control structures in COBOL, we have a methodology of program design. The next section deals with how to resolve the problem into structured constructs. This section considers how to give effect to the three structures in COBOL. (This may seem to be the wrong way round, but I think you will have better insight into the next section if you know beforehand precisely where it is leading.)

If structure charts, as opposed to flowcharts, are used, there is no danger of violating the limited control structures allowed. The structure diagrams may be embedded in one another as in Fig. 25. Study this figure before continuing with the text.

It is a moot point whether 'calculate decade growth factor' and 'set starting population' belong where they are or at the start of 'Print a page of results'. Equally, 'set decade to current year + 10...' could be shifted into the main diagram; indeed, the whole of 'Print a page of results' could be shifted into the inner block of the main diagram. All these variants are logically equivalent; which is preferred is discussed at the end of the next frame.

K4   SEQUENCE AND IF..THEN..ELSE

Sequence

This is obviously straightforward since all imperative statements in COBOL are executed in sequence. A point to be clear about, though, is that when the basic COBOL verbs have conditional phrases appended (making them conditional statements, not imperative statements) the logic from the condition onwards belongs to the next class of control structure, the if..then..else.

Population Explosion (see Practical Exercise 1, Appendix A)

Calculate surface area		
Repeat until end of file		
	Read growth rate	
	Y End of file? N	
		Calculate decade growth factor
		Set starting population
		Do: Print a Page of Results
Stop run		

Print a Page of Results

Set decade to current year +10, print headings			
Repeat until decade = current year +210 or size error occurs			
	Calculate new population		
	Y Size error? N		
	Print the error message	Calculate new density	
		Y Size error? N	
		Print the error message	Print a line of results
	Add 10 to decade		

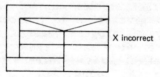 X incorrect

Fig. 25: Illustrating how the three structure diagrams may be placed inside each other, or kept separately as subroutines. Each rectangular diagram must be substituted wholly for a rectangle in another diagram, or must be entirely separate; the inset at foot shows an example that is not allowed.

The conditional variants of the basic verbs covered in Part 1 are:

    arithmetic verbs with SIZE ERROR clause
    READ with AT END clause
    WRITE with AT END-OF-PAGE clause.

If..then..else

A COBOL IF..ELSE sentence corresponds exactly to the if..then..else structure. If there is nothing to be done on the 'false' leg, the ELSE part of the sentence is omitted. If there is nothing to be done on the 'true' leg, the NEXT SENTENCE phrase can be deployed; e.g. IF LINECOUNT LESS THAN 60 NEXT SENTENCE ELSE PERFORM NEWPAGE.

The conditional variants of the basic verbs also correspond to an if..then structure but unfortunately in standard COBOL they have no 'false' leg. ELSE in standard COBOL matches only IF. (Some non-standard compilers match ELSE to any condition, e.g. READ .. AT END .. ELSE... It is now proposed that COBOL should provide else legs for SIZE ERROR etc. by allowing a NOT clause after the condition, e.g. ADD .. ON SIZE ERROR .. NOT SIZE ERROR ...) The present standard version of the language leaves a problem when there is something to be done, as there often is, on the 'false' leg of a basic verb.

A plain solution for use with simple cases (i.e. when the basic verb is not itself subordinate to a condition) involves setting a 'flag' data item to signal the outcome of the conditional phrase in the basic verb. This flag can then be tested using an IF sentence, effectively giving a 'false' leg to the condition. For example (using T for True and F for False):

```
            MOVE "F" TO SE-FLAG.
            COMPUTE POP ROUNDED = POP * GROWTH-FACTOR
            ON SIZE ERROR
                  MOVE "T" TO SE-FLAG.
            IF SE-FLAG = "T"
                  WRITE ALINE FROM ERROR-MESSAGE AFTER 2
            ELSE
                  :
                  :
```

This next example, illustrating a point from the program specified in frame J3, shows a way of dealing with an if..then..else embedded in an end-of-file if..then..else.

```
            MOVE "F" TO EOF-FLAG.
            READ TABLE-RECORD
            AT END
                  MOVE "T" TO EOF-FLAG.
            IF EOF-FLAG = "F"
                  IF TABLESUB LESS THAN 26
                        ADD 1 TO TABLESUB
                        MOVE TABLEREC TO W-S-TABLEREC(TABLESUB)
                  ELSE
                        DISPLAY "TABLE FILE INVALID"
                        STOP RUN.
```

If you are not perfectly happy about this example, draw the structure diagram for it and satisfy yourself about the precise meaning.

When the basic verb with the conditional clause itself appears in a conditional sentence, we have an embedded condition in which the subordinate condition has no 'false' leg available. Since the full stop terminates the scope of ALL the conditions, we cannot get out of this quite as simply as before. Consider, for the continuation of the first example above, working from the structure diagram of Fig. 25:

```
            :
            IF SE-FLAG = "T"
                  WRITE ALINE FROM ERROR-MESSAGE AFTER 2
            ELSE
                  COMPUTE DENSITY ROUNDED = POP / SURFACE-AREA
                  ON SIZE ERROR
                        MOVE "T" TO SE-FLAG.
```

```
          IF SE-FLAG = "T"
              WRITE ALINE FROM ERROR-MESSAGE AFTER 2
          ELSE
              MOVE...(prepare detail line)
              WRITE ALINE FROM DETAIL-LINE AFTER 2.
          :
```

The problem here is that the second IF sentence is executed even if the first IF condition is true, **contrary** to the structure diagram. The consequence in this example is that the error message is printed twice when POP overflows.

Although it is a general solution to this problem to remove all duplicate use of flags (e.g. by defining POP-SE-FLAG, DENSITY-SE-FLAG) and to retest all the conditions in the second sentence, e.g.

```
          :
          IF POP-SE-FLAG = "T"
              NEXT SENTENCE
          ELSE
              IF DENSITY-SE-FLAG = "T"
                  WRITE ALINE FROM ERROR-MESSAGE AFTER 2
              ELSE
                  MOVE...
                  WRITE ALINE FROM DETAIL-LINE AFTER 2.
          :
```

this gets rather tiresome. The difficulty is that the conditions being retested always give rise to a NEXT SENTENCE on the true leg, since their aim is to skip over all the code on the original false leg. Although the code could be reduced by eliminating the NEXT SENTENCEs as a result of negating the conditions, this solution is still a rather roundabout one.

There are two further general solutions, (a) the forward GO TO and (b) putting the conditional statement out-of-line.

In the forward GO TO approach, the common activity at completion of the conditional actions must be identified and labelled. In Fig. 25, this is the action 'add 10 to decade' – let us label this ADD-TEN. Now the retesting of conditions in the example can be avoided by GOing TO the label at the end of the nest of conditions, i.e.

```
          :
          MOVE "F" TO SE-FLAG.
          COMPUTE POP ROUNDED = POP * GROWTH-FACTOR
          ON SIZE ERROR
              MOVE "T" TO SE-FLAG.
          IF SE-FLAG = "T"
              WRITE ALINE FROM ERROR-MESSAGE AFTER 2
              GO TO ADD-TEN.
          COMPUTE DENSITY ROUNDED = POP / SURFACE-AREA
          ON SIZE ERROR
              MOVE "T" TO SE-FLAG.
          IF SE-FLAG = "T"
              WRITE ALINE FROM ERROR-MESSAGE AFTER 2
              GO TO ADD-TEN.
          MOVE...
          WRITE ALINE FROM DETAIL-LINE AFTER 2.
      ADD-TEN.
```

```
        ADD 10 TO DECADE.
            :
```

In both of the IF sentences here, an ELSE could replace the terminal full stop without changing the logic. However, because the GO TOs are branching forward to the next paragraph, everything after the GO TO and before the next paragraph must be contained on the 'false' leg, so the ELSE is redundant.

The forward GO TO has introduced an opportunity to clean up this code. Since the ELSE has been made redundant, we no longer have to contrive an IF sentence that gives us an ELSE. Other things being equal, we can do away with everything to do with flags and recode the example:

```
            :
        COMPUTE POP ROUNDED = POP * GROWTH-FACTOR
        ON SIZE ERROR
            WRITE ALINE FROM ERROR-MESSAGE AFTER 2
            GO TO ADD-TEN.
        COMPUTE DENSITY ROUNDED = POP / SURFACE-AREA
        ON SIZE ERROR
            WRITE ALINE FROM ERROR MESSAGE AFTER 2
            GO TO ADD-TEN.
        MOVE ...
        WRITE ALINE FROM DETAIL-LINE AFTER 2.
    ADD-TEN.
        ADD 10 TO DECADE.
            :
```

Other things are not actually equal in the example of Fig. 25 since the size error flag is needed to signal termination of the repetition. There is still a need to set a flag when a size error occurs; this can be done in the SIZE ERROR legs above.

If there is no common activity at completion of the conditions, a dummy paragraph containing the EXIT verb must be supplied, to be the destination of the forward GO TO. Since this case arises only when the conditions are part of a block which is being repeated (or which for some other convenience is being performed as a subroutine), an example is deferred to the next frame, which deals with repetitions.

The alternative general solution involved putting the subordinate conditional statement out-of-line. Going back to the original example, this solution is

```
            :
        MOVE "F" TO SE-FLAG.
        COMPUTE POP ROUNDED = POP * GROWTH-FACTOR
        ON SIZE ERROR
            MOVE "T" TO SE-FLAG.
        IF SE-FLAG = "T"
            WRITE ALINE FROM ERROR-MESSAGE AFTER 2
        ELSE
            PERFORM CALC-DENSITY.
        ADD 10 TO DECADE.
            :
    CALC-DENSITY.
        COMPUTE DENSITY ROUNDED = POP / SURFACE-AREA
        ON SIZE ERROR
```

```
            MOVE "T" TO SE-FLAG.
      IF SE-FLAG = "T"
            WRITE ALINE FROM ERROR-MESSAGE AFTER 2
      ELSE
            MOVE ...
            WRITE ALINE FROM DETAIL-LINE AFTER 2.
      :
```

The use of a separately-compiled program (see Section U) to perform the functions of the subroutine (CALC-DENSITY) is a special case of this general solution. A separately-compiled program might be used where facilities were good for program linkage, where the function of the subroutine was perfectly plain and clear, perhaps with some opportunity to re-use it with other programs, and where it made sense to test the program as a separate entity. The last three criteria hardly support making CALC-DENSITY into a separate program.

Whether the GO TO or the out-of-line subroutine solution is to be preferred is a matter of the facts of the particular case. Broadly, the strength of structured programming lies in the way it reduces the span of attention needed to comprehend a program. The span of attention possible is in turn dependent on human short-term memory capacity – this varies somewhat from one person to another. The programmer should aim to make easy the span of attention needed to comprehend his program, both for himself and for any future reader.

Span of attention is reduced in structured programming by permitting independent consideration of the blocks. In Fig. 25, for example, 'Print a page of results' can be considered independently of 'Population explosion' provided one appreciates that the growth factor and starting population have been initialised. These two variables can be thought of as parameters or arguments which communicate between the main program and the subroutine. If many such parameters (say, more than three) have to be passed mentally in order to understand the program, span of attention is being stretched. This indicates a need to look for a simplification. In Fig. 25, if 'calculate decade growth factor' and 'set starting population' are shifted out of the main program into the subroutine, only the growth rate need be communicated as a parameter. Since this reduces the number of parameters (from 2 to 1) this is a preferred solution.

There is an important qualification that must be made to the idea of independent consideration. A block can be independently considered only if the meaning of each operation in the block is perfectly clear. When one of the operations is to perform a subroutine, the precision of meaning depends in part on the choice of words used to describe the subroutine – the subroutine name. This is within the control of the programmer. He should take care to call a subroutine by a name which describes its purpose accurately. If he cannot think up a suitably precise name, this may be a warning that the subroutine has an inappropriate scope.

The basic operations done by COBOL verbs may be considered perfectly clear, since they are defined in the COBOL language manual. An equivalent precision is rarely achieved with subroutine operations even when care is taken with the name. For example, we have already seen two different interpretations of the subroutine 'Print a page of results' – the interpretation of Fig. 25 and the adjusted interpretation above. A perfect comprehension of someone else's program is achieved only by understanding it in terms of basic operations. Although the author of it may understand perfectly the main program of Fig. 25, the reader must also take in the subroutine. The need to take in the subroutine increases the span of attention called for, and tends to defeat the idea of independent consideration. Except in the case of a subroutine whose purpose is very well understood (because, for example, it is a standard or very familiar subroutine or it performs a function, such as a mathematical function, which is widely recognised) it should be a programming objective to limit the depth of nesting of subroutines.

The point of this discourse is to argue that the forward GO TO solution is the preferred one in the case in question. But there may be cases, when the subroutine function is better defined or when the destination of the GO TO is excessively distant and therefore stretches attention, where the subroutine solution is better.

Exercise

1   Many programmers like to include a fourth construct in their structured program design, the 'case' construct (also called 'selection'). In principle, this is a list of actions to be taken according to the value of some variable; an example is given in Fig. 26.

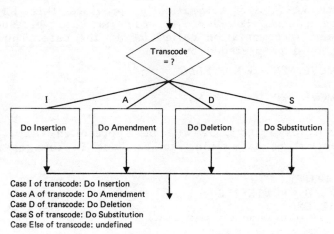

Fig. 26: Frame K4. Exercise 1. The case construction.

This construct can be represented by another structured programming construct - how?

2   What alternative ways can you see for implementing a case construct in COBOL (a) when the case variable is alphanumeric, (b) when the case variable is an integer in the range 1 to n where n is the number of cases? Which alternative is best?

K5   REPEAT..UNTIL

This construct will be taken, in this text, to be exactly equivalent to the COBOL verb PERFORM..UNTIL (and in suitable cases its variant PERFORM..VARYING..FROM..BY..UNTIL). The repetition blocks in Fig. 25

can be expressed respectively

    PERFORM READ-GROWTH-ETC UNTIL EOF-FLAG = "T"

and

    PERFORM CALC-POP-AND-PRINT VARYING DECADE FROM
    current-year+10 BY 10 UNTIL DECADE = current-year+210
    OR SE-FLAG = "T".

Although the test for equality to 'current year + 210' is evidently thoughtful, a test for 'not less than 200' would require smaller span of attention since it refers to data in the problem. The 'not less than' style, though, should not be used if it results from sloppy thinking about the terminating condition.

The logic behind any iteration should be thought of in these steps:

1   Establish initial conditions

2   Make the test for completion

3   Do the operation

4   Increment the control variables if called for

5   Repeat from step 2.

The PERFORM..VARYING.. automatically provides this logic and is therefore recommended. However, it may fail to provide all the initialisation and incrementation called for in the case. Thus the above two examples should be preceded by

    MOVE "F" TO EOF-FLAG

and

    MOVE "F" TO SE-FLAG

respectively.

Referring again to Fig. 25, it will be appreciated that when end of file is reached, there is nothing to be done in the repeated block. Thus:

    READ-GROWTH-ETC.
        READ GROWTHFILE
        AT END
            MOVE "T" TO EOF-FLAG.
        IF EOF-FLAG = "F"
            COMPUTE GROWTH-FACTOR ROUNDED = ...
            MOVE 4000000000 TO POP
            PERFORM PRINT-A-PAGE-OF-RESULTS.

The complication here will arise if a size error clause is added to the COMPUTE statement, as was recommended in frame C3. Of course, this complication would be removed if the meaning of 'Print a page of results' were enlarged as discussed in the last frame — but let us stick with the above version for the sake of example.

There is no instruction to label for a forward GO TO, so an EXIT paragraph must be added, as discussed in frame D5. This leads to a need to use the PERFORM..THRU variant; to avoid this, a repeated block can be made into a SECTION. When a SECTION is PERFORMed, all the paragraphs through to the last in the section are executed; control returns after execution of the last paragraph, just as with a PERFORM..THRU which nominated the first and last paragraphs in the section.

The inner block of our example could now be completed:

```
        READ-GROWTH-ETC SECTION.
        RG.
            READ GROWTHFILE
            AT END
                MOVE "T" TO EOF-FLAG
                GO TO RG-EXIT.
            COMPUTE GROWTH-FACTOR ROUNDED = ....
            ON SIZE ERROR
                DISPLAY "PROGRAM ERROR IN RG - ABORTED"
                STOP RUN.
            MOVE 4000000000 TO POP.
            PERFORM PRINT-A-PAGE-OF-RESULTS.
        RG-EXIT.
            EXIT.
```

The use of STOP RUN in an out-of-line paragraph, as here, should be confined to terminations considered 'abnormal'.

It is often the case in commercial programming that a special action is required if an input file is empty. This has the effect of distinguishing the first READ instruction from the others. (That is, if end of file is discovered on the first READ, take the special action. Otherwise, process the record. When end of file is discovered on a subsequent READ, take the normal end-of-file action.)

This case is handled by issuing the first READ instruction in-line and putting subsequent READs in an iterated block. Since a record will have been read on entry to the subroutine, the subroutine logic must first process the record just input, then read the next record. It is a happy circumstance that this eliminates the forward GO TO associated with end of file in the subroutine (and therefore the need for an EXIT paragraph and therefore the justification for a SECTION). Consider for example the population explosion with the new requirement that a message is to be sent to the operator if the input file is empty. (This example also illustrates the adjusted meaning of 'Print a page of results'.)

```
        PROCEDURE DIVISION.
        MAIN SECTION.
        M1.
            OPEN INPUT GROWTHFILE.
            MOVE "F" TO EOF-FLAG.
            READ GROWTHFILE
            AT END
                MOVE "T" TO EOF-FLAG.
            IF EOF-FLAG = "T"
                DISPLAY "EMPTY GROWTHFILE - ABORTING"
            ELSE
                OPEN OUTPUT PRINTFILE
                PERFORM PROCESS-GROWTHRATE UNTIL EOF-FLAG = "T"
                CLOSE PRINTFILE.
            CLOSE GROWTHFILE.
            STOP RUN.
        PROCESS-GROWTHRATE.
            PERFORM PRINT-A-PAGE-OF-RESULTS.
            READ GROWTHFILE
            AT END
                MOVE "T" TO EOF-FLAG.
```

```
PRINT-A-PAGE-OF-RESULTS.
    COMPUTE GROWTH-FACTOR ROUNDED = ....
    ON SIZE ERROR
        DISPLAY ....
        STOP RUN.
    MOVE 4000000000 TO POP.
    :  ) print
    :  ) headings
    MOVE "F" TO SE-FLAG.
    PERFORM CALC-POP-AND-PRINT VARYING DECADE FROM ....
    BY 10 UNTIL DECADE = .... OR SE-FLAG = "T".
CALC-POP-AND-PRINT SECTION.
    :
```

The initialisation of GROWTH-FACTOR and POP has been placed to conform with the discussion to date. The only amendment I would now make would be to move these down after the printing of the headings, to conform with the good general principle that variables used as parameters should be initialised as close as possible to the point where the subroutine is invoked. Although this change alters the logic slightly when a size error occurs, it is assumed that this particular size error results in an abnormal termination and the status of the headings in this case (i.e. whether they are to be printed or not) is undefined.

Exercise

1   Fig. 27 illustrates another construction advanced as desirable for structured programming, the do-once-then-repeat..until. Give two ways in which this can be achieved using only the basic constructs.

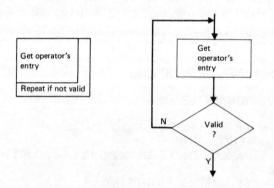

Fig. 27: Frame K4, Exercise 1

(In other texts, the PERFORM..UNTIL   is known as do..while or while..do. This does not fit COBOL very well since either the while or the UNTIL condition requires negation to be implemented, and this increases attention span. In some quarters, repeat..until is taken to mean the construct of Fig. 27; in others, this is known as a do..until or a do–while–do.

This is an unhappy state of affairs. Which verb (repeat, do, etc.) is used is not really important. A sensible rule would be that if the condition is mentioned first (until condition do.., while not condition repeat..) then the test is intended to be first; and if the condition is mentioned last (do..until condition, etc.) then the test is intended to be last. But this idea is not widespread and in this text any mention of 'until' will imply 'test first', COBOL–fashion.)

2   Some very small compilers do not support the UNTIL variant of the PERFORM verb. On most computers, the PERFORM uses quite a lot more computer time than GO TO and, in rare cases where a program has a very tight loop executed many thousands of times, it may be desirable to tune by using GO TO instead of PERFORM. In general, how would you code a program if you had to use GO TO in place of PERFORM?

3   Write the code to read and store the TABLE file of frame J3, following the guidelines of this section.

4   Structured programming is sometimes equated with GO TO–less programming. This is not quite the viewpoint of this section, but there are restrictions on the scope of GO TOs if the guidelines here are followed. Can you identify them?

ANSWERS - SECTION K

Frame K1

1   Most people readily agree that (c) is most important and that (b) is least important; and that (d) is more important than (e). My argument on objective (f) is that if the things listed cannot be done, objectives (c) and (d) will tend to be defeated. So I place it second most important.

That leaves the relative merits of (a) and (d) to be discussed. The costs of developing a program are large enough to make (d) more important if (a) is not a pressing need. With that proviso, my list: (c) (f) (d) (a) (e) (b).

Frame K2

1   The line printer. If the display device is the programmer's VDU, there is a greater chance in most installations that the display will not be checked as thoroughly as it would have been had it appeared on hard copy.

The operator's console should be used only for very small quantities of data, and then only for data that the operator might be expected to act upon or to record. If the displayed variable is in a loop, a very large quantity of print–out might result; you might instruct the operator or the operating system to terminate the program after so many pages or seconds. You could also make the DISPLAY conditional on a counter.

Frame K4

1   See Fig. 28 overleaf.This is obviously not so satisfactory when the number of cases is large.

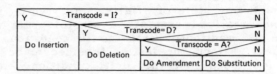

Fig. 28: Answer to Exercise 1, frame K4

2   (a) (i) IF TRANSCODE = "I"
                   PERFORM INSERTION
               ELSE
                   IF TRANSCODE ="D"
                       PERFORM DELETION
                   ELSE
                       IF TRANSCODE ="A"
                           PERFORM AMENDMENT
                       ELSE
                           PERFORM SUBSTITUTION.
        (ii) IF TRANSCODE = "I"
                 PERFORM INSERTION.
             IF TRANSCODE = "D"
                 PERFORM DELETION.
             IF TRANSCODE = "A"
                 PERFORM AMENDMENT.
             IF TRANSCODE = "S"
                 PERFORM SUBSTITUTION.
     (b)   GO TO 1 2 N DEPENDING ON CASE.
         1.   PERFORM PROCESS-1.
               GO TO COLLECTOR.
         2.   PERFORM PROCESS-2.
               GO TO COLLECTOR.
         N.   PERFORM PROCESS-N.
         COLLECTOR.

Answer (a)(ii) is very plain, and attractive when efficiency is not
a consideration. The efficiency of (a)(ii) can be increased by
adding a forward GO TO to a collecting paragraph, and sequencing
the sentences in the order of likelihood of being used. If the other
methods are used, an explanatory comment is called for.
  There is of course a subtle difference in the logic of (a)(i) and
(a)(ii) above (what?); I have assumed this difference is not
important.

Frame K5

1

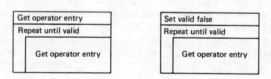

Fig. 29: Answer to Exercise 1, frame K5

2   I would design the program using structured constructs (as if PERFORM..UNTIL were available). Wherever a PERFORM..UNTIL would appear, I would put in a plain PERFORM in a little loop corresponding to the five step iteration.

    If further tuning is desired, the statements in the performed paragraph can be substituted for the plain PERFORM. This may entail introducing a collector paragraph and another for a forward GO TO to get out of the iteration. Since there is considerable loss of clarity with this tuning, the golden rule is: do not tune unless essential to do so, and then put in the PERFORM..UNTIL as a comment.

3
```
    OPEN INPUT TABLE
    READ TABLE
    AT END
        DISPLAY "TABLE FILE EMPTY"
        STOP RUN.
    MOVE "F" TO EOF-TABLE.
    PERFORM PROCESS-TABLEREC VARYING TABLESUB FROM 1 BY 1
    UNTIL TABLESUB GREATER THAN 26 OR EOF-TABLE = "T".
    CLOSE TABLE
    IF EOF-TABLE NOT = "T"
        DISPLAY "TABLE FILE INVALID"
        STOP RUN.
    :
PROCESS-TABLEREC.
    MOVE TABLEREC TO W-S-TABLEREC(TABLESUB).
    READ TABLE
    AT END
        MOVE "T" TO EOF-TABLE.
```

4   Forward GO TOs are always to some common collector. You never find forward GO TOs leap-frogging over one another. A backward GO TO, if used at all, will either be contained completely inside or completely outside the range of any other backward GO TO (or performed block).

L Structured program design

L1 RECOGNISING DATA STRUCTURES

The previous section dealt with translating structured programming constructs into COBOL code. This section deals with translating the problem into structured programming constructs.

M. Jackson in his book *Principles of Program Design* (Academic Press, 1975) highlighted the relationship between data structures and program structures. In order to decide on the program structure, the programmer must first comprehend the data structures involved in the program. The data structures referred to are usually the input and output files, although in rarer cases an internal table needs to be analysed.

The method explained in this section is therefore:

1   analyse the data in the problem
2   produce a **data** structure diagram from this analysis
3   produce a **program** structure of the type described in section K
4   produce the COBOL program.

In commercial programs, the data structures can often be represented simply by a hierarchy of three elementary constructs: sequence, selection and repetition. Jackson's diagramming blocks for these three structures are illustrated in Fig. 30.

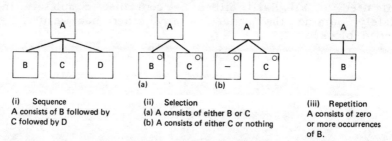

(i)   Sequence
A consists of B followed by
C folowed by D

(ii)   Selection
(a) A consists of either B or C
(b) A consists of either C or nothing

(iii)   Repetition
A consists of zero
or more occurrences
of B.

Fig. 30: Data structures. By increasing the number of optional boxes in item (ii), we have a 'case' data structure.

In the method described here, any box may have any other construct substituted for it. If, for example, the repetition was to consist of one or more occurrences of B, this may be described in either of the ways illustrated in Fig. 31.

The highest level of data structure is usually the file. The occurrence of record types in the file is illustrated by appending data structure blocks subordinate to the file. Fig. 32 illustrates some cases we have met already (the dashed lines in this figure are explained in the next frame).

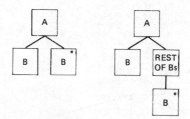

Fig. 31: Illustrating the case where A is followed by one or more occurrences of B. Either of these constructions is allowed.

Note that although there is only one type of TRANSREC, the valid records are to be processed differently from the invalid records. Whenever a record arises which is to be the subject of different treatment from the others, it will help to treat it as a different record type for the purpose of the data structure diagram.

Exercise

1   Draw the data structure diagram for the Student Attendance problem (Appendix B).

L2   DERIVING PROGRAM STRUCTURE IN A SIMPLE CASE

Set out the input and output data structures concerned in the problem (see Fig. 32). Sometimes, as is the case with the validation problem, the program goes in phases, in which case one can consider the phases independently. A phase is generally marked by the opportunity to close one file (or more) prior to opening another file (or more). Thus the storing of the TABLE file can be considered independently of the processing of the TRANS file.

Next draw arrows showing all one-to-one correspondences between an input box and an output box (see dashed lines in Fig. 32). Thus one TRANS file produces one VALTRANS file and one ERROR REPORT file. One VALID TRANSREC produces one VALTRANSREC, and one INVALID TRANSREC produces one ERROR GROUP.

Now our aim is to produce a **program** structure diagram (Section K) which accounts for all the boxes of the **data** structure diagram. As we build elements in the program structure diagram, we shall tick off the boxes in the data structure diagram. We shall build the program structure diagram by working through the **input** file data structure; whenever there is a box, we shall 'process' it. If it is a sequence box with an arrow emanating from it, we shall 'process' it to 'produce' the output. When it is an iteration, we shall 'repeat..until..'. When it is a selection, we shall use 'if..then..else', as illustrated below.

First step

Process TRANS to produce VALTRANS and ERROR REPORT

This is a statement of the whole program phase operation. The rest of the analysis will be an amplification of this operation. Tick off TRANS, VALTRANS and ERROR REPORT.

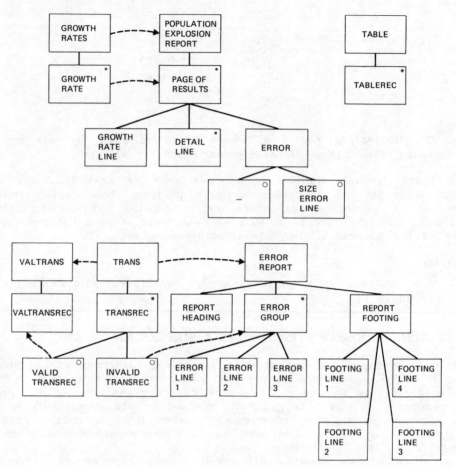

Fig. 32: Data structures involved in the Population Explosion exercise (Appendix B) and the Validation program (frame J3). Note that although TABLE is invalid if it is empty, the validation program is expected to handle this invalidity, so the program must expect zero or more occurrences of TABLEREC. The error report must have a heading and a footing; the body of the report may be empty. The validation specification is ambiguous as to whether or not ERROR REPORT is to appear if TABLE is invalid; probably better that it doesn't. This makes ERROR REPORT an optional file, but there is no need to record its optionality in the diagram, which must be taken as showing its structure should it appear.

Next step

| Repeat until end-of-file of TRANS |
| Process TRANSREC |

Fig. 33: Program structure relating to TRANSREC

Tick off TRANSREC. The next step, the selection, is subordinate to the iteration:

```
Repeat until end-of-file of TRANS
    Process TRANSREC
    Y                           Valid?                        N
    Process VALID TRANSREC      Process INVALID TRANSREC
    to produce VALTRANSREC      to produce ERROR GROUP
```

Fig. 34: Program structure after dealing with the selection

Tick off VALID TRANSREC, VALTRANSREC, INVALID TRANSREC and ERROR GROUP.

We have exhausted the input boxes and must now account for any unticked output boxes (produce...). The output boxes will be accounted for in one of three ways:

(a) as an operation before (or after) an operation already defined
(b) as an amplification of an operation already defined
(c) by means of a do..whenever or possibly some other method.

The last case is dealt with in the next frame.

If the output is a selection or an iteration, it must be produced under the control of the corresponding structured construct, as before. An amplification can either be put in a separate structure diagram (as a subroutine) or substituted for the original operation.

Applying this to Fig. 32 it is plain that REPORT HEADING is produced just once **before** the process defined by Fig. 34, and REPORT FOOTING is produced just once **after** it. All the other boxes are a sequence amplification of ERROR GROUP and REPORT FOOTING respectively. Thus the complete program phase structure diagram derived for the validation program in Fig. 32 is as in Fig. 35.

```
Process TRANS to produce VALTRANS and ERROR REPORT
    Produce REPORT HEADING
    Repeat until eof TRANS
        Process TRANSREC
        Y                           Valid?                    N
        Process VALID TRANSREC      Process INVALID TRANSREC
        Produce VALTRANSREC         Produce ERROR GROUP
    Produce REPORT FOOTING
```

```
Produce ERROR GROUP              Produce REPORT FOOTING
    Produce ERROR LINE 1            Produce FOOTING 1
    Produce ERROR LINE 2            Produce FOOTING 2
    Produce ERROR LINE 3            Produce FOOTING 3
                                    Produce FOOTING 4
```

Fig. 35: Structure diagram of the second phase of the validation program

Given the method of translating structure diagrams into code explained in the previous section, you are probably already in a position to code this program. However, let us continue in this methodical fashion for the sake of example.

Fig. 36 shows the data structures and program structure corresponding to the first phase of the program, treating the working-storage table and possible error message as output data structures.

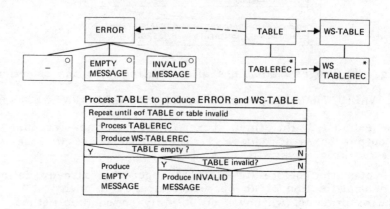

Fig. 36: The first phase of the validation program. The second phase is done only if the table is valid. Thus in the empty box derived in this figure should be inscribed 'Process TRANS to produce VALTRANS and ERROR REPORT'. If the second phase were not conditional in this way, a third program structure could be used to tie the two phases of the program together. This would comprise only the two sequence operations, Process TABLE... and Process TRANS...

We must now get down to detail. Let us assume that we have defined in working storage the records REPORT-HEADING, ERROR-LINE-1 through ERROR-LINE-3, FOOTING-1 through FOOTING-4 and WS-TABLEREC OCCURS 26 TIMES. The records TABLEREC, TRANSREC and VALTRANSREC can be defined in the File Section since they do not have any constants to be established in them by the program. We shall also need a File Section record for ERROR-REPORT - say, ALINE.

We can also expect that we shall need a flag data item for each condition tested in the program structure diagram, where the condition does not reference an input data item directly. It may be possible to eliminate some of these flags later on, when we come to clean up the code as explained in the next frame, but for the time being let us assume the worst. Inspection of Figs 35 and 36 produces the following list of flags:

```
        EOF-TABLE          PIC X
        TABLE-INVALID      PIC X
        TABLE-EMPTY        PIC X
        EOF-TRANS          PIC X
        TRANSREC-VALID     PIC X
```

We are already in a position to write the skeleton of our Procedure Division, concentrating on control structures and flags. (The numbers in this example will be explained very shortly.)

```
        PROCEDURE DIVISION.
        PROCESS-TABLE SECTION.
        PROC-TABLE.
```

```
                MOVE "F" TO EOF-TABLE.
                MOVE "F" TO TABLE-EMPTY.
  1             READ TABLE
                AT END
                    MOVE "T" TO EOF-TABLE
                    MOVE "T" TO TABLE-EMPTY.
                MOVE "F" TO TABLE-INVALID.
  3, 4, 5       PERFORM PROCESS-TABLEREC UNTIL EOF-TABLE = "T"
                OR TABLE-INVALID = "T".
  2             IF TABLE-EMPTY = "T"
                    DISPLAY "TABLE FILE EMPTY"
                ELSE
                    IF TABLE-INVALID = "T"
                        DISPLAY "TABLE FILE INVALID"
                    ELSE
                        PERFORM PROCESS-TRANS.
  28                :
            PROCESS-TABLEREC SECTION.
            PROC-TABLEREC.
                    :
            PRODUCE-WS-TABLEREC.
  6                 :
                READ TABLE
                AT END
                    MOVE "T" TO EOF-TABLE.
            PROCESS-TRANS SECTION.
            PROC-TRANS.
  7             PERFORM PRODUCE REPORT-HEADING.        13
  19            MOVE "F" TO EOF-TRANS.
  9             READ TRANS
                AT END
                    MOVE "T" TO EOF-TRANS.
  11            PERFORM PROCESS-TRANSREC UNTIL EOF-TRANS = "T".
  10, 12        PERFORM PRODUCE-REPORT-FOOTING.
  8                 :
            PROCESS-TRANSREC SECTION.
            PROC-TRANSREC.
                MOVE "T" TO TRANSREC-VALID.
  17, 14            :
                IF TRANSREC-VALID = "T"
                    PERFORM PROCESS-VALID-TRANSREC
                    PERFORM PRODUCE-VALTRANSREC
                ELSE
                    PERFORM PROCESS-INVALID-TRANSREC
                    PERFORM PRODUCE-ERROR-GROUP.
                READ TRANS
                AT END
                    MOVE "T" TO EOF-TRANS.
            PROCESS-VALID-TRANSREC SECTION.
                    :
            PRODUCE-VALTRANSREC SECTION.            18
                    :
            PRODUCE-ERROR-GROUP SECTION.
            PROD-ERROR-GROUP.
  20            PERFORM PRODUCE-ERROR-LINE-1.
```

```
              PERFORM PRODUCE-ERROR-LINE-2.
              PERFORM PRODUCE-ERROR-LINE-3.
          PRODUCE ERROR-LINE-1 SECTION.
15, 21        :
          PRODUCE-ERROR-LINE-2 SECTION.              22
              :
          PRODUCE-ERROR-LINE-3 SECTION.
16, 23        :
          PRODUCE-REPORT-FOOTING SECTION.
              PERFORM PRODUCE-FOOTING-1.             24
              PERFORM PRODUCE-FOOTING-2.             25
              PERFORM PRODUCE-FOOTING-3.             26
              PERFORM PRODUCE-FOOTING-4.             27
```

The next step is to make a list of as many sentences as possible, being all those that are expected to be included in the program and which have not already been dealt with. These include:

1   OPEN INPUT TABLE.
2   CLOSE TABLE.
3   MOVE 1 TO TABLESUB.
4   ADD 1 TO TABLESUB.
5   IF TABLESUB = 27 MOVE "T" TO TABLE-INVALID.
6   MOVE TABLEREC TO WS-TABLEREC(TABLESUB).
7   OPEN OUTPUT ERROR-REPORT.
8   CLOSE ERROR-REPORT.
9   OPEN INPUT TRANS.
10 CLOSE TRANS.
11 OPEN OUTPUT VALTRANS.
12 CLOSE VALTRANS.
13 WRITE ALINE FROM REPORT-HEADING AFTER 2.
14 IF TRANS-UPDATE-CODE NOT = "I" OR "A" OR "D"
        MOVE "*" TO POSSIBLE-STAR-COL-2
        MOVE "F" TO TRANSREC-VALID.
    and all the other validation sentences.
15 MOVE TRANS-UPDATE-CODE TO ERROR-UPDATE-CODE
    and all the other moves preparing ERROR-LINE-1.
16 MOVE TRANS-ADDRESS(3) TO ERROR-LINE-3.
17 MOVE SPACES TO ERROR-LINE-2.
18 WRITE VALTRANSREC FROM TRANSREC.
19 MOVE 2 TO LINECOUNT.
20 ADD 4 TO LINECOUNT.
21 WRITE ALINE FROM ERROR-LINE-1 BEFORE 1.
22 WRITE ALINE FROM ERROR-LINE-2 BEFORE 1.
23 IF LINECOUNT LESS THAN 63
        WRITE ALINE FROM ERROR-LINE-3 BEFORE 2
    ELSE
        WRITE ALINE FROM ERROR-LINE-3 BEFORE PAGE.
    MOVE ZERO TO LINECOUNT.
24 WRITE ALINE FROM FOOTING-1 BEFORE 1.
25 WRITE ALINE FROM FOOTING-2 BEFORE 1.
26 WRITE ALINE FROM FOOTING-3 BEFORE 1.
27 WRITE ALINE FROM FOOTING-4 BEFORE 1.
28 STOP RUN.
29 MOVE TRANS-ADDRESS(2) TO ERROR-LINE-2-ADDR.

You might have considered sentences slightly different from mine, but
```
```

these minor variations are not significant. Whether BEFORE or AFTER is chosen for WRITE commands is quite arbitrary, but once any choice has been made then the other choices must conform to get the desired printer spacing.

Note that this analysis treats the check upon the credit code as just another IF sentence like those in item 14; obviously there is more to it but we can neglect this aspect for the moment provided we are clear that failure of this check will result in an asterisk being moved to column 10 and the flag being set false. Similarly the move of the credit limit is treated for the time being just like any other moves of item 15.

It is now necessary to put these sentences into the appropriate place in the skeleton program. To find where to place a given sentence, ask yourself the question 'I must do this operation every time I ...?' and the answer should be provided by a procedure name you have already defined. For example, sentence 1 – I must do this every time I .. process-table. Sentence 14 – I must do this every time I process-transrec. Having located the procedure, it is usually straightforward to insert the sentence in the correct place in the skeleton. Files are usually opened at the last opportunity and closed at the first opportunity. Try to avoid disconnecting the parameter initialisation from the subroutine calls. The item numbers are annotated against the skeleton above to show completion of this operation.

The numbers on the left of the skeleton statements indicate that the sentence is to be inserted before the line. The numbers on the right indicate that the single sentence contains everything included in the procedure on the left and could replace it.

Items 4 and 5 have been placed with item 3 out of recognition that 3, 4 and 5 together make a PERFORM..VARYING..UNTIL.. construction. If this were not recognised, item 4 would have to be placed at the end of PROCESS–TABLEREC and item 5 at the outset of PROCESS–TABLEREC, with arrangements made for exit if the condition were true.

The definition, initialisation and update of the footing line totals has been omitted from the example – they are left as an exercise for the reader.

When you have experience of organising programs in the rather mechanical fashion explained here, you will be in a good position to try out the more direct approach of Structured English, as explained in the next frame.

Exercise

1   Follow the skeleton and annotation of this frame to rewrite the example. It will be seen that TABLESUB = 27 means the same as TABLE-INVALID = "T" and this can be used to eliminate the special flag. The introduction of the preliminary READ TABLE, which was not considered in the structure diagram, also allows the TABLE-EMPTY flag to be deleted. See if you can do this.

Where a PERFORMed paragraph or section has only one imperative statement in it, substitute the statement for the PERFORM. Where a procedure has no sentences in it, eliminate it. If the program emerges with only one paragraph per section, eliminate the sections.

L3   STRUCTURED ENGLISH AND THE DO..WHENEVER

Once insight into the meaning of structured programming has been gained by the use of the structure diagrams, it is quite easy to represent program structure by Structured English, as explained below. This has the advantage of being much easier to amend than a diagram. Structured English may be used either in top-down fashion by a systems analyst who wishes to specify the objectives of a program, or in analytical fashion by a programmer who wishes to design a program.

To write Structured English, it is best if you use a sheet of paper with vertical rules (computer listing paper turned through 90° will usually do). Each rule, or margin, is used to denote the scope of the structured constructs. Sequence operations are written on successive lines against a margin. Statements subordinate to an 'If' or an 'Else' are written indented, with the else aligned on the same margin as the if, in the manner of the programming examples given throughout this book. However, there is no full stop; the scope of an if or else is limited by the appearance of another statement further down on the same margin, or by the physical end of the procedure. Similarly, an iteration has the iterated statements indented by one margin and the scope is shown by a return to the margin or the physical end of the procedure. (CODASYL have proposed that COBOL should include explicit scope terminators such as END-IF, END-PERFORM, which will enable COBOL programs to be coded in an almost identical manner, without full stops being needed.) A subroutine may be performed, in which case the subroutine procedure name is enclosed in quotes in the calling procedure and underlined at the head of the called procedure. Leave at least one blank line or the word 'End' between procedures.

The following example is the Structured English equivalent of Figs 35 and 36.

Validation program

Process TABLE to produce ERROR and WS-TABLE
Repeat until eof TABLE or table invalid
    |Process TABLEREC
    |Produce WS-TABLEREC
If table empty
    |Produce EMPTY-MESSAGE
Else
    |If table invalid
    | |Produce INVALID-MESSAGE
    |Else
    | |Do 'Process TRANS to produce VALTRANS and ERROR REPORT'

Process TRANS to produce VALTRANS and ERROR REPORT
Produce REPORT HEADING
Perform until eof TRANS
    |Process TRANSREC
    |If TRANSREC valid
    | |Process VALID TRANSREC
    | |Produce VALTRANSREC
    |Else
    | |Process INVALID TRANSREC

```
|     |Do 'Produce ERROR GROUP'
Do 'Produce REPORT FOOTING'

Produce ERROR GROUP
Produce ERROR-LINE-1
Produce ERROR-LINE-2
Produce ERROR-LINE-3

Produce REPORT FOOTING
Produce FOOTING-LINE-1
Produce FOOTING-LINE-2
Produce FOOTING-LINE-3
Produce FOOTING-LINE-4
```

This can, of course, be used to produce a program skeleton exactly as before. It will be realised that Structured English leads to the same organisation of the text as the structure diagrams, except that the 'selection' operations are stacked one above the other instead of side-by-side.

A common complication in program design by the method of frame L2 is that an output box remains unticked after the Structured English is produced from the data structure diagram. This problem can be overcome with a Do..whenever.. construct (this is not widely recognised as a structured programming construct). The Do..whenever.. is conceived by considering the unticked box and asking the question 'I want to produce this output whenever I ...?' The answer supplied should be a complete statement of all the conditions under which the output is to be produced.

Suppose in the validation problem it had been a requirement to produce a page heading on each page of the ERROR REPORT in which an ERROR GROUP appeared. The data structure of ERROR REPORT could be amended as in Fig. 37.

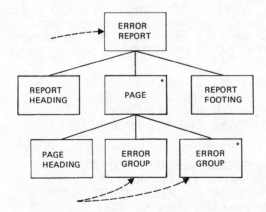

Fig. 37: Revised structure of ERROR REPORT

We now have two blocks containing the words ERROR GROUP. The dashed lines show the 'forked' arrow that comes from INVALID TRANSREC, indicating that a given TRANSREC will correspond either to the first ERROR GROUP in a PAGE or to a subsequent one. Thus, we will still want to process INVALID TRANSREC to produce ERROR GROUP. The same program structure diagram/Structured English will result, and both boxes containing ERROR GROUP can be ticked. Produce REPORT HEADING and Produce REPORT FOOTING are handled as before. This leaves Produce PAGE and Produce PAGE HEADING to be handled by Do..whenever constructs. 'I want to produce PAGE whenever..there is an ERROR GROUP to be produced **and** (it is the first ERROR GROUP of the report **or** I wrote the last line of the previous ERROR GROUP within five lines of page end).' In Structured English:

```
Whenever there is an ERROR GROUP to be produced
     |If it is the first ERROR GROUP of the report or the last line
     |of the previous ERROR GROUP was within 5 lines of page end
     |     |Produce PAGE
```

Obviously we need some data by which to recognise the conditions – we have to invent FIRST-ERROR-GROUP flag and we would have to invent LINECOUNT had we not done so already. Tick off the PAGE box.

Continuing with the remaining unticked box, 'I wish to produce PAGE HEADING whenever..I produce PAGE.' In other words, Produce PAGE HEADING is an operation always done after Produce PAGE or it is an amplification of Produce PAGE. This leads to the conclusion:

```
Whenever there is an ERROR GROUP to be produced
     |If first error group or linecount greater than 61
     |     |Produce PAGE
     |     |Produce PAGE HEADING
```

To implement a Do..whenever.., inspect every place in the program where the 'whenever' condition(s) are or could be satisfied, and insert a sentence to match the Structured English logic. Any flags or variables invented to create a testable condition in the program will also give rise to further sentences (MOVE "T" TO FIRST-ERROR-GROUP, MOVE "F" TO FIRST-ERROR-GROUP, MOVE 0 TO LINECOUNT, ADD 1 TO LINECOUNT) that need to be treated in the manner already explained.

It is plain with this example that the 'whenever' belongs in the procedure called PRODUCE-ERROR-GROUP, where we need an opening sentence as follows:

```
          IF FIRST-ERROR-GROUP = "T" OR
          LINECOUNT GREATER THAN 61
               PERFORM PRODUCE-PAGE
               PERFORM PRODUCE-PAGE-HEADING.
```

After simplification, this code could emerge as follows:

```
          IF FIRST-ERROR-GROUP = "T" OR
          LINECOUNT GREATER THAN 61
               MOVE "F" TO FIRST-ERROR-GROUP
               MOVE ZERO TO LINECOUNT
               WRITE ALINE FROM PAGE-HEADING AFTER PAGE
               ADD 1 TO LINECOUNT.
```

With this approach, the previous operation 23 can be simplified to WRITE ALINE FROM ERROR-LINE-3 BEFORE 2; and of course there is another obvious simplification possible in the above code.

Incidentally, there is an argument against simplification of code, on the grounds that it tends to defeat the connection between the program structure and the data structure and as a result the program is less easily maintained. A counter-argument is that an unsimplified program may call for a greater span of attention in order to be understood, and this may be a cause of programmer error.

The Do..whenever.. does not automatically cater for all unticked outputs. For example, the output sequence may be in contradiction to the input sequence - perhaps the input needs to be resequenced. When there is no place in the program to insert the 'whenever' logic, or if no 'whenever' can be conceived in the context of the program as developed so far, some more fundamental change is required - but this takes us more onto the topic of system design rather than program design.

To summarise, the recommended steps in program design are:

1   Draw data structure diagrams and mark correspondences

2   Derive Structured English specification from the input file and correspondences, adding Do..whenevers for unticked outputs

3   Derive program skeleton neglecting Do..whenevers

4   Add to the skeleton all the sentences not to do with 'whenevers'

5   Add 'whenever' data items and sentences

6   Review, and simplify if it helps.

As an alternative to step 2, it will be found feasible after practice to write the Structured English specification directly. Nevertheless a design methodically derived from the data structure diagram will probably be easier to maintain.

Exercise

1   Write a Structured English specification of the Population Explosion problem. Do it (a) by derivation from the data structures; (b) by reference to Fig. 25 (remember to minimise the parameters). How do you explain the difference?

2   Write a Structured English specification of the student attendance problem (see Exercise 1, frame L1).

3   Write a Structured English specification of the Poem problem (Appendix B).

L4   MULTIPLE INPUT FILES

When there are multiple input files in a problem, draw the data structures and correspondences as before. Choose one file - the transaction file - to govern the procedure and derive the program structure that results from processing this file. If there are multiple transaction files, treat the problem as if it were two programs or two phases, the first to process the transaction files to produce a merged transaction file, the second to process the merged transaction file to produce the other outputs.

A typical problem calls for a transaction file to produce a report, to which corresponding master records also contribute. There may be many transactions for a given master, but only one master for a given transaction. The handling of the master may be outlined thus:

```
Whenever a transaction is to be processed
     |If the transaction id is not the same as the current master id
     |    |Get as current master the master with id equal to the
     |    |transaction id
     |    |If there is no such master
     |    |    |...
```

If the master is a sequential one with records ordered in ascending id's, the transaction records being similarly sequenced, then this outline becomes

```
Whenever a transaction is to be processed
     |Repeat until master id not less than trans id or eof master
     |    |Read master
     |If master id greater than trans id or eof master
     |    |...
```

It will be seen that both of these outlines give the clue as to where to put Process MASTER and thereby tick off an input master record box. As with transaction files, implementation of the second version is helped if one master record is read at the outset of the program; then Process MASTER is put under the control of the Repeat..until.., the last action of Process MASTER being READ MASTER AT END MOVE "T" TO EOF-MASTER.

The case of the sequential input master being updated by transactions to produce a sequential output master can also be analysed with 'whenever' logic, e.g.

```
Whenever a master is to be read in (not being the first master)
     |Write out the current master
```

This gives us somewhere to put Produce MASTEROUT.

If the transactions include those which delete a master, we want to include something like

```
If the transaction type indicates deletion
     |Delete master
```

When the master file is being updated by copying it forward, this operation is achieved, once it is established that the current master id is equal to the current transaction id, by skipping over the input master with a second read:

```
If transaction type indicates deletion
     |Read old master
```

This is a case where the current master is not to be written out when a master is to be read in; the 'whenever' above needs to be modified:

```
Whenever a master is to be read in (not being the first master) and it
is not a read to effect a deletion
     |Write out the current master.
```

The program in Appendix A is an example of an update by copy forward.

ANSWERS – SECTION L

Frame L1

1   See Fig. 38.

Frame L2

```
1    PROCEDURE DIVISION.
     PROCESS-TABLE.
         OPEN INPUT TABLE.
         READ TABLE
         AT END
             DISPLAY "TABLE FILE EMPTY"
             STOP RUN.
         PERFORM PROCESS-TABLEREC VARYING TABLESUB FROM 1 BY 1
         UNTIL EOF-TABLE = "T" OR TABLESUB GREATER THAN 26.
         CLOSE TABLE.
         IF TABLESUB GREATER THAN 26
             DISPLAY "TABLE FILE INVALID"
             STOP RUN.
         PERFORM PROCESS-TRANS.
         STOP RUN.
*
     PROCESS-TABLEREC.
         MOVE TABLEREC TO WS-TABLEREC(TABLESUB)
         READ TABLE
         AT END
             MOVE "T" TO EOF-TABLE.
*
     PROCESS-TRANS.
         OPEN OUTPUT ERROR-REPORT.
         MOVE 2 TO LINECOUNT.
         WRITE ALINE FROM REPORT-HEADING BEFORE 2.
         OPEN INPUT TRANS.
         MOVE "F" TO EOF-TRANS.
         READ TRANS
         AT END
             MOVE "T" TO EOF-TRANS.
         OPEN OUTPUT VALTRANS.
         PERFORM PROCESS-TRANSREC UNTIL EOF-TRANS = "T".
         CLOSE TRANS.
         CLOSE VALTRANS.
         PERFORM PRODUCE-REPORT-FOOTING.
         CLOSE ERROR-REPORT.
*
     PROCESS-TRANSREC.
         MOVE SPACES TO ERROR-LINE-2.
         MOVE "T" TO TRANSREC-VALID.
         IF TRANS-UPDATE-CODE NOT = "I" OR "A" OR "D"
             MOVE "*" TO POSSIBLE-STAR-COL-2
             MOVE "F" TO TRANSREC-VALID.
         :
         IF TRANSREC-VALID = "T"
             WRITE VALTRANSREC FROM TRANSREC
         ELSE
             PERFORM PRODUCE-ERROR-GROUP.
*
     PRODUCE-REPORT-FOOTING.
         WRITE ALINE FROM FOOTING-1 BEFORE 1.
         WRITE ALINE FROM FOOTING-2 BEFORE 1.
```

```
            WRITE ALINE FROM FOOTING-3 BEFORE 1.
            WRITE ALINE FROM FOOTING-4 BEFORE 1.
   *
      PRODUCE-ERROR-GROUP.
            ADD 4 TO LINECOUNT.
            PERFORM PRODUCE ERROR-LINE-1.
            PERFORM PRODUCE-ERROR-LINE-2.
            PERFORM PRODUCE-ERROR-LINE-3.
   *
      PRODUCE-ERROR-LINE-1.
            MOVE TRANS-UPDATE-CODE TO ERROR-UPDATE-CODE
            :
            WRITE ALINE FROM ERROR-LINE-1 BEFORE 1.
   *
      PRODUCE-ERROR-LINE-2.
            MOVE TRANS-ADDRESS(2) TO ERROR-LINE-2-ADDR.
            WRITE ALINE FROM ERROR-LINE-2 BEFORE 1.
   *
      PRODUCE-ERROR-LINE-3.
            MOVE TRANS-ADDRESS(3) TO ERROR-LINE-3
            IF LINECOUNT LESS THAN 63
                  WRITE ALINE FROM ERROR-LINE-3 BEFORE 3
            ELSE
                  WRITE ALINE FROM ERROR-LINE-3 BEFORE PAGE.
```
(Again, the updating of footing totals is neglected.)

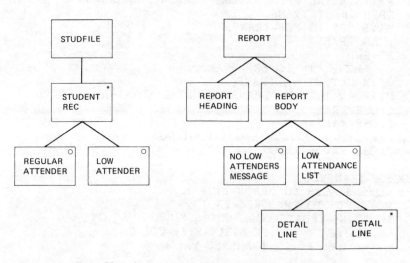

Fig 38: Answer to Exercise 1, frame L1

Frame L3

1   (a) Process GROWTHRATES to produce POPULATION EXPLOSION REPORT
        Until end of file of GROWTHRATES do
              |Process GROWTHRATE
              |Do 'Produce PAGE OF RESULTS'

        Produce PAGE OF RESULTS

Produce GROWTH RATE LINE
Repeat varying decade from current year + 10 by 10 until
decade = current year + 210 or size error occurs
    |Produce DETAIL LINE
Do 'Produce ERROR'

Produce ERROR
If size error has occurred
    |Produce SIZE ERROR LINE

(b) Population explosion
Calculate surface area
Until end of file do
    |Read growth rate
    |If not end of file
    | |Do 'Print a page of results'
Stop run

Print a page of results
Set decade to current year + 10, print headings
Calculate decade growth factor
Set starting population
Until decade = current year + 210 or size error occurs, do
    |Calculate new population
    |If size error occurs
    | |Print the error message
    |Else
    | |Calculate the new density
    | |If size error occurs
    | | |Print the error message
    | |Else
    | | |Print a line of results
    |Add 10 to decade

   The difference is that (a) is the skeleton program design derived
in analytical fashion and makes no attempt to embrace all the
purposes of the program. It corresponds to a programmer's design
when he is given an unstructured specification. Version (b) could
be the analyst's structured specification of the program – but it
still needs a little amplification to be a full specification
(e.g. how is surface area to be calculated?).
   Since the size error terminates the repetition in version (b),
there is a good argument to be made that the operation 'Add 10 to
decade' is more appropriately placed under the control of the last
'Else'; there is no need to increment the decade if a size error has
occurred. However, since the state of 'decade' is undefined in the
problem if a size error occurs, it is not wrongly placed where it is
and of course it conforms more closely to PERFORM..VARYING..UNTIL.

3   Get a colleague to check your answer.

M Documentation

M1 PROGRAM DOCUMENTATION

Two main documents show in detail what a program does:

The Program Specification, being file and record descriptions, procedure definitions in Structured English, decision tables or similar expressions of program objectives, and

The Program Listing.

The first of these is more accurately a **design** document, prepared before coding commences. It is often prepared by a systems analyst rather than a programmer. Although nearly all installations require that the Program Specification be brought up to date to reflect the current status of the program, such updating is often done 'after the event'. In consequence, there may be discrepancies between the specification and the listing. The latter, therefore, is the only truly reliable statement of what a program does. It is to the listing that programmers turn when considering modification or correction of the detail of the program.

For this reason, the front line of documentation should be the program listing. Not only is the listing the most credible of the available documents, it is also comparatively painlessly and automatically updated by the programmer.

Although it is easy to justify program documentation as an aid to later program modification, there is another more telling reason which is less obvious. A programmer who adopts consistent habits of documentation such as those described here will be working in a less error-prone fashion than one who does not. Since it is impossible fully to test a program after construction, it is vital that the development method should be robust. The documentation is an aid to maintaining integrity of purpose during the refinement of the problem into program code.

For small-to-medium sized programs, a very good strategy for program development takes three steps:

1   Write a detailed definition in Structured English and have a colleague inspect and agree the detail of this specification

2   Systematically code from the Structured English and have a colleague inspect and agree the detail of the coding

3   Systematically test the program as explained in Section N and have a colleague inspect and agree the scope of testing and test results.

With large programs, it may be desirable to make a Structured English specification at an even higher level, perhaps defining programs which can be separately compiled and tested for later linking together (Section U). This also needs to be checked out before being systematically enlarged into the more detailed specifications.

A COBOL program written in a straightforward way does not alone produce a listing which adequately satisfies these additional **explanatory** requirements we are imposing. The following frames are concerned with suggestions for modifying the listing so that these requirements are met.

M2 IDENTIFICATION DIVISION ENTRIES

The start of the program is a suitable place to correct the deficiency of the listing in showing

1   the place of this program in the suite

2   the overall objectives of the program

3   the overall design of the program

4   the logic of the program in plainer language than COBOL code.

If there is a good standard of systems documentation in force (see, for example, Chapters 6 and 12 of *Systems Analysis*, published by Edward Arnold in the UK and by Little, Brown in the USA) the first two of these might be met by a cross-reference to other documents. Failing this, a simple narrative can be included:

```
*INPUTS       - PARTS TRANSACTION FILE "PARTRANS" PRODUCED FROM
*               PROGRAM PAR002VET
*             - OLD PARTS MASTER FILE "PARTMASTER" PREVIOUSLY
*               OUTPUT FROM THIS PROGRAM
*OUTPUTS      - NEW PARTS MASTER FILE "PARTMASTER"
*             - AMENDMENTS MADE FILE "PARTAMENDS", PASSED TO
*               PROGRAM PAR004PRINT
*PROCESSING   - THE PARTRANS FILE CONTAINS AMENDMENTS, DELETIONS
*               AND INSERTIONS AND IS SORTED INTO PART-NUMBER
*               ORDER. THE SORTED FILE IS USED TO UPDATE THE OLD
*               PARTS MASTER TO PRODUCE A NEW PARTS MASTER.
*               ERRORS CAUSED BY INCONSISTENCY OF TRANSACTIONS
*               WITH MASTERS ARE LISTED, WHILE ACCEPTED TRANS
*               ACTIONS ARE RECORDED ON THE AMENDMENTS-MADE FILE,
*               TOGETHER WITH THE NEW STATUS OF THE MASTER
*               RECORD, FOR SUBSEQUENT PRINTING. CONTROL COUNTS OF
*               TRANSACTION RECORDS (BY TYPE OF TRANSACTION) AND
*               MASTER RECORDS ARE ACCUMULATED AND LISTED.
```

The next two requirements, to show the overall design and logic of the program, can be met by including the Structured English specification. If some of the logic has been described by decision tables or state tables (see Section P) it is usually feasible to include these in the listing as well.

When the process is composed of separately-compiled programs (Section U), the name and purpose of each program should be listed in the main program. It will also help to show how the program is organised into a hierarchy of paragraphs and sections - see frame M4.

Exercise

1   The programmer may direct the compiler to throw to the head of a new page of the listing by placing an oblique stroke "/" in column 7. Why is this useful when the documentation practice is to

annotate the Identification Division as outlined here?

2   Most installations adopt a standard system of allocating program
     names. These systems usually aim at (a) ensuring that each
     program has a unique name and (b) identifying the system to which
     the program belongs. Why?

3   Of what practical value is it to record the program author and date
     compiled on the program listing?

M3   DATA DIVISION ENTRIES

Documentation in the Data Division centres around **name conventions** and
supplementary information.
Name conventions have two objectives:

1   to aid location of the Data Division entry for a particular data
     item when it is referenced in the Procedure Division, e.g. so that
     its picture can be established

2   to give meaning to a data item.

Of many possible schemes to achieve the first objective, a workable
and consistent one uses a two-character prefix to each data name. This
is an overkill on small programs, but it begins to make sense as
programs get larger.
The first letter shows in which section of the Data Division the data
item is defined:

F = File Section
R = Report Section
W = Working-Storage Section, etc.

The second letter of the prefix is used to identify the record in which
the data item appears. The records are lettered in the sequence in
which they are coded. If there are few data items in a section, the
second letter of the prefix can be dropped. A complete example is given
in Appendix A.
The suggested name conventions assume that the programmer has
discretion to name the data items. In a well-organised data processing
department, the systems analysts may have built up a dictionary or
catalogue of all the data used in the system, and they may have
defined the names of all the files, records and data elements. If this is
the case, the programmer should use the same names in the File Section.
If duplicate names arise when following this convention (e.g. when a
sequential master file is to be updated by copying it forward) a
reasonable way out is to add a suffix -I or -O to distinguish the input
data items from the output data items.
In the Working-Storage Section, some records will arise naturally out of
association with an input or output record type. The remaining data
items need to be organised into records by the programmer. The
following guidelines will help this process:

1   put into a common record all those data items which are meant to
     be globally accessible in the program, i.e. items which are used in
     the main procedure and subroutines

2   put into a common record all those data items identified as being
     passed as parameters when a subroutine is called (i.e. one record

for each PERFORM that passes a parameter)

3   put into a common record all those data items identified as being
local to a subroutine, i.e. used only within the subroutine (one
record per subroutine that requires any local data element).

Meaning is given to the data by the choice of good names, and it is
largely a matter of common sense. This usually makes data names
longer, but by any reckoning DUE–DATE–OF–NEXT–PAYMENT is to be
preferred to DDONP.
A spin–off from prefixing is that accidental use of reserved words is
avoided. A spin–off from meaningful names is that mis–spelling in the
Procedure Division is less likely.
Supplementary information should aim to fill the information gaps which
the COBOL language leaves. Thus, Data Division entries can tell you, of
an item,

1   its size and type (PICTURE)
2   its initial value (VALUE)
3   its internal storage format (USAGE)
4   its purpose (if you have picked a meaningful name)
5   the meaning of its values if it is a flag or code (if you use
condition names – see frame Q4)
6   what it is subscripted by if it is a table (if you use INDEXED BY
– see frame O5).

COBOL entries do not tell you

1   its purpose (if this is not entirely clear from the name)
2   the range of values it can have (if this is less than the full range
allowed by its PICTURE)
3   the meaning of its values if it is a flag or code and you have not
used condition names
4   what it is subscripted by if it is a table and you have not used
INDEXED BY.

This supplementary information should be given in a comment
immediately following the data description entry. The skeleton of this
comment would be

      *   purpose
      *   RANGE range of values
      *   code MEANS meaning (as often as required)
      *   INDEXED BY subscript name

The programmer should consider writing this comment after each data
description entry, omitting irrelevant portions. This is a sort of quality
control check, since if the programmer has chosen wisely a comment will
rarely be required. The program in Appendix A, for example, called
only for a comment on WA–ERROR–MESSAGES whose use was a little more
involved than usual.
If a data dictionary exists in which the purpose, range etc. of data
items is recorded, there is not much point in repeating this information
in the program.

Exercise

1   Write the data description entries and comment for a table of twelve
three–character month names in working storage, to be used to
translate a numeric month for printing out on a page heading.

M4   PROCEDURE DIVISION ENTRIES

The main suggestions for ease of reading are:

1   write one statement per line;
2   do not write on the same line as a paragraph name;
3   follow the indentation conventions for conditional statements;
4   if nesting more than about 3 or 4 deep, consider using a forward GO TO or out-of-line subroutine instead, or consider documenting by comments the analysis which went into the deeply nested statements;
5   use blank lines to highlight the program blocks;
6   use paragraph names which describe the procedures in the paragraph;
7   use a procedure name prefix which will help location of the procedure.

A good prefixing system for procedures in a structured program uses a two-part prefix. The first part is a letter showing the level at which the paragraph, block of paragraphs or section is called. The main procedure is level A, and it PERFORMS level B procedures. A level C procedure is PERFORMed by a level B procedure, and so on. The second part is a serial number uniquely identifying the procedure and serving to help locate it in a large listing. The procedures should be coded in the listing in order of their prefixes. If a procedure block consists of a section or group of paragraphs, all the paragraphs in the block should have the same prefix.

Thus, in a program in which no procedures are re-used in different places, the program control hierarchy will always be along the following lines:

```
A
    B1
        C1
        :
        Cn
    B2
        Cn+1
        :
        Cn+m
    B3
        Cn+m+1
        :
    B4
    :
```

When a procedure is re-used, it is suggested that it is coded at a level corresponding to its highest-level use. The prefix which would have been allocated to it in its other use should be omitted from the procedures. This may sound a little complicated, but I am sure if you try it you will come to see that it makes a lot of sense.

There is an argument against re-use of procedures, as follows.   A re-used procedure is used in at least two different contexts. If it is modified in one of these contexts, the modification may corrupt it for use in the other context. Procedures should either be duplicated, or the documentation should make the re-use plain.

The hierarchy of control should be documented in the Identification

Division comments to aid program maintenance. This can be done simply by listing out the names of the procedure blocks indented according to their level. It helps if in this list the prefixes omitted in the procedures on account of re-use are now included and cross-referenced to the block where the code appears. The program in Appendix A gives an example of this method.

Exercise

1   Derive procedure name prefixes for the program appearing as the answer to Exercise 1, frame L2.

ANSWERS - SECTION M

Frame M2

1   The listing can be organised so that each major component of the commentary and procedures appears on a fresh page. Splitting a Structured English specification or decision table over a page can be avoided. (No Structured English procedure should be longer than a page. Create more subroutines if necessary to meet this ideal.)

2   (a) Every program must have a unique name so that it can be entered in and retrieved from the installation's library of programs – see Section U.
    (b) The other programs in the suite can be readily identified and located if the listings are filed in program-name order. This can be helpful in understanding the listing or in tracing the consequences of an amendment.

3   Author - might be handy to know who the original programmer was if the program goes wrong or needs amendment.
    Date compiled - if more than one version of the listing has been filed, this will identify the current version.

Frame M3

1   03 WD-TABLE-CONTENTS   VALUE etc.
            05 WD-ALPHA-MONTH OCCURS 12 TIMES PIC XXX.
    *   USED TO TRANSLATE NUMERIC MONTH FOR REPORT
    *   HEADING;
    *   INDEXED BY FC-NUMERIC-MONTH

Frame M4

1   A1-PROCESS-TABLEREC
        B1-PROCESS-TABLEREC
        B2-PROCESS-TRANS
            C1-PROCESS-TRANSREC
                D1-PRODUCE-ERROR-GROUP
                    E1-PRODUCE-ERROR-LINE-1
                    E2-PRODUCE-ERROR-LINE-2
                    E3-PRODUCE-ERROR-LINE-3
            C2-PRODUCE-REPORT-FOOTING

N Program testing

N1 AIM OF FUNCTIONAL TESTING

Testing of computer procedures may be considered from three points of view; the user's, the analyst's and the programmer's.

The user wishes to establish that the program is a good fit to his organisation's requirements. The user is the only one who can ultimately judge whether or not the program produces the desired results because he is the only one (I assume) who can conclusively decide what the 'desired results' are.

The systems analyst has tried to comprehend the desires of the user, but he may have done this imperfectly. He will seek to establish that the program matches up to the specification which he assisted the user to produce, and that it works as intended when run in a suite with other programs and human procedures.

The programmer has tried to comprehend the desires of the systems analyst and user, but he may have done this imperfectly. He will seek to establish that the program works in accordance with his understanding of the specification. If, at the program testing stage, it is found that the specification is at fault, it will be very much more expensive to correct the fault than if it had been detected at specification time.

The three parties may also have different viewpoints when it comes to formulation of test data. The test data is submitted to search out hypothetical faults in the program; each party has different reasons for these hypotheses, as follows.

The user may consider the whole computer system a black box. His choice of test data may come entirely from his understanding of what is important to him and the organisation. For example, he may choose data concerning his most important customer. Though the programmer may be unable to conceive of any reason why his program should behave differently for the most important customer, as opposed to any other customer, the user's test data should not be dismissed for this reason. His data probably covers the circumstances of greatest expected loss and this alone is a justification. The user may have other valid reasons for selecting test data, e.g. he remembers an event which caused difficulty with the old system last year and he thinks the same transaction should be tried with the new system.

The systems analyst may also consider the program a black box, but he probably has insights into computer programs in general and may hypothesise a different sort of fault to those imagined by user or programmer. For example, he may know that zero amounts or blank fields are often not processed as intended, or sometimes the intention for such cases is not clear from the specification. Test data conceived by the systems analyst can be a worthwhile addition to that of user and programmer.

The programmer considers testing in full knowledge of the processes of his program. Knowing the exact structure of the program, he is in a position to postulate faults which would escape the attention of analyst and user; for example, overflow on working storage variables, table overflow, incorrect arithmetic sign. The programmer's test data should be concerned with exploring the robustness of the program at its limits. If it works correctly with the limiting cases, it is very likely (especially with commercial programs) to work for all cases in between. The user should participate in certifying the correctness of the results, even those produced by the programmer's test data.

The aim of functional testing is to improve confidence in the program's functional correctness. Obviously all three parties should submit test data; the programmer's test data is just one step on the way to confidence. The programmer should concentrate on devising tests appropriate to his special knowledge of the program structure (and if the programmer is also the analyst or user, he should try to think like analyst or user in addition). Each test should explore some new facet of the program. Each test should be checked out to see if the results are correct. If the programmer succeeds in making each of his tests check something different, he will have an added incentive to verify all the results.

Testing a program is a necessary, but not sufficient, way to build confidence in it. A typical commercial program deals with hundreds of thousands of different possible input values, and it is out of the question to test them all. As important as the confidence that comes from testing is that which comes from using a robust method of program design (such as that of Sections K and L), from desk-checking, and from peer inspection of design and code (see frame M1).

Formal methods have been advanced for proving the correctness of programs, but these are difficult and expensive to apply in other than simple cases. In the absence of formal proof, close desk-checking inspection of the operations of the program, with a view to being informally convinced of its correctness, is called for. Experienced programmers have a knack of recognising which parts of their programs are not completely straightforward, and mentally tracing the program with test data which allows review of correctness.

There is a sound psychological basis for supposing that detailed inspection of a program by a fellow programmer may reveal faults which escaped the original programmer's attention, as well as experimental evidence to support this. The original programmer gets set or fixed on one particular interpretation of the program, which he has difficulty in standing back from. A fresh mind has not the same constraint.

Exercise

1   Here is a question to think about. When a test exposes a fault in a program, and you fix the fault, should your confidence in the program be (a) increased, (b) reduced?

N2 MINIMALLY-THOROUGH TESTING

The programmer cannot 'completely' test a program as if it were a black box, since that would imply that every possible combination of input data values, in every possible sequence, should be offered to it. This is a vast number even for quite trivial programs.

A target level of testing is required which is capable of being reached and which gives a reasonable degree of confidence – a 'thorough' test. Although I prefer to leave undefined exactly what is meant by a 'thorough' test, I can define a **minimally-thorough** test and put forward other tests which should be considered for a given program. A thorough test may then be loosely defined as a minimally-thorough test made by the programmer, together with selected other tests made by programmer, analyst and user.

A minimally-thorough test is a test such that every simple condition in the program is executed in both its outcomes (true and false) where possible. 'Where possible' is stipulated because there may be conditions included in the program, one of whose outcomes cannot be made to happen with any possible input data. The reason for impossibility may be either logical contradiction or practical impossibility caused by the quantity of data that would be required. An example is given in frame K4 where a defensive SIZE ERROR clause was added to a COMPUTE statement. There is no known input value which will cause the size error; the SIZE ERROR clause results from following a belt-and-braces philosophy.

A similar position arises on rare occasions when there is a logic error on the programmer's part and some portion of the code is unreachable – an attempt to do minimally-thorough testing will expose such errors. Another case occurs when a program is totalling fields in records which exist in undefined quantities in a file. The programmer may set the size of the total field such that he believes that there is no practical possibility of size error occurring; but since there is no size of total field which will eliminate the theoretical possibility of overflow, it is proper to include a SIZE ERROR clause, mainly to trap possible logic errors. The 'size error true' condition which results from admitting this clause might as well be considered as arising from an impossible set of input data.   Neglecting such cases, minimally-thorough testing as defined above ensures that there is no statement in the program which is not executed at least once during testing. Note that 'simple condition' in the definition includes conditional phrases such as SIZE ERROR as well as conditions in IF sentences.

If an identical condition appears in more than one place, every occurrence of it must be exercised. To create the set of test cases, place a T or an F against any defensive condition, showing which is the outcome for which no test can be created. Then specify a test input, and place a T or an F against each condition exercised by it, to show the branch that the test will cause the computer to take. Now look for any conditions that do not have both a T and an F, and specify a further test which will reach the condition and cause the untested branch to be taken. Again place a T or an F against all the conditions not already so marked which are now exercised by the tests. Continue until all conditions have both a T and an F. For each test case created, record your prediction of the result.

Sometimes a condition in a program cannot be exercised without more test data than you are presently prepared to supply, e.g. page overflow on a large page. An interim test can be made by suitably changing the condition, e.g. reducing the number of lines per page. Nevertheless, the program should be tested with the proper condition before it is finally accepted for production work.

Exercise

1   Specify minimally-thorough tests for the first section of the validation program whose Procedure Division is outlined in frame L2 (the record layouts are given in frame J3). An empty TRANS file will suffice for this exercise.

2   How can you avoid creating 800-character records during the preliminary testing of the POEM program (Appendix B)?

N3   OTHER TESTS

Another idea for construction of test cases with knowledge of program structure is that of exploring the program with minimum and maximum values of input data and minimum and maximum values that exercise the conditions. The argument is that if the program works with these extreme values, it is likely to work for all cases in between since most commercial programs have regular (technically, monotonic) processes.

In practice it is difficult to follow this idea to the limit and pursuing it does not always add to confidence. For example, size errors usually result in abnormal termination in commercial programs. If so, there does not seem much point in exercising the size error conditions with values that only just cause a size error and with values that will cause the largest possible size error. Nevertheless, it does seem a fair general rule to consider using maximum/minimum values and to judge each case on its merits.

To generate extreme test cases, inspect each numeric field in the input record layouts. Create tests in which each of these is given the smallest and largest values for which results are defined. Often these will be the values allowed by the PICTURE of the item (e.g. A PIC S99; smallest value of A −99, largest value of A +99). Sometimes results are specified to be 'undefined' when input values go outside a certain range (e.g. because a previous program has validated the data to be within the range). In this case, choose the smallest and largest values in the range for which the results are defined. Now inspect each relation condition comparing numeric data in the program and ensure that test cases are included which give rise to the smallest and largest values to exercise the condition in both its outcomes (e.g. IF A GREATER THAN 50; test cases for A=−99, A=49, A=50, A=+99). When the relation condition is 'equality', e.g. IF A = 50, there must be a test case where A = 50; the unequal outcome may be tested with minimum and maximum values of A.

When the condition is a loop terminator (e.g. a count) there is usually only one value which can be created to terminate the condition. So be it.

Other types of test to consider are those which would expose the following faults:

1   Zero faults. Test data in which numeric input is zero should be included. Consider also non-zero test data which produces a zero result, e.g. transactions which leave a zero account balance.

2   Overflow faults. Possible overflow of numeric fields, strings, tables or filespace.

3   Empty file faults. If the operating system permits input files to be empty of records, does the program handle this case correctly?

4   Case sequence faults. If the treatment of one input record may depend on how the previous record was processed, or if different record types exist in the input, consider the permutations.

5   File mismatch faults. For example, a transaction for which there is no master.

6   End-of-file faults. Particularly when a master file is being updated by copying it forward, a test should be included to ensure that insertions before the end of the old master, and after the end of the old master, as well as insertions within the old master, are correctly handled. Similar consideration should be given to deletions, particularly a deletion of the last record on the old master. The same type of idea may apply to some table-handling operations.

7   Rounding faults. Particularly important with any sort of compound interest calculation since insufficient precision in working storage variables may lead to error in a significant digit of the result. The test should cover the longest period of compounding and the results should be checked by hand or with a calculator (but beware, many cheap calculators are inaccurate when many digits of precision are called for).

8   Cycle faults. When an output file is to be re-input into the same program at next execution, this cycle must be tested at least once.

Exercise

1   Suggest the test data for the Population Explosion program (Appendix A).

N4   SELF-AUDITING PROGRAMS

An additional technique is to plan the program to be self-auditing. The idea is to arrive at the results by two different methods, as a check on the program logic. This is the same idea as that known to accountants as 'cross footing'. How it is done depends on the exact nature of the program; here are a couple of examples.

Suppose a transaction file can add to or delete from a master file. Every time the program reads a transaction, it should add 1 to a transaction count, and similarly every time it reads or writes a master it should add 1 to an old or new master count. At the point where it determines that the transaction is an addition, it should add 1 to an addition count, while on the remaining path it should add 1 to a deletion count. At the end of the program it should check that

transaction count = addition count + deletion count

and that

new master count = old master count + addition count – deletion count.

It is important that there is no branch instruction written between the instruction that adds to the count and the instruction which performs the operation it is counting.

For another example, consider a program which reads records containing a value and a code, and which is to accumulate totals of the values by code plus a grand total. You should add the value to the grand total as soon as the record is read (i.e. no branch instructions between the READ and the ADD – this may mean making the ADD conditional on the READ not having detected end of file) and then proceed to add the value to the appropriate total by code. At the end of the program, it should add up all the totals and check they agree with the grand total. (There would be little point in this particular check, though, if you were using very high-level facilities such as the SUM clause described in frame S3.)

 This may strike you as overkill, considering that once the program is tested the self-audit procedures will be redundant. Remember, though, that commercial programs typically have life of many years and are frequently revised and maintained. Your audit routine will tend to confirm that future amendments have been made satisfactorily.

ANSWERS – SECTION N

Frame N1

1   Rationally, you could be influenced either way. The safest philosophy is to let each fault that you find **reduce** your confidence in the program. If you find more than two or three faults in a program, you should consider re-writing it from scratch, following a robust program design method.

  Perhaps this answer surprises you; I have certainly met a lot of programmers who follow the converse philosophy. The point is that there is an enormous number of possibilities which are supposed to be correctly processed by the program. Any number of possibilities could be incorrectly processed, but your test data can consider only a relative handful of these. Before you do the testing, you have a certain level of belief (estimate of probability) that these untested possibilities are processed correctly. Each test **passed** by your program tends to confirm that it is robust and should increase your belief that the untested possibilities are correctly processed. Conversely, each test **failed** tends to confirm that the program is not robust and should reduce your belief that the untested possibilities are correctly processed.

  This reduced confidence may be partly or wholly counteracted by the increased confidence that should be had when the bug is fixed. But there is a good chance that the programmer will let his confidence rise on account of this by more than is justified, so I think it better to err on the cautious side and neglect this aspect.

Frame N2

1   The simple conditions in the first section are (READ TABLE) AT END; EOF-TABLE = "T"; TABLE-INVALID = "T"; TABLE-EMPTY = "T"; TABLE-INVALID = "T" (second occurrence). No impossible outcomes. Tests are as follows.

 Run 1. Empty TABLE file.
 Outcomes: AT END true; EOF-TABLE = "T" true; TABLE-EMPTY = "T" false.
  Predicted result: message "TABLE FILE EMPTY".

 Run 2. TABLE file has one record containing A9999999 (the data is

arbitrary). TRANS file empty.
Outcomes not previously tested: AT END false; EOF–TABLE = "T" false; TABLE–INVALID = "T" false; TABLE–EMPTY = "T" false; TABLE–INVALID = "T" (second occurrence) false.
Predicted result: report with heading and footing lines, no invalid records, zeros in all footing totals.

Run 3. Table file has 27 records with arbitrary data.
Outcomes not previously tested: TABLE–INVALID = "T" true; TABLE–INVALID = "T" (second occurrence) true.
Predicted result: message "TABLE FILE INVALID".

2   Reduce the record size to a more convenient one, say 80 characters. To prevent the possibility of the program dealing only with the special case where the input record size was equal to the output record size, reduce the line length to, say, 60 characters. A program which dealt satisfactorily with 80 character input and 60 character output may be expected to behave properly when these constants are changed to 800 and 80 respectively; but this expectation will still need a final test, of course.

Frame N3

1   Test 1: Empty file.
    Test 2: Three records,

    0000
    1001 (or any other data using the least significant digit; make a prediction of the final population and density)
    9999 (expect size error)

Award yourself full marks if you deduced that one of the size errors (in either population or density) must be impossible.

O Techniques of table and data manipulation

O1 INSPECT

The INSPECT verb can be used to manipulate the individual characters contained in a data item.

$$\underline{\text{INSPECT}} \text{ identifier-1 } \underline{\text{TALLYING}} \text{ identifier-2 } \underline{\text{FOR}} \left\{ \begin{array}{l} \underline{\text{ALL}} \\ \underline{\text{LEADING}} \end{array} \right\} \text{ literal-1}$$

Suppose you have a six-character field called NUM containing ____27. If you wished to establish how many leading spaces there are, you could define an item to hold the answer, say SPACE-COUNT, and then code MOVE ZERO TO SPACE-COUNT, INSPECT NUM TALLYING SPACE-COUNT FOR LEADING SPACES. Note that INSPECT just adds the tally to identifier-2; it is up to the programmer to establish the proper initial value for this item.

The ALL variation will give you a count of all the 'literal-1's' that are in the field, whether leading or not. The BEFORE INITIAL variation (see Appendix D) will give a count of the number of characters that precede 'literal-1'. For example, if you have a field SURNAME, 20 characters long, which contains a person's surname followed by spaces, and you wish to establish how long the surname is, you could write MOVE ZERO TO SPACE-COUNT, INSPECT SURNAME TALLYING SPACE-COUNT FOR CHARACTERS BEFORE INITIAL SPACE. The answer will again be in SPACE-COUNT.

When the REPLACING version is used (Appendix D), every 'literal-3' will be replaced by 'literal-4'. If NUM contains ____27 and you code MOVE ZERO TO SPACE-COUNT, INSPECT NUM TALLYING LEADING SPACES REPLACING LEADING SPACES BY ZEROS, then SPACE-COUNT will contain 4 and NUM will contain 000027.

Tallies and replacements can be made both before and after a particular value in the field concerned; each occurrence of a particular string of characters in the field (as opposed to a single character) can be tallied, or replaced by another string; more than one tallying or replacing operation can be achieved. I do not propose to deal with all these alternatives, but I would like to develop a particular example as an introduction to concepts to follow.

Suppose you received a large quantity of data which has been recorded on a different computer from yours. Computers made by different manufacturers (or even by the same manufacturer at different times) may use different internal codes for representing the characters. Sometimes nearly all the characters have different codes, sometimes most of the characters have the same code but there are some special characters that are different.

Suppose data from the other computer contains a $ sign, but the code for $ on the other machine is the code for £ on yours. When your computer reads the data, all the $ signs will be (mistakenly) read as £

signs. The task facing you will be to replace the erroneous £ signs with $ signs in your computer's code; that way you will have the correct data.

You could say INSPECT INPUT-RECORD REPLACING ALL "£" BY "$". However, one advantage of the INSPECT verb is that you can make more than one character substitution in one sentence. Suppose your problem is as follows:

Data from other computer	Read in by your computer as
$	£
*	!
?	*
!	(
)	?

You can put this whole code translation table into a single INSPECT statement:

```
INSPECT INPUT-RECORD REPLACING ALL
"£" BY "$"
"!" BY "*"
"*" BY "?"
"(" BY "!"
"?" BY ")".
```

(If there is to be a substantial translation of data from an incompatible computer, a better solution may be to use the CODE-SET facilities of COBOL if these are available; consult the reference manual. Also, CODASYL have proposed an extension, INSPECT..CONVERTING.., which may better suit this case.)

Exercise

1   You are about to write a record called OUT-REC which will be read in by another machine. The codes of the two machines are the same, except as follows:

Output from your machine	Read in by other machine as
;	.
.	;
*	=
=	/
/	*
#	)
&	(
)	#
(	&

Amend the data in OUT-REC so that it will be correctly read in by the other machine. This exercise is not as straightforward as you might at first think.

O2   TABLE LOOK-UP

We have already met the concept of a table. It consists of repeated elements of data described by an OCCURS clause.

Let us take the problem of exercise 1 in frame O1 by way of example. The codes to be output by your machine are the **target** codes; the codes

in the original data are the **source** codes. To achieve translation from
the source codes into the target codes, we can write the relevant parts
of the program as follows:

```
01    OUT-REC.
      02    OUT-CH            PIC X OCCURS 100 TIMES.
WORKING-STORAGE SECTION.
01    TABLES.
      02    SOURCE-TABLE      VALUE ".;=/*)(#&".
      03    SOURCE-CH    PIC X OCCURS 9 TIMES.
      02    TARGET-TABLE      VALUE ";.*=/#&)(".
01    SUBSCRIPTS COMP SYNC RIGHT.
      02    DATASUB           PIC 999.
      02    TABLESUB          PIC 99.
PROCEDURE DIVISION.
:
(prepare output record)
      PERFORM B1-TRANSLATE-REC.
:
B1-TRANSLATE-REC.
      PERFORM C1-TRANSLATE VARYING DATASUB FROM 1 BY 1
      UNTIL DATASUB = 101.
C1-TRANSLATE.
      PERFORM D1-LOOKUP VARYING TABLESUB FROM 1 BY 1
      UNTIL OUT-CH(DATASUB) = SOURCE-CH(TABLESUB)
      OR TABLESUB = 10.
      IF TABLESUB LESS THAN 10
          MOVE TARGET-CH(TABLESUB) TO OUT-CH(DATASUB).
D1-LOOKUP.
```

D1-LOOKUP is a dummy paragraph with no actions.
The first character of OUTREC is compared with the first, second, third
etc. character in SOURCE-TABLE. If no match is found (i.e. when
TABLESUB reaches 10), the character does not need translation. If a
match is found, the corresponding character in TARGET-TABLE is
substituted. Then the next character in OUTREC is selected, under the
control of the first PERFORM..VARYING, and the process is repeated until
all characters have been translated.

There are other ways of achieving a similar objective. For example, on
some machines the internal code of the character to be translated can be
treated instead as an equivalent (binary) number. Since every code is
different, each will give rise to a unique number, which can be used
directly as a subscript to access the target code (the target table will
have to contain the complete character set).

Frame 05 shows you how to do table lookup without a dummy paragraph
when the SEARCH verb is available.

Exercise

1   (Quite hard.) You are reading cards which were punched on a
    machine which coded the first nine letters of the alphabet in your
    codes 1 to 9, and vice versa. In addition, the code which you read
    as * meant a run of three zeros on the other machine. The record
    you read in is 80 characters long, but it could grow to 240
    characters after translation (if it was all asterisks). The
    translated record is to be built in a 240-character record in
    working storage called NEW-REC; the original record is to be called

IN-REC.
Write code to achieve the translation.

O3 TABLE ORGANISATION

When a large table is being searched for an item, and there are many items to be found, it is clear that there may be a great deal of processing time involved in the searching. Imagine that you need to translate 50,000 records, each containing 1000 characters, from another computer's code into your own. Using the table search described in frame O2, a total of 50 million searches would be made of the table. If the table was 60 characters long, and each character had equal probability of being in the input data, on average 30 characters in the table would be inspected before the right one was found. Even on a large modern computer, the amount of time needed to do 1,500 million comparisons will probably be measured in hours rather than minutes. When a large table and large files are involved, therefore, it can be desirable to find faster methods of searching.

When the items in a table are inspected one after the other, usually from left to right, this is said to be a **sequential** search. A simple trick to speed up a sequential search is to sequence the items in the table in descending order, from left to right, according to the frequency with which they are needed. Putting the most frequently encountered items at the beginning of the table will mean that on average fewer items will be inspected before the one needed is found.

For example, suppose in the above case two of the items in the input that needed translation were zero and space, and that 40% of all the characters in the input were zeros and 30% spaces. Putting zero and space first and second in the table would mean

40% of searches would require 1 comparison
30% of searches would require 2 comparisons
30% of searches would require 2 + (60 - 2)/2 = 31 comparisons on average.

The overall average number of comparisons would therefore be

$$\frac{40 \times 1 + 30 \times 2 + 30 \times 31}{100} = 10.3$$

There is no exercise for this frame, but you might like to look back to the next-to-last paragraph of frame O2 where the self-indexing method of table look up is briefly described. Where this technique can be used, no comparisons are needed.

O4 THE BINARY CHOP OR LOGARITHMIC SEARCH

This is a technique of table searching which, if all the items have equal frequency of being needed, guarantees the fewest possible number of comparisons are made (when self-indexing is not possible).

The items in the table are sequenced in ascending order of value, e.g.

| AC | AY | CR | DE | EL | LE | TR | YO |

Fig. 39: TABLE-1 (Two-character town codes)

Let us assume that a town code has been read in on the input data and needs translating into the town name given in another table:

| ACTON | AYR△△ | CREWE | DERBY | ELY △△ | LEEDS | TRURO | YORK△ |

Fig. 40: TABLE-2 (Five-character town names)

Let the number of items in the table be **N** (=8, in TABLE-1). Inspect the item **N/2** (=4) from the beginning (=DE). Assuming this is not the desired item, the search continues as follows: if the desired item is greater than the item just inspected, this means that the whole of the left-hand side of the table must be irrelevant. Inspect the item **N/4** (=2) positions to the **right** of the item last inspected (=LE).

Let us imagine that the desired item is EL, which is **less** than the item last inspected; this means that the whole of the right-hand quarter of the table is irrelevant. Therefore, we inspect the item **N/8** (=1) positions to the **left** of the item last inspected. In this way the location of the item is determined.

In general, you will see that the first comparison eliminates half the table, the second comparison a further quarter, the third a further eighth, and so on. The maximum number of comparisons needed to locate an item in a table of **N** items is $\log_2$ **N**, while the average number is less than this.

Exercise

1   (Quite hard.) A card contains a two-digit town code in CD-TWN which is to be translated as follows:

Code	Town	Code	Town
DI	DISS	AC	ACTON
CR	CREWE	AY	AYR
DE	DERBY	ES	ESHER
RY	RYE	EP	EPSOM
CO	CORBY	LE	LEEDS
AS	ASTON	KE	KELSO
YO	YORK	TR	TRURO

Assume that the code in the card is known to be valid. Draw a flowchart to perform a binary chop search to translate this code. Try describing the process in Structured English if you wish; this is the sort of problem where in practice one might use both a flowchart and Structured English to try to check out that the definition of the procedure is correct. Dry run your procedure with code TR and one or two others to make sure it works (you may have a truncation problem when the number of items in the table is not a power of 2; one way around this problem is to make the number of items a power of 2 and place the largest COBOL value possible in the spare items at the right of the table).

Consider the COBOL statements needed to perform the search (you can do it with only one table in this example – can you see how?).

O5   SEARCH

Larger compilers also provide an automatic means of searching a one dimension table. There are a number of options, but the basic method is as follows:

1   The name of the subscript ('index-name') which is to be used with the table is declared by an INDEXED BY clause in the data description entry for the table, e.g.

```
01    TABLE.
      02    TABLE-ITEM PIC XX OCCURS 100 TIMES
            INDEXED BY TAB-INDEX.
```

The index-name specified is not declared elsewhere in the Data Division; the compiler creates a suitable data item. This index is automatically updated when a SEARCH is made.

2   The desired initial value of the subscript is achieved by the SET verb. This desired initial value is usually 1 to ensure that the table search starts with the first item in the table, e.g.

```
      SET TAB-INDEX TO 1.
```

3   The table is searched by an instruction of the following form:

SEARCH identifier AT END imperative-statement-1

WHEN condition-1 $\left\{ \begin{array}{l} \text{imperative-statement-2} \\ \text{NEXT SENTENCE} \end{array} \right\}$

The identifier specified must be the one that was given the INDEXED BY clause in the Data Division, e.g.

```
      SET TAB-INDEX TO 1.
      SEARCH TABLE-ITEM
      AT END
          PERFORM ITEM-NOT-FOUND
      WHEN TABLE-ITEM(TAB-INDEX) = INPUT-CODE
          NEXT SENTENCE.
```

An automatic binary chop search can be achieved with the SEARCH ALL variation. In this case, the table sequence must also be specified, e.g.

```
      02    TABLE-ITEM PIC XX OCCURS 100 TIMES
            ASCENDING KEY IS TABLE-ITEM
            INDEXED BY TAB-INDEX.
```

To institute a binary chop search, we could say:

```
      SEARCH ALL TABLE-ITEM
      AT END
          PERFORM ITEM-NOT-FOUND
      WHEN TABLE-ITEM(TAB-INDEX) = INPUT-CODE
          NEXT SENTENCE.
```

The complete formats of SEARCH and SET verbs are given in Appendix D. The use of INDEXED BY is recommended for table operations, even when SEARCH is not being used, but the programmer must be careful not to let the value of the subscript go outside the range of the table bounds. This is not allowed, except when the subscript is the item referred to in the VARYING clause of a PERFORM..VARYING.

06   TWO DIMENSION TABLES

These are found when a repeated item appears within another item which is itself repeated, i.e. when one OCCURS clause is subordinate to another OCCURS clause. For example, suppose a manufacturer supplies parts to overseas agents, area distributors and contractors with a different rate of discount depending on the nature of the part and the class of purchaser, as follows:

			Parts	
Purchaser	Motors	Panels	Wheels	Other
Overseas agent	35%	30%	30%	30%
Area distributor	30%	25%	20%	20%
Contractor	10%	5%	5%	0%

Imagine that a program is to prepare an invoice for a customer from an order record which, apart from the gross cost of the order, contains two single digit items coded as follows:

PURCHASER-CODE	PART-TYPE
1 = Overseas agent	1 = Motors
2 = Area distributor	2 = Panels
3 = Contractor	3 = Wheels
	4 = Other

We can now code the relevant parts of the program to apply the discount as follows:

```
WORKING-STORAGE SECTION.
01   DISC-TABLE VALUE "353030303025202010050500".
    02   ROW OCCURS 3 TIMES.
        03   DISCOUNT OCCURS 4 TIMES PIC V99.
```

This describes a table of 3 rows and 4 columns; the first four items in the VALUE clause are the discounts for each column of the first row of the table, the next four are the discounts for each column of the second row, and so on. As mentioned before, it would probably be better to set out the values against 12 filler items to aid maintenance – this is a rather unsatisfactory feature of COBOL, and the CODASYL committee are making new recommendations for methods of initialising tables.

An individual item can be located with two subscripts, the first for the row and the second for the column. Motor parts for overseas agents have the discount in the first row, third column; this is DISCOUNT(1,3). Panels for area distributors would take DISCOUNT(3,4). The contents of the VALUE clause can be imagined to be split up like this:

35	30	30	30	30	25	20	20	10	05	05	00

ROW (1)   ROW (2)   ROW (3)

Fig. 41: Contents of DISC-TABLE

Within a row, each item is described as follows

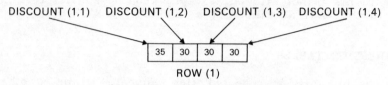

Fig. 42: Contents of ROW(1)

In this example, the value of PURCHASER-CODE correctly describes the desired row, and the value of PART-TYPE correctly describes the desired column; i.e. the table is self-indexed by these items. Procedure Division statements might include:

    MULTIPLY GROSS-COST BY DISCOUNT(PURCHASER-CODE, PART-TYPE)
    GIVING DISCOUNT-AMOUNT ROUNDED.

Exercise

1   Suppose, in the example in the text, PURCHASER-CODE took the values 0, 1, 2, 3. How would you have to amend the program?

2   In the same program as the example in the text, a record has been defined as follows:

    01 PRINTLINE.
        02   ROW-OUT OCCURS 3 TIMES.
            03   FILLER   PIC XX.
            03   DISC-OUT   PIC 0.99B OCCURS 4 TIMES.
    There are two PICTURE 9 items in working storage called ROW-SUB and COL-SUB. Write statements which will move each DISCOUNT into the corresponding DISC-OUT field. (Hint: consider writing the statement PERFORM FILL-ROW VARYING ROW-SUB FROM 1 BY 1 UNTIL ROW-SUB = 4. In FILL-ROW could be another PERFORM statement which will move individual fields.)

3   A program has a large table which is to be used to accumulate totals:

    01   TABLE-1.
        02   ROW   OCCURS 100 TIMES INDEXED BY ROW-SUB.
            03   TOTAL   OCCURS 5 TIMES PIC S9(4)V99 COMP
                         INDEXED BY COL-SUB.

Each total is to have an initial value of zero, but a value clause cannot be used with an item that OCCURS. Moreover, TOTAL has been given computational usage, which on many machines will mean that moving zeros to the group item TABLE-1 will NOT result in the individual TOTALs containing zero. Code must be written to clear each table item to zero. Write statements to achieve this.

O7   STRING

The verbs STRING and UNSTRING – although at first sight rather formidable – make for much easier manipulation of data in some cases. The complete formats are given in Appendix D; I shall try to explain the use of these verbs and illustrate some of their potential, but a knowledge of these verbs is not essential to the rest of the text.

The STRING verb, stripped to bare essentials, is of the form

$$\underline{\text{STRING}} \quad \begin{Bmatrix} \text{identifier-1} \\ \text{literal-1} \end{Bmatrix} \begin{bmatrix} \text{identifier-2} \\ \text{literal-2} \end{bmatrix} \ \dots \ \underline{\text{DELIMITED}} \ \text{BY} \ \begin{bmatrix} \text{literal-3} \\ \underline{\text{SIZE}} \end{bmatrix}$$

$\underline{\text{INTO}}$ identifier-3.

The ideal use of the verb occurs when you wish to collect together a number of fields to make one long string of characters in a new field. This typically arises when some message is to be sent to a VDU screen as part of a dialogue with which the terminal user interacts.

For example, suppose you had records as follows:

```
01   SCREEN-LINE              PIC X(60).
01   PART-RECORD.
     02   PART-NUMBER         PIC 9(4).
     02   BIN-NUMBER          PIC 99.
     02   PART-DESCRIPTION    PIC X(20).
```

Further suppose that the contents of these fields called PART-NUMBER, BIN-NUMBER and PART-DESCRIPTION happened to be 8076, 16 and "TUBULAR STEEL._____" respectively. These fields could be edited into LINE-OF-PRINT by:

```
MOVE SPACES TO SCREEN-LINE.
STRING
"PART: "
PART-NUMBER
" DESCRIPTION: "
PART-DESCRIPTION
" BIN: "
BIN-NUMBER
DELIMITED BY SIZE INTO LINE-OF-PRINT.
```

The DELIMITED BY SIZE clause simply means that the whole of the sending field will be added to the string that is formed. Thus, after execution of this statement, SCREEN-LINE will contain:

PART: 8076 DESCRIPTION: TUBULAR STEEL._____BIN: 16

Unlike the MOVE verb, STRING does not automatically pad out the right hand end of the receiving field with spaces; hence the preliminary MOVE in the example.

Next suppose that what you would really like to do is to make the line appear as a continuous sentence by closing up the literal " BIN: " so that it follows immediately after the last letter of the description. If the description text was always terminated by a full stop, this could be achieved by

```
MOVE SPACES TO SCREEN-LINE
STRING
"PART: "
PART-NUMBER
" DESCRIPTION: "
DELIMITED BY SIZE
PART-DESCRIPTION
```

```
                    DELIMITED BY "."
                    " BIN: "
                    BIN-NUMBER
                    DELIMITED BY SIZE INTO SCREEN-LINE.
```

The delimiter itself is not moved. Thus, the result of this statement will be

   PART: 8076 DESCRIPTION: TUBULAR STEEL BIN: 16

The delimiter can be a sequence of characters if desired. If a delimiter is not encountered while the move is taking place, the whole of the sending field is added to the string being formed.

It will be seen that when the moves are not DELIMITED BY SIZE, the actual number of characters strung together in the receiving field is not constant. The programmer can establish the number of characters strung together by using the POINTER option, which references an elementary data item which is to contain the number of the next available position in the receiving field, counting from the left (i.e. the actual number of characters moved to the field, plus 1). For example if an item NEXT-CH PIC 999 USAGE COMP had been defined, we could code:

```
                    MOVE 1 TO NEXT-CH.
                    MOVE SPACES TO SCREEN-LINE.
                    STRING
                    "PART: "
                    PART-NUMBER
                    " DESCRIPTION: "
                    DELIMITED BY SIZE
                    PART-DESCRIPTION
                    DELIMITED BY "."
                    " BIN: "
                    BIN-NUMBER
                    DELIMITED BY SIZE INTO SCREEN-LINE POINTER NEXT-CH.
```

After execution of this statement, NEXT-CH would have the value 46. When a pointer has been specified, the receiving field accepts characters starting at the position indicated by the pointer field; hence the need to establish an inital value for NEXT-CH in the example. The pointer option is particularly valuable if you wish to add further to a previously formed string. To continue the example:

```
                    STRING " OUT OF STOCK"
                    DELIMITED BY SIZE INTO LINE-OF-PRINT POINTER NEXT-CH.
```

would - assuming the value of NEXT-CH had not been changed in any way - produce the result

   PART: 8076 DESCRIPTION: TUBULAR STEEL BIN: 16 OUT OF STOCK

Finally, there may be cases where the receiving field is too short to accept the desired string. This condition can be detected by the OVERFLOW keyword - see Appendix D.

08 UNSTRING

The purpose of the UNSTRING verb is to take a string of characters in a sending field and distribute it as shorter strings in receiving fields. For example, suppose we had the following fields in the Data Division:

```
      02   NEXT-CH               PIC 999 COMP.
      02   NO-OF-LINES           PIC 9 COMP.
01   INPUT-ADDRESS               PIC X(150).
01   PRINTABLE-ADDRESS.
      02   NAME                  PIC X(40).
      02   ADDR-LINE-1           PIC X(40).
      02   ADDR-LINE-2           PIC X(40).
      02   ADDR-LINE-3           PIC X(40).
      02   ADDR-LINE-4           PIC X(40).
```

The record called INPUT-ADDRESS contains a name and address with an oblique stroke separating each line. No line is longer than 40 characters; there may be two, three or four lines of address following the name. We wish to get each line into the corresponding field in PRINTABLE-ADDRESS and we wish to know how many lines there are. This can be achieved by UNSTRING as follows.

```
      MOVE ZERO TO NO-OF-LINES.
      UNSTRING INPUT-ADDRESS DELIMITED BY "/" INTO
      NAME
      ADDR-LINE-1
      ADDR-LINE-2
      ADDR-LINE-3
      ADDR-LINE-4
      TALLYING IN NO-OF-LINES
      ON OVERFLOW
            PERFORM TOO-MANY-LINES.
```

The OVERFLOW condition arises if all the receiving fields are used and there are still unconsidered characters left in the sending field. The TALLYING option arranges a count of the number of receiving fields affected; note that it is necessary for the programmer to arrange the desired initial value in the item that accumulates the tally. Data is sent to the receiving fields in accordance with the rules for MOVEs (the sending field to be treated as alphanumeric), so there is no need to initialise the receiving fields.

There is a POINTER option, as with STRING, and more than one delimiter may be specified by joining delimiters with OR. The delimiter itself can be saved, if desired, by the DELIMITER IN clause. Let us suppose that, in the previous example, the end of the last line of address was indicated by an asterisk instead of the oblique stroke. Assuming suitable items had been defined in the Data Division, all of these options can be illustrated by a routine to print out the name and address on subsequent lines.

```
      MOVE ZERO TO NO-OF-LINES.
      MOVE 1 TO NEXT-CH.
      MOVE SPACE TO SAVED-DELIMITER.
      PERFORM PRINT-A-LINE UNTIL SAVED-DELIMITER = "*".
      ADD NO-OF-LINES TO LINE-COUNT etc.
            :
PRINT-A-LINE.
      UNSTRING INPUT-ADDRESS DELIMITED BY "/" OR "*" INTO
      LINE-OF-PRINT
      DELIMITER IN SAVED-DELIMITER
      POINTER NEXT-CH
      TALLYING NO-OF-LINES.
```

WRITE LINE-OF-PRINT BEFORE ADVANCING 1 LINE.

A delimiter may be preceded by the word ALL, in which case several consecutive occurrences of the delimiter will be treated as a single occurrence. If there is no data to be moved by the UNSTRING statement (e.g. as a result of consecutive delimiters when ALL is not used), the receiving field is filled with spaces if it is alphanumeric, zeros if it is numeric. If the programmer wishes to know how many characters have been transferred to the receiving field, this can be achieved with the COUNT IN option (see Appendix D).

ANSWERS – SECTION O

Frame O1

1   Imagine there is a semi-colon in OUT-REC; to get the other machine to read this as a semi-colon, you will have to output it as a full stop. Therefore, semi-colons need to be translated into full stops.
    Applying the same logic to each character, we get:

```
INSPECT INPUT-RECORD REPLACING ALL
";" BY "."
"." BY ";"
"*" BY "/"
"=" BY "*"
"/" BY "="
"#" BY ")"
"&" BY "("
")" BY "#"
"(" BY "&".
```

Frame O2

1   Of the many possible answers, this one follows closely on the text.

```
01   IN-REC.
     02   IN-CH        PIC X OCCURS 80 TIMES.
WORKING-STORAGE SECTION.
01   FILESUBS      COMP SYNC RIGHT.
     02   INRECSUB     PIC 99.
     02   NEWRECSUB    PIC 999.
01   TABLES.
     02   SOURCE-TAB   VALUE "ABCDEFGHI123456789".
          03   SOURCE-CH   PIC X OCCURS 18 TIMES.
     02   TARGET-TAB   VALUE "123456789ABCDEFGHI".
          03   TARGET-CH   PIC X OCCURS 18 TIMES.
     02   TABLESUB     PIC 99 COMP SYNC RIGHT.
01   NEW-REC.
     02   NEW-CH       PIC X OCCURS 240 TIMES.
PROCEDURE DIVISION.
: (get input record)
     PERFORM B1-TRANSLATE-REC UNTIL EOF-INFILE = "T".
:
B1-TRANSLATE-REC.
     MOVE SPACES TO NEW-REC.
     MOVE 1 TO NEWRECSUB.
     PERFORM C1-TRANSLATE VARYING INRECSUB FROM 1 BY 1
```

```
            UNTIL INRECSUB = 81.
            READ INFILE
            AT END
                MOVE "T" TO EOF-INFILE.
    C1-TRANSLATE.
            IF IN-CH(INRECSUB) = "*"
                PERFORM D1-MOVE-ZERO 3 TIMES
            ELSE
                PERFORM E1-LOOKUP VARYING TABLESUB FROM 1 BY 1
                UNTIL TABLESUB = 19
                OR IN-CH(INRECSUB) = SOURCE-CH(TABLESUB)
                IF TABLESUB LESS THAN 19
                    MOVE TARGET-CH(TABLESUB) TO NEW-CH(NEWRECSUB)
                    ADD 1 TO NEWRECSUB
                ELSE
                    MOVE IN-CH(INRECSUB) TO NEW-CH(NEWRECSUB)
                    ADD 1 TO NEWRECSUB.
    D1-MOVE-ZERO.
            MOVE ZERO TO NEW-CH(NEWRECSUB).
            ADD 1 TO NEWRECSUB.
    E1-LOOKUP.
```

Frame O4

1   Let the table contain 16 items, the last two being HIGH-VALUES.

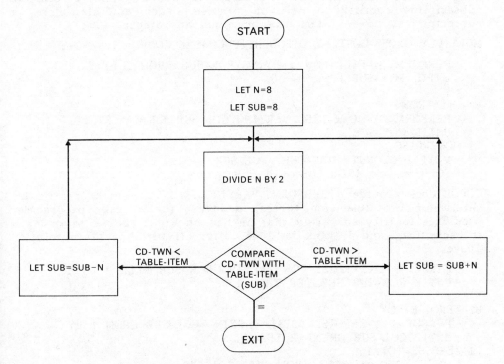

Fig. 43: Answer to Exercise 1, frame O4

```
WORKING-STORAGE SECTION.
01   TABLE    VALUE "ACTONASTONAYR   CORBYCREWEDERBYDISS EPSOM"
-            "ESHERKELSOLEEDSRYE   TRUROYORK ".
     02 FILLER    PIC X(10)    VALUE HIGH-VALUES.
```

```
01   TABLE-2 REDEFINES TABLE.
     02   TOWN-NAME OCCURS 16 TIMES.
          03   TABLE-ITEM   PIC XX.
          03   FILLER       PIC XXX.
01   SEARCH-AIDS COMP SYNC RIGHT.
     02   N                 PIC 99.
     02   SUB               PIC 99.
PROCEDURE DIVISION.
     :
     MOVE 8 TO N.
     MOVE 8 TO SUB.
     PERFORM B1-SEARCH-TABLE UNTIL CD-TWN = TABLE-ITEM(SUB).
     MOVE TOWN-NAME(SUB) TO ...
     :
B1-SEARCH-TABLE.
     DIVIDE 2 INTO N.
     IF CD-TWN LESS THAN TABLE-ITEM(SUB)
          SUBTRACT N FROM SUB
     ELSE
          ADD N TO SUB.
```

Frame 06

1 You would have to add 1 to PURCHASER-CODE to bring it into the range desired for use as a subscript. COBOL offers a **relative** subscripting facility to help in problems such as this. Here, a subscript may be any item plus or minus an integer, e.g.

```
MULTIPLY GROSS-COST BY DISCOUNT(PUCHASER-CODE + 1,PART-TYPE)..
```

2
```
     PERFORM B1-FILL-ROW VARYING ROW-SUB FROM 1 BY 1
          UNTIL ROW-SUB = 4.
     :
B1-FILL-ROW.
     PERFORM C1-MOVE-DISC VARYING COL-SUB FROM 1 BY 1
          UNTIL COL-SUB = 5.
C1-MOVE-DISC.
     MOVE DISCOUNT (ROW-SUB, COL-SUB)
     TO DISC-OUT (ROW-SUB, COL-SUB).
```

COBOL does provide a PERFORM..VARYING..AFTER.. which specifically caters for two dimension tables. However, the average programmer uses this facility so rarely that he has an uphill battle to re-learn it each time, and I think he'd be better off with the plain solution above.

3
```
     PERFORM B1-ZEROISE-ROW VARYING ROW-SUB FROM 1 BY 1
          UNTIL ROW-SUB GREATER THAN 100.
     :
B1-ZEROISE-ROW.
     PERFORM C1-ZEROISE-TOTAL VARYING COL-SUB FROM 1 BY 1
          UNTIL COL-SUB GREATER THAN 5.
C1-ZEROISE-TOTAL.
     MOVE ZERO TO TOTAL(ROW-SUB, COL-SUB).
```

P Programming interactive dialogues

P1 GENERAL GUIDELINES

A dialogue can be a simple thing to program when it is a series of questions and answers without much branching logic. On the other hand, it can be a very complicated program when the user has a lot of choices and the dialogue can be diverted down many different paths. Two features of commercial interactive programming that make it difficult are (a) exercising control over the visual display hardware when this has a lot of built-in features, and (b) exercising control over the program flow when the choices are complicated.

Unfortunately, there is no standard answer to item (a). Visual display units come with a wide variety of features such as reverse video, bold text and underlining, screen protect, X-Y cursor addressing, screen clear, flashing fields, audible signals, etc. These features are usually invoked by outputting to the VDU control symbols stored in the program, but the actual symbols vary from device to device. Further, manufacturers have not in practice chosen standard methods for dealing with VDUs in COBOL (although CODASYL is considering standard screen management facilities); most allow simple teletype-like operations using READ and WRITE, some use ACCEPT and DISPLAY for input and output (frame Q3), some treat the display as a record on a relative file which can be read from or written to (frame T3), some use the COMMUNICATIONS SECTION facilities of standard COBOL (not covered in this text). Many commercial programming departments use modified versions of COBOL, or special screen formatting and data entry utility programs, to assist with interactive programming. You are advised to study the technical manuals for the particular equipment you are using.

The next three frames are concerned with particular methods of controlling the flow of interactive programs. For simplicity a teletype-like display is assumed in frame P2 and P3, and a display with X-Y cursor addressing in frame P4.

Programmers are often expected to play a larger part in the analysis and design of interactive procedures. For suggestions about choosing suitable dialogues and designing screen layouts, see Chapters 8 and 9 of my book *Systems Analysis*. The following checklist may also help:

1   Allow for case shift variants in replies

2   Organise large menus into a tree

3   Consider hard copy menus

4   Give experienced users a chance to abbreviate or take short cuts

5   Consider different levels of help, or different lengths of explanatory messages, for users of different experience

6   Let users customise their view of the system if possible

7   Keep the dialogue style, method of work and meaning of codes, keywords, etc. standard throughout the system

8   Give quick response to each input

9   Do not make the user rely upon memory

10   Consider producing hard copy instead of/in addition to a display

11   Keep records of system and user responses for later improvements (e.g. numbers of transactions, frequency with which different choices are made, frequency of errors)

12   Give as much thought to error conditions as to the main dialogue

13   Choose words carefully

14   Avoid cluttered screens

P2   THE MENU DIALOGUE

The menu is an easy dialogue to program and is particularly suited to inexperienced users. Its main disadvantage is that it may be slow compared with other dialogue styles, especially if the terminal device is slow in operation.

Menus tend to be verbose so to keep to the concise style of this book I have to choose an unrealistically short example. Suppose we have a master menu as follows:

Menu 1
Do you want to
    1. enter a transaction
    2. print a file
    3. ask a question?

A response of '1' prompts the further menu:

Menu 1.1
Select type of transaction:
    1. invoice
    2. payment
    3. change master file detail

while a response of '2' to the master menu results in the display:

Menu 1.2
Select file to be printed:
    1. invoices this month
    2. payments this month
    3. customer master

and so on.

Let us suppose that in this system a blank response indicates that the user does not wish to continue with the menu and is to be returned to the next higher menu. A response that is neither blank nor a digit in the range of the menu is an error response. After successful completion of a lowest-level operation (at a 'leaf' of the tree of selections) the last menu offered is to be repeated. Thus, the user can 'back up' the tree of menus by entering successive blank entries when he is offered a menu he does not want.

This hierarchical branching logic is clearly a 'case' construction. In essence the program is of the form:

Menu 1
Repeat until blank response
    |Repeat until response is valid
    | |Display menu
    | |Get response
    | |Evaluate response
    | |When 1
    | | |Perform 'Menu 1.1'
    | |When 2
    | | |Perform 'Menu 1.2'
    | |When 3
    | | |Perform 'Menu 1.3'
    | |When blank
    | | |no action
    | |Else
    | | |Response not valid

Menu 1.1
Repeat until blank response
    |Repeat until response valid
    | |Display menu
    | |Get response
    | |Evaluate response
    | |When 1
    | | |Perform 'Enter-invoice'
    | |When 2
    | | |Perform 'Enter-payment'
    | |When 3
    | | |Perform 'Change-master'
    | |When blank
    | | |no action
    | |Else
    | | |Response is not valid

and so on.
(The Evaluate..When.. style of dealing with the case construct here corresponds to a proposed EVALUATE verb in COBOL.)

Obviously each response not specifically stated to be not valid is a valid response. Also it should be appreciated that error actions need to be added to the Else case. The outline supposes that the menu is to be re-output on each occasion; if this is not the case, the 'display menu' action should be repositioned just before the inner 'repeat' instruction, and the error actions will have to include repositioning the cursor at the data entry point after displaying the error message.

It should also be appreciated that the word 'response' in this example is **local** to each procedure, i.e. response in Menu 1 means the Menu 1 response, whereas response in Menu 1.1 means the Menu 1.1 response. The following general rules should be observed when using Structured English for program design:

1   References to names of files or data items in files centrally documented, e.g. in a data dictionary, are global unless declared to be local

2   References to other data items are local unless declared to be global

3   Local items which are to be passed as parameters should be placed in brackets after the subroutine reference.

If response were declared to be global in this example, this would have the effect that a blank entry at any point would take the user right back to the top of the tree and exit from the program.

With most computer systems, the text of dialogues is better stored on backing storage accessible to the program rather than embodied as constants in the program. This is because it is usually easier to edit a data file than to change a program and recompile it, and dialogue wordings often need successive refinements while they are being tried out with users. One possibility is to have each menu as a record on a file (direct access is probably best - see Section T), while another possibility is to have each menu as a file and each selection as a record on that file. The latter method is the more flexible approach if the operating system gives suitable support for the large quantity of files that may result, and it also makes it easier to build a general-purpose menu handling system.

With a general-purpose menu handling system, there is only one program to be written to handle the display of menus and the gathering of responses. Each menu item record must include the message to be displayed for the item and the action that is to be taken if the item is selected. This will be either presentation of a further menu (naming the menu file) or taking a 'leaf' action (naming the program), or both. With this strategy, the programming of a hierarchical menu dialogue is resolved simply to the creation of a set of data files for the menus and writing the leaf programs (the leaf programs can be executed by inter-program communication - see Section U).

Exercise

1   Amend the example of this frame so that the dialogue returns to the main menu (Menu 1) if the user types the letter M in response to any menu selection request.

Practical

1   Write a Structured English specification of a general-purpose menu handler. Implement it. (If you wish to keep things simple, restrict the menu selection choices to the digits 1, 2, 3 etc. and blank. You will need to limit the number of selections allowed on a given menu.)

P3   STATE TRANSITION TABLES

Interactive dialogues often involve interpretation of strings of characters entered at the keyboard (this sort of problem more rarely arises with batch systems). Many of these problems can be solved with the UNSTRING and INSPECT facilities already explained. There is also quite a large class of problems which can be solved by state transition tables. The main advantage of these tables is that they help to clarify a complex problem prior to coding.

Suppose that in an interactive program a visual display operator is to enter a data item 'value of sale'. Further, although 10 character positions are to be allowed for the data item, the data can be of any length up to 10 characters, including an unspecified number of leading and trailing spaces. The amount may not be arithmetically signed (+ or −). At least one digit must be present, and a decimal point may optionally be present. An integer is to be interpreted as 'dollars' unless it is followed by the symbol ¢, in which case it is to be interpreted as 'cents'. The symbol ¢ is not allowed when a decimal point is present.

To construct a state transition table for this case, identify all the characters or classes of characters which are significant to the interpretation of the data − space, digit, decimal point, symbol ¢, any other character. These are the characters which cause a change of state as described later. All digits are lumped together in the class 'digit' because there is no different treatment required for any particular digit. Similarly any character other than space, digit, decimal point and cent symbol will give rise to an error state.

In this case there is one other significant state of the input, namely the state where the field is completely full as a result of ten characters having been entered.

The input states and characters are used to label the columns of the table. Now, to construct the table, label the first row with the initial state (e.g. 'Before any significant digit') and enter in the table under each column an arbitrary number to represent the row of the new state. Use the same number, of course, if two different inputs lead to the same new state. Label the second row, and continue in this fashion until all entries are complete, except for those states considered terminal.

Fig. 44 shows the table that results.

CURRENT STATE \ INPUT	Space	Digit	Decimal point	Symbol "¢"	Any other character	End of data
1. Before any significant digit	1	2	3	6	6	6
2. Digits before decimal point	5	2	3	5	6	7
3. Expecting first digit after decimal point	5	4	6	6	6	7
4. Expecting second digit after decimal point	5	5	6	6	6	7
5. After end of entry	5	6	6	6	6	7
6. Error						
7. Finished						

Fig. 44: State transition table showing the new current state that results from the specified input character or input state

In preparing the state transition table, there are likely to be states arising which were not clearly dealt with in the narrative specifications (e.g. may the decimal point be the last non-space character entered?). These points should be referred to the analyst or user for clarification.

In the example, to keep it short, states have been lumped together which could have been differentiated if called for. For example, there is only one 'error' state; different sorts of error could have been identified by having states 'Error – invalid character present', 'Error – embedded space', 'Error – blank entry', etc. (see also the next frame). Similarly we could have had states like 'Finished and the field contains integer dollars', 'Finished and the field contains integer cents', etc.

Implementation of a program from a state table has straightforward possibilities, but which is the best approach depends on the circumstances. An approach to consider is described below. This may seem a little complicated, but once understood I think you will not want to do it another way.

The columns are considered to be numbered 1, 2, 3 etc., and the states (= rows) are also numbered 1, 2, 3 etc. The state table is stored as data and the input character is converted, by means of a lookup table (see frames 02 and 05), into the column number. The procedure is then as follows.

Validate sale value
Set state to 1
Input (or index) first character
Repeat until state = 6 or 7
     |Convert input character to column number
     |Set state to table-entry (row = state, column = column number)
     |If state not = 6 or 7
     | |Input (or index) next character

This approach leads to reasonably easy maintenance provided the maintaining programmer also understands the method, and the state transition table is documented.

Exercise

1   What change would you need to make to Fig. 44 if the decimal point were not allowed to be the last non-space character in the input?

P4 STATE TABLE TO CONTROL DIALOGUE PROGRESS

Cases often arise in interactive dialogues where it is desired to exercise control in a non-hierarchical way. For example, consider the following possible service to a user who wishes to consider investment choices.

Please respond to each of the following four questions. Respond with a ? for the item you wish to find; enter the value of the other three items. Only one ? is allowed in the answers.

Number of years of investment (whole years) = ...
Amount of principal to be invested = £.......
Annual rate of interest (compounded annually) = ...%
Maturity value of investment = £........

Press RETURN after each of your entries.
Press RETURN in answer to any question if you have made a mistake and wish to start again at question 1.

zzzzzzzzzzzzzzzzzzzzzzzzzzzzzzzzzzzzzzzzzzzzz

The whole of the screen is to be presented at the outset (except the line of z's, which show the location of the result and error message area). The cursor is moved to the first dot of the first question. After the user's valid entry, the cursor is positioned at the first dot of the next question, and so on. After the last entry, a message is written, being one of these four corresponding to the '?':

Number of years required is ZZ9
Principal required is ££,£££,££9
Rate of interest needed is ZZ9.999%
Maturity value is ££,£££,££9

If a size error occurs, the message will be:

The answer is too large to report. Please enter new data.

If the user's data is not valid, a suitable error message is displayed in the message line and the cursor is repositioned at the first dot of the entry concerned. If the user's entry is empty (indicated by the entry of RETURN alone, with this particular equipment) the screen is re-presented and the cursor repositioned for question 1.

To rearrange this problem so that it is amenable to a hierarchical solution can be very pedestrian. In this example, it would require one menu offering four choices of query type, and for each query type there would be a different dialogue asking for the three values needed to answer that type of query.

The state table solution is similar in principle to that described in the previous frame, the only difference being that in addition to a new state being determined by an entry in the table, each current state/input combination also calls for an **action** to be taken before continuing to the next state.

Fig. 45 shows a state table for our problem. In addition to the new state, each item of the table has been labelled with an action number. This is only to help you understand the implementation of the state table; the action number is not included in the table stored in the program.

CURRENT STATE		"?" 1	Valid numeric response to question 2	Any other case 3	Empty 4
1.	Before no-of-years question	A1, 2	A2, 3	A3, 1	A4, 1
2.	? found, before principal question	A5, 2	A6, 4	A7, 2	A8, 1
3.	? not found, before principal question	A9, 4	A10, 5	A11, 3	A12, 1
4.	? found, before rate question	A13, 4	A14, 6	A15, 4	A16, 1
5.	? not found, before rate question	A17, 6	A18, 1	A19, 5	A20, 1
6.	? found, before maturity question	A21, 6	A22, 1	A23, 6	A24, 1

INPUT CASE

Fig. 45: State transition table for the investment dialogue

Just as before, it is necessary to work methodically through the table, analysing the transitions from the current state to the next state, but in addition the action to be taken at each stage needs to be noted. For brevity the list of actions is omitted but has been incorporated into the Structured English specification of the program which follows.

Investment query program
Repeat until no-more-queries
    |Display text on screen
    |Cursor to number-of-years field
    |Set state to 1
    |Get input case
    |Repeat until query-answered
    | |Do 'Convert input case to column-no'
    | |Do 'Carry out action' (state, column-no, query-answered)
    | |Exit if query-answered
    | |Set state to table entry (state, column-no)
    | |Get input case
    |Display "Do you have another query? Answer Y or N"
    |If answer is "N"
    | |No-more-queries

Convert input case to column-no
Evaluate user's response
When "?"
    |Set column-no to 1
When space
    |Set column-no to 4
When valid numeric response to question
    |Set column-no to 2
Else
    |Set column-no to 3

Carry out action (state, column-no, query-answered)
Evaluate state and column-no
When 1 and 1
    |Set query-type to 1
    |Cursor to principal field
When 1 and 2
    |Cursor to principal field
When 1 and 3
    |Write invalid data message
    |Cursor to number-of-years field
When 2 and 1
    |Write ? already entered message
    |Cursor to principal field
When 2 and 2
    |Cursor to rate field
When (2 and 3) or (3 and 3)
    |Write invalid data message
    |Cursor to principal field
When 3 and 1
    |Set query-type to 2
    |Cursor to rate field
When 3 and 2
    |Cursor to rate field
When 4 and 1

```
     |Write ? already entered message
     |Cursor to rate field
When 4 and 2
     |Cursor to maturity field
When (4 and 3) or (5 and 3)
     |Write invalid data message
     |Cursor to rate field
When 5 and 1
     |Set query-type to 3
     |Cursor to maturity field
When 5 and 2
     |Calculate maturity
     |If size error
     |     |Write result too large message
     |Else
     |     |Write maturity message
     |Query-answered
When 6 and 1
     |Write ? already entered message
     |Cursor to maturity field
When 6 and 2
     |Evaluate query-type
     |When 1
     |     |Calculate years
     |     |If size error
     |     |     |Write result too large message
     |     |Else
     |     |     |Write years message
     |When 2
     |     |Calculate principal
     |     |If size error
     |     |     |Write result too large message
     |     |Else
     |     |     |Write principal message
     |When 3
     |     |Calculate rate
     |     |If size error
     |     |     |Write result too large message
     |     |Else
     |     |     |Write rate message
     |Else
     |     |Program logic error
     |Query-answered
When 6 and 3
     |Write invalid data message
     |Cursor to maturity field
Else
     |Cursor to principal field
```

If implementing the case construction by means of GO TO..DEPENDING ON ACTION-NO, the ACTION-NO in this case can be computed by (state − 1) * 4 + 1.

State transition tables can be used to exercise larger control over dialogues, e.g. control over successive screen presentations. A complicated dialogue may call for control, at different stages or at different levels of analysis, by state tables, menus and structured constructs. The programmer who masters all three techniques is in a position to solve any commercial text-based dialogue problem.

Practical

1   Implement the investment query program on your equipment.

ANSWERS – SECTION P

Frame P2

1   Declare entry-is-M global in Menu 1. Amend the opening statement of each subordinate menu to Repeat until blank response or entry-is-M. In each subordinate menu, take no action on case response = "M".

Frame P3

1   Change the 5 in row 3, column 1, to a 6.

Part 3
Further COBOL

Q Programmer aids and sundries

Q1 COPY

The format of this verb is simply

COPY text-name

where text-name is the name of some pre-written COBOL statements which have been stored on a library accessible to the COBOL compiler. This library is usually held on magnetic disk.

For example, suppose you had arranged for the following coding to be inserted in the library under the name STANDARD-CARDLIST

```
SELECT CARDIN ASSIGN TO CARD-READER.
SELECT PRINTOUT ASSIGN TO PRINTER.
```

If you wished to write a program using these file names and devices, you could write the FILE-CONTROL paragraph of the program as follows:

```
FILE-CONTROL. COPY STANDARD-CARDLIST.
```

The compiler will look up the statements in the library and insert these so that your program will be compiled as if you had written in full

```
FILE-CONTROL.    SELECT CARDIN ASSIGN TO CARD-READER.
                 SELECT PRINTOUT ASSIGN TO PRINTER.
```

COBOL allows you to change a name or word appearing in library statements by using the word REPLACING, e.g.

```
FILE-CONTROL. COPY STANDARD-CARDLIST REPLACING
              CARDIN BY CARDFILE
              PRINTOUT BY PRINTFILE.
```

This would be compiled as:

```
FILE-CONTROL.    SELECT CARDFILE ASSIGN TO CARD-READER.
                 SELECT PRINTFILE ASSIGN TO PRINTER.
```

COBOL also allows you to make text substitutions of any sort (even comments), e.g. COPY STANDARD-CARDLIST REPLACING << PRINTER >> BY <<PRINTER RESERVE 3 AREAS >> would produce

```
FILE-CONTROL.    SELECT CARDIN ASSIGN TO CARD-READER.
                 SELECT PRINTOUT ASSIGN TO PRINTER
                 RESERVE 3 AREAS.
```

There remains the issue of how to get the standard entries onto the library in the first place. This is not done by the standard COBOL compiler; manufacturers provide a utility program which inserts entries into the library.

In a department that maintains a central catalogue or dictionary of all data items in files, it can be a good idea to establish the file and record descriptions in the library so that they can be copied into programs. Other than this, COPY has rather limited use in practice, but the concept of the library is important for other programming work.

Q2   DEBUGGING AIDS

There are several facilities to assist with fault finding. Before these facilities were standardised, many manufacturers offered debugging aids of their own invention (and still do). The facilities are of three types: debug lines, trace facilities and monitoring facilities.

Debug lines are lines of source code which are inserted into a program during testing but which are not intended to be part of the finished program. Any line with a "D" in column 7 is a debug line which is basically treated as a comment by the compiler, but which can be 'activated' by the programmer at compilation time and execution time.

At compilation time, the compiler can be asked to compile the debug lines by adding the phrase WITH DEBUGGING MODE to the entry in the SOURCE-COMPUTER paragraph. In the absence of this phrase, debug lines will be treated as comments.

At execution time, the computer operator can arrange for the computer to execute the debug lines, or not, as required. This is done by means of commands through the operating system.

Trace facilities aim to list out the paragraph names or line numbers in the order they are executed by the program.

Monitoring facilities aim to show how the value of a particular item changes as the program proceeds.

Debug lines should be included in programs to verify the correctness of assertions considered when writing the source program. Apart from this usage, programmers who have mastered structured program design rarely need to call on these facilities.

Q3   OPERATOR COMMUNICATION

A message can be passed to the computer operator during execution of the program by the DISPLAY verb. This is simply the word DISPLAY followed by a string of variables and/or literals, e.g.

        DISPLAY "NO OF RECORDS READ = " REC-COUNT.

If REC-COUNT contained 01273, the message

NO OF RECORDS READ = 01273

would appear on the 'display device', i.e. the peripheral device designated for displays. This is often the computer operator's console display or the display from which execution of the program was initiated. With some computers the display device can be explicitly stated.

Similarly, information can be obtained from the operator with the ACCEPT verb. This is the word ACCEPT followed by a single identifier of some element of data in the Data Division. The machine stops and whatever the operator types is entered in the variable, e.g.

        DISPLAY "ENTER 2-DIGIT RUN NUMBER".
        ACCEPT RUN-NO.

Again, with some computers, the device is explicitly stated. Whatever the operator keys is entered left-justified in the accepting field, so with numeric fields there may have to be some juggling with the data if the operator does not enter the full number of digits in the item.

The ACCEPT statement has a second format.

$$\underline{ACCEPT} \text{ identifier } \underline{FROM} \quad \left\{ \begin{array}{l} \text{DATE} \\ \text{DAY} \\ \text{TIME} \end{array} \right\}$$

The DATE option puts a six digit date in the form YYMMDD into the identifier specified. DAY gives a five digit Julian date, YYDDD. TIME gives an eight digit time in hours (24 hour clock system), minutes, seconds and hundredths of a second.

Q4   CONDITION NAMES

Quite a handy documentation aid is the level-88 condition name. Here a name (condition-name) is assigned to certain values of data in an elementary item. If, at execution time, the item contains the stated value, the condition-name will be true; otherwise, it will be false. The truth of the condition-name can be tested in an IF statement statement in the Procedure Division. For example:

```
02   ERROR-FLAG   PIC X.
     88   VALID-RECORD      VALUE IS "F".
     88   INVALID-RECORD    VALUE IS "T".
  :
PROCEDURE DIVISION.
  :
     PERFORM B1-VALIDATE-REC.
     IF INVALID-RECORD
        PERFORM B2-PRINT-ERRORS.
```

The last sentence has the same effect as if it said

```
     IF ERROR-FLAG = "T"
        PERFORM B2-PRINT-ERRORS.
```

Condition-names can be associated with any elementary item. A range of values can be assigned by the THRU option,

```
02   QUANTITY-ORDERED    PIC 9(4).
     88   SMALL-QUANTITY   VALUE IS 0 THRU 100.
     88   LARGE-QUANTITY   VALUE IS 101 THRU 9999.
```

The range of values may overlap if desired. (A welcome proposal from CODASYL is that a sentence such as SET VALID-RECORD TRUE will have the same effect as MOVE "F" TO ERROR-FLAG.)

Q5   STOP

I haven't bothered to explain this verb before because its purpose is reasonably plain. There are two versions

```
STOP literal.
STOP RUN.
```

In the first case, the machine stops executing the program and the literal is displayed on the display device. The operator can re-start the program from the point it stopped, if he so decides.

In the second case, the program terminates completely, handing control of the computer back to the operating system.

R Sorting

R1   SORTING CONCEPTS

The purpose of a sort is to place the records of a file into a certain order. Suppose you had a file of records as follows:

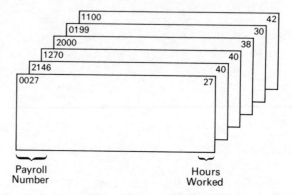

Fig. 46: TIME-CARDS file

and you wished to match these against a master file on magnetic tape which contained employee records in payroll number order (one record per employee). Clearly the TIME-CARDS file must be resequenced into the same order as the master file.

In this example, you could easily achieve this by hand. But if the file were large, you must get the computer to do the sorting for you. How the computer achieves this is quite complex and beyond the scope of this text – it is sufficient to understand that there is a program provided with the computer which will read in an unsorted file and produce a sorted file in accordance with your instructions.

In this example, the payroll number is called the **key field** of the sort, i.e. it is the field which contains the data which determines whereabouts in the file the record should be located. The file could be sorted either into ascending order (lowest numbered record at the start of the file) or descending order (highest number at the start of the file).

Sorting TIME-CARDS on a computer would work broadly like this. The records are read in (the 'first pass') and transferred to a work-file on backing storage. The records in the work file are shuffled about until they are in sequence, finally being output (the 'last pass') onto a device you have specified, e.g. magnetic disk.

During the first pass the records are read into the computer in their original order. During the last pass they are output in key sequence, making the sorted file.

Exercise

1   If TIME-CARDS was sorted using hours-worked as the key field, descending order, which record would appear first on the file?

R2   MAJOR AND MINOR KEYS

Sometimes it is desired to sort a file on more than one key field. Suppose the management wanted a report of hours worked in descending value of hours. There may be many employees who have worked the same number of hours, and the report is to list these employees in ascending payroll number. The hours worked is the **major** key field and the payroll number is the **minor** key field for this sorting operation. You need to sort TIME-CARDS on ascending payroll number within descending hours worked. This will mean that the first record on the file after it is sorted will be that of the employee who has worked the most hours; if more than one employee has worked this number of hours, the employee with the lower payroll number will appear first. The last record on the sorted file will be for the employee who worked the least hours; if more than one employee has worked this number of hours, the highest numbered employee will appear last.

Key fields with numeric pictures are compared algebraically, i.e. negative numbers are lower than positive numbers. All other fields are compared character-by-character according to the 'collating sequence' of the computer. An ASCII collating sequence can be invoked by declaring PROGRAM COLLATING SEQUENCE IS STANDARD-1 in the OBJECT-COMPUTER paragraph of the Configuration Section; otherwise the collating sequence native to the machine will be used (these vary). Facilities exist to invoke non-standard collating sequences - consult the reference manual.

Care must be taken when sorting alphanumeric fields that the resulting order is the desired one. There can be some strange effects; for example, with some collating sequences, a sort on an alphanumeric field that was declared to be signed numeric when the data was created may result in the negative numbers being sorted higher than the positive numbers.

R3   THE SORT VERB

In its simplest form, the SORT verb is used to sort an input file to create a sorted output file. Both files are defined with conventional FD entries.

An extra working file must also be defined, with an SD entry (Sort-file Description). This file is purely an intermediate file which is used to achieve the sort. The SD entry is followed by the record description (01) entries. The file name specified in an SD entry must be SELECTed and ASSIGNed just as any other file, but some manufacturers make special provision for the name of the device to which a sort-file is assigned. In use, the verb might appear:

```
FILE SECTION.
SD   WORKFILE.
```

```
            01    TIMEWORK.
                  02    PAYROLL-NO        PIC X(4).
                  02    FILLER            PIC X(74).
                  02    HOURS-WORKED      PIC 99.
            FD    TIMECARDS.
            01    TIME-CARD-IN            PIC X(80).
            FD    SORTED-TIME-CARDS.
            01    TIME-CARD-OUT           PIC X(80).
            PROCEDURE DIVISION.
            A1.
                  SORT WORKFILE ON
                  DESCENDING HOURS-WORKED
                  ASCENDING PAYROLL-NO
                  USING TIMECARDS
                  GIVING SORTED-TIME-CARDS.
                  STOP RUN.
```

This program simply prepares the sorted output file SORTED-TIME-CARDS for use by a subsequent program, e.g. a program to produce the management report. The keys are specified major first, minor last, i.e. in decreasing significance (this may bear no relation to the order they appear in the record). The keys are all fields in the record belonging to the sort-file. It is as if TIME-CARD-IN is moved to TIMEWORK to be sorted and then moved to TIME-CARD-OUT after sorting. The keywords USING and GIVING specify the names of the unsorted input file and the sorted output file respectively.

Note that the sort-file is not opened. This is done automatically. Practice varies between manufacturers as to whether or not the other files need to be opened and/or closed (one system does not require them to be opened, but requires the output file to be closed with lock if it is to remain after the program is completed).

Had the management required the report with ascending hours worked, as well as ascending payroll number, we could have prepared the sorted file with

```
            SORT WORKFILE
            ON ASCENDING KEY HOURS-WORKED PAYROLL-NO
            USING TIMECARDS
            GIVING SORTED-TIME-CARDS.
```

Exercise

1   A magnetic disk file contains unsequenced 100-character records for books in a library. The author's name is in the first 20 characters, classification in the next 10 characters and title in the remaining characters. Sketch out Data Division and Procedure Division entries to sort this file into title within author within classification (ascending).

2   Will the resulting file be in the sequence the librarian expects?

R4   OWN CODING - FIRST PASS

In the preceding frame, the output file contained exactly the same data as the input file. Only the sequence differed. Suppose you wished to modify, delete or add to the records input to the sort?

To do this, you need to introduce your own coding into the logic of the first pass of the sort. This will save writing and running a separate program to create a modified input file for the sort. This can be achieved by specifying INPUT PROCEDURE IS section-name in place of the USING option in the SORT sentence. Section-name is the name of a section in the Procedure Division which contains your own coding for the first pass.

In this section, you read the input file in the usual non-sort way. You prepare the modified or amended record in the data record of sort-file. When the record is ready, you code RELEASE record-name, where record-name is the name of the sort-file record. If you wish to delete a record, you simply do not release it to the sort.

Imagine, for the example in frame R3, it was desired to prepare a sorted output file only for employees who had worked more than 40 hours. The records for all other employees are to be omitted. With the same Data Division entries, this could be achieved by writing:

```
PROCEDURE DIVISION.
A1-MAIN SECTION.
A1.
      OPEN INPUT TIMECARDS.
      SORT WORKFILE
      ON ASCENDING KEY HOURS-WORKED PAYROLL-NO
      INPUT PROCEDURE IS B1-FIRST-PASS-CODING
      GIVING SORTED-TIME-CARDS.
      CLOSE TIMECARDS.
      STOP RUN.
B1-FIRST-PASS-CODING SECTION.
B1.
      PERFORM C1-PROCESS-TIME-CARD-IN UNTIL EOF-TIMECARDS.
C1-PROCESS-TIME-CARD-IN SECTION.
C1.
      READ TIMECARDS RECORD
      AT END
           Set EOF-TIMECARDS true.
      IF NOT EOF-TIMECARDS
           MOVE TIME-CARD-IN TO TIMEWORK
           IF HOURS-WORKED GREATER THAN 40
               RELEASE TIMEWORK.
```

A better method would have been to define the hours worked field in the input record and inspect its value there, without moving it to the sort record. This would also allow you to use the option RELEASE TIMEWORK FROM TIME-CARD-IN, thereby eliminating the MOVE instruction.

Exercise

1   Modify your answer to question 1, frame R3, so that records with all blanks in the classification field do not appear in the output file.

R5   OWN CODING – LAST PASS

Just as you can control records on the first pass with RELEASE, so you can get hold of records on the last pass with the RETURN statement. In this case, you specify OUTPUT PROCEDURE is section-name instead of the

GIVING clause in the SORT sentence.

Suppose in the example of frame R3 it was desired to prepare not only the report of employees whose hours worked exceeded 40 but also a complete sorted file of the time records of all employees. Assuming a suitable print file and record had also been described, we could code:

```
      OPEN OUTPUT SORTED-TIME-CARDS PRINTFILE.
      SORT WORKFILE
      ON ASCENDING KEY HOURS-WORKED PAYROLL-NO
      USING TIMECARDS
      OUTPUT PROCEDURE IS B1-LAST-PASS-CODING.
      CLOSE SORTED-TIME-CARDS PRINTFILE.
      STOP RUN.
  B1-LAST-PASS-CODING SECTION.
  B1.
      PERFORM C1-PROCESS-TIMEWORK UNTIL EOF-WORKFILE.
  C1-PROCESS-TIMEWORK SECTION.
  C1.
      RETURN WORKFILE
      AT END
          Set EOF-WORKFILE true.
      IF NOT EOF-WORKFILE
          WRITE TIME-CARD-OUT FROM TIMEWORK
          IF HOURS-WORKED GREATER THAN 40
              WRITE PRINTLINE FROM TIMEWORK.
```

Exercise

1   RELEASE takes the sort-file record name while RETURN takes the sort-file file name. Why?

R6   THE MERGE VERB

This allows two or more files, which are already in the same sequence, to be merged together to form a new file.

The MERGE verb works on a sort-file in the same way as SORT, and the syntax of the two verbs is practically identical, except that MERGE cannot have own-coding on the first pass. The complete format is given in Appendix D.

ANSWERS - SECTION R

Frame R1

1   The record for payroll number 1100.

Frame R3

```
1   FILE SECTION.
    SD   SORTWORK.
    01   BOOKREC.
         02   AUTHOR-NAME      PIC X(20).
         02   CLASSIFICATION   PIC X(10)
         02   BOOK-TITLE       PIC X(70).
    FD   BOOKS-IN.
```

```
01   BOOK-IN              PIC X(100).
FD   BOOKS-OUT.
01   BOOK-OUT             PIC X(100).
PROCEDURE DIVISION.
A1.
     SORT SORTWORK
     ON ASCENDING KEY CLASSIFICATION AUTHOR-NAME BOOK-TITLE
     USING BOOKS-IN
     GIVING BOOKS-OUT.
     STOP RUN.
```

2   Probably not. The file will be in the order dictated by the collating sequence of the computer. The librarian would probably want the file sequenced according to the indexing rules of his library. The latter do all sorts of things the computer does not, e.g. 'ignoring' spaces, expanding abbreviations to full words (Dr to be filed under 'doctor'), translating numbers into words ('2001 – a space odyssey' to be filed under 'twothousandandone').

Frame R4

1
```
     SORT SORTWORK ASCENDING KEY etc.
     INPUT PROCEDURE IS B1-DROP-BLANKS
     GIVING TAPE-OUT.
        :
B1-DROP-BLANKS SECTION.
B1.
     Until eof-books-in
         Read books-in record
         At end
              Set eof-books-in true
         Else
              If classification not = spaces
                   RELEASE BOOKREC FROM BOOK-IN.
```

Frame R6

1   See frame G2, question 3.

S The Report Writer

S1 BACKGROUND

The Report Writer feature employs concepts which are quite different from most other COBOL concepts. For this reason, COBOL courses often omit any mention of it, and the result is that many COBOL programmers do not learn how to use it.

The main difference is that the Report Writer is mainly a **declarative** language, i.e. the programmer declares what results he wants and lets the machine worry about how to achieve these. Other aspects of COBOL are mainly **procedural**, i.e. the programmer has to stipulate exactly **how** the results are achieved. Although it may seem obvious that the declarative style is desirable, in practice it is not very flexible. The Report Writer is very good for straightforward reports, but it tends to get rather complicated for anything out of the ordinary.

There are so many facilities in the feature that to cover them all in detail would be like learning a new programming language. My aim here is to provide a foundation on which the student can build from the reference manual if desired.

The aim of the Report Writer is to make it easier to produce reports on the line printer. Its value rests in the fact that many reports take the same shape. They start of with **headings**, followed by lines of **detail** with **total** lines at some **control break**. To write the report in conventional COBOL requires standard procedures like numbering the pages, counting the lines, repeating the headings on each fresh page, making sure there are spaces between the data items. The Report Writer handles all these things automatically, with only the minimum of procedural statements by the programmer.

S2 A TYPICAL REPORT: FD OF A REPORT FILE

Suppose your task is to prepare a Sales Analysis report from sales records which contain the following information

Col	1	Area code
	2–5	Salesman number
	6–11	Date of sale DDMMYY
	12–17	Value of sale 9(4)V99.

The file of records for a month is held in ascending salesman number within area. The desired report has the following appearance:

```
           MONTHLY SALES ANALYSIS          PAGE  1
AREA      SALESMAN   DATE OF SALE    AMOUNT
1          1001       01 01 83        27.46
1          1001       07 01 83       100.00
```

```
          SALESMAN TOTAL              127.46
1            1002     01 01 83         50.00
1            1002     21 01 83        100.00
          SALESMAN TOTAL              150.00
          AREA TOTAL                  277.46
             :
             :
          GRAND TOTAL                9900.46
```

There are three control breaks in this report – change of salesman number, change of area number and end of report.

If the report is to be produced by the Report Writer, the File Section of the program will be

```
          FILE SECTION.
          FD   PRINTFILE     REPORT IS SALES-ANALYSIS.
          FD   SALES         VALUE OF IDENTIFICATION "SALES".
          01   SALES-RECORD.
               02   AREA-CODE       PIC 9.
               02   SALESMAN-NO     PIC 9999.
               02   SALE-DATE       PIC 9(6).
               02   SALE-VALUE      PIC 9(4)V99.
```

Note that PRINTFILE is given a REPORT IS clause. The report, given the programmer-defined name SALES-ANALYSIS, is described in the Report Section.

S3   THE REPORT SECTION

The report layout and control breaks are defined in the Report Section, which is the last section in the Data Division. The description comprises an RD clause (report description), which specifies the control breaks, followed by level 01 entries to describe the lines of the report.

The report description for our example could be

```
          REPORT SECTION.
          RD   SALES ANALYSIS
               CONTROLS ARE FINAL, AREA-CODE, SALESMAN-NO
               PAGE LIMIT 55 LINES.
```

The CONTROLS ARE clause defines the control breaks in major-to-minor order, i.e. the most significant control break first (the one that prints last) and the least significant control break last (the one that prints first). FINAL is a keyword for the control break that occurs at the end of the report. PAGE LIMIT tells the Report Writer to throw to a new page and print out heading lines when the line number specified is reached.

The RD entry is followed by 01 entries for the lines. These differ from the usual 01 entries in several respects:

1   They can be given a TYPE. TYPE PAGE HEADING means the line is a page heading to be printed automatically on each new page. TYPE DETAIL means the line is a detail line, to be printed under the control of the Procedure Division. TYPE CONTROL FOOTING followed by a control break data-name means the line is a total line, to be printed automatically when the control break occurs.

2   Names of records and fields can be omitted. Only the detail line

usually needs a name.

3   The LINE clause specifies how the paper is to be advanced. LINE 1 means print on the first line, LINE PLUS 1 means print one line after the previous line, LINE PLUS 2 means print with double spacing, and so on.

4   The fields in the record are specified to start in a particular column of the page by a COLUMN clause. Fillers are not needed; the Report Writer automatically inserts spaces between the fields.

5   It is not necessary to move data to the fields. The SOURCE clause is used to state where the data comes from.

6   Totals can be accumulated in a field by the SUM clause.

The entries for our example will show the use of these features in practice.

```
        01   TYPE PAGE HEADING.
             02   LINE 1.
                  03   COLUMN 11    PIC X(22).
                       VALUE "MONTHLY SALES ANALYSIS".
                  03   COLUMN 40    PIC X(4)      VALUE "PAGE".
                  03   COLUMN 45    PIC Z9        SOURCE PAGE-COUNTER.
             02   LINE 2.
                  03   COLUMN 1     PIC X(46)
                       VALUE "AREA        SALESMAN    DATE OF SALE      "
    -                  "AMOUNT".
    01   SALES-LINE    TYPE DETAIL        LINE PLUS 1.
         02   COLUMN 2           PIC 9         SOURCE AREA-CODE.
         02   COLUMN 11          PIC 9(4)      SOURCE SALESMAN-NO.
         02   COLUMN 20          PIC 99B99B99 SOURCE SALE-DATE.
         02   COLUMN 34          PIC ZZZ9.99 SOURCE SALE-VALUE.
    01   TYPE CONTROL FOOTING       SALESMAN-NO
         LINE PLUS 1.
         02   COLUMN 9             PIC X(14)
              VALUE "SALESMAN TOTAL".
         02   COLUMN 33            PIC Z(4)9.99 SUM SALE-VALUE.
    01   TYPE CONTROL FOOTING       AREA CODE
         LINE PLUS 1.
         02   COLUMN 9             PIC X(10)
              VALUE "AREA TOTAL".
         02   COLUMN 32            PIC Z(5)9.99 SUM SALE-VALUE.
    01   TYPE CONTROL FOOTING       FINAL
         LINE PLUS 1.
         02   COLUMN 9             PIC X(11)
              VALUE "GRAND TOTAL".
         02   COLUMN 31            PIC Z(6)9.99 SUM SALE-VALUE.
```

In this example,

1   PAGE-COUNTER is a reserved word for the page counter which is automatically updated by the Report Writer.

2   The first record describes two lines which are to be printed on the page heading.

3   The second record describes the detail line, which is printed under the control of statements in the Procedure Division (see next frame).

4   The last three records describe the lines to be printed out at the control break specified, i.e. change of salesman, change of area and final.

The SUM clause means that the total of all the preceding SALE-VALUES which have been printed out is to be accumulated in the field concerned, i.e. every time a detail line is printed, SALE-VALUE is added in to the fields in columns 33, 32 and 31 respectively in the last three records. This breaks the usual rule about not using an edit-picture item for arithmetic, but the Report Writer caters for this. These fields are automatically cleared back to zero when the lines they are in are printed out.

Exercise

1   The SUM clause can also be used with the name of a total field accumulated for a less significant control break – providing, of course, that field has been given a name. This can save the machine doing a lot of additions when accumulating the higher level totals. Amend the example in this frame so that the area total is summed from the salesman total and the grand total is summed from the area total. Also arrange for the total lines to come with double, triple and quadruple line spacing respectively.

S4   PROCEDURE DIVISION ENTRIES

Three special verbs are provided to handle the report. These are

1   INITIATE report-name, which initialises the page counter and arranges for the heading to be printed before the first detail line.

2   GENERATE record-name, which arranges for the printing of the detail line (all other lines are printed automatically).

3   TERMINATE report-name, which arranges for the final control break to be handled. This counts as a control break for all the control fields.

Applying these to our example, the entire Procedure Division would appear as follows.

```
PROCEDURE DIVISION.
A1-PRODUCE-REPORT.
      OPEN OUTPUT PRINTFILE.
      INITIATE SALES-ANALYSIS.
      OPEN INPUT SALES.
      PERFORM B1-PROCESS-SALES-RECORD UNTIL EOF-SALES.
      CLOSE SALES.
      TERMINATE SALES-ANALYSIS.
      CLOSE PRINTFILE.
      STOP RUN.
B1-PROCESS-SALES-RECORD.
      READ SALESCARDS RECORD
      AT END
            set EOF-SALES true
      else
            GENERATE SALES-LINE.
```

These are all the statements required to write the report as described in frame S2.

There is no exercise for this frame, but it would be instructive to consider the coding needed to produce the identical results of this example without using the Report Writer feature.

ANSWERS - SECTION S

Frame S3

```
1   01   TYPE CONTROL FOOTING      SALESMAN-NO
         LINE PLUS 2.
         02   COLUMN 9    PIC X(14)      VALUE "SALESMAN TOTAL".
         02   MANTOT        COLUMN 33    PIC Z(4)9.99 SUM SALE-VALUE.
    01   TYPE CONTROL FOOTING      AREA-CODE
         LINE PLUS 3.
         02   COLUMN 9    PIC X(10)      VALUE "AREA TOTAL".
         02   AREATOT       COLUMN 32    PIC Z(5)9.99 SUM MANTOT.
    01   TYPE CONTROL FOOTING      FINAL
         LINE PLUS 4.
         02   COLUMN 9    PIC X(11)      VALUE "GRAND TOTAL".
         02   COLUMN 31   PIC Z(6)9.99 SUM AREATOT.
```

If you wanted double and triple spacing to come both before and **after** the first two types of total line, this could be achieved by coding after 02 MANTOT...

```
         02   LINE PLUS 1.
```

and after 02 AREATOT...

```
         02   LINE PLUS 2.
```

The automatic line advance for the next line printed will ensure the double and triple spacing respectively.

If only two blank lines are desired between the salesman total line and the area total line, the area total line advance would have to be reduced from 3 to 2. Similarly the final total line advance needs to be reduced from 4 to 2.

T Direct access files

T1 THE DISK PACK AND DRIVE

A disk drive records information on the surfaces of a disk platter. The nature of the platters found in practice varies widely, ranging from the $5\frac{1}{4}$ inch flexible diskette capable of holding a few tens of thousands of characters to rigid multiple platters mounted on a common spindle, capable in total of storing hundreds of millions of characters. There are about $\frac{1}{2}$ million characters in this book.

Fig. 47 illustrates a multi-platter system with read-write heads attached to a moving access arm. Some systems have a fixed arm and supply a read-write head for every track on the disk.

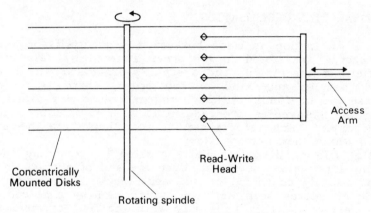

Fig. 47: The disk pack

With the disk rotating, data is transmitted through the write head and magnetically recorded on the surface in a circular track. Drives typically record on between 80 and several hundred tracks. With a multi-platter system, the tracks accessible on all the platters without moving the access arm are called a cylinder.

It will be appreciated that any record can be accessed directly, providing its position is known, as follows:

1   Move the comb of read-write heads to the appropriate position (this is called a seek). This step is omitted in the case of a head-per-track drive.

2   Select the required track (called a head switch). This step is un-necessary in the case of a single-platter drive.

3   Wait for the disk to rotate until the desired record is under the read-write head (a search).

4   Transfer the data record.

These physical operations are undertaken automatically by the operating system. As will be explained shortly, from the point of view of the program logic these operations do not concern the programmer. But programmers are often expected to be able to estimate how much time will be taken up in accessing records on files, and for this purpose a knowledge of the characteristics of the backing storage device is needed.

Exercise

1   How many cylinders would there be on a 200-track disk pack used with a moving-head drive?

2   About how much data can be held on a cylinder of a 6-platter (10 surface) disk pack with 8000 characters per track?

3   About how much data can be held on a 6-platter disk pack with 400 cylinders and 8000 characters per track?

4   Is the data on the inner tracks recorded with more, less or the same density as data on the outer tracks?

T2   SEQUENTIAL FILE ORGANISATION

Sometimes a distinction is made between a sequentially-organised file, in which records are stored in the order dictated by data recorded in some key field of the record, and a serially-organised file in which the records are not in any kind of key order. There is no difference between these two in COBOL. Although the difference may affect the logic of the program, both cases are sequential files to COBOL, meaning that the only order in which records can be read back into the machine is the order in which they were written.

A sequential file on disk is usually created by recording the records one after the other along a track. When the end of a track is reached, recording is usually continued on the next track on the same cylinder. This technique reduces seek activity, which can be time consuming; a seek to the next cylinder is made only when the first cylinder is full of data. A seek to an adjacent cylinder usually takes a few milliseconds. Many systems record data simultaneously through more than one write head, increasing the rate of data transfer.

Several files may be held on one disk pack (provided, of course, the files are small enough). Each is usually allowed to occupy a specified number of tracks or cylinders, i.e. the start of the file is at the first record on the first track of the first cylinder allocated to the file, while the physical end of the file is at the end of the last track of the last cylinder so allocated. If the actual data in the file requires fewer tracks than those allocated, the logical end of the file will fall before the physical end of file. (The terminology of file allocation varies widely, with the unit of allocation being variously called an area, a page, an extent. Sometimes this unit does not correspond to the size of a track or cylinder. Sometimes the size of the unit of allocation is under the control of the programmer.)

If records are added at the end of the file (this is allowed in COBOL by declaring OPEN EXTEND file-name before writing to the file), the file may need more space than that allocated. With most computer systems, the operating system will automatically allocate more space. The method of telling the operating system how much space to reserve in the first instance, and how much additional space to reserve each time the previous allocation beomes full, is not standard. Most systems allow the programmer to stipulate the maximum space that may be occupied by the file. If this space is exceeded, an error condition has arisen.

We write the File-control statement for a straightforward sequential file on disk:

```
FILE-CONTROL.
    SELECT EXAMPLE-DISK-FILE ASSIGN TO DISK.
```

The keyword DISK varies according to the type of computer. A disk file described in this way is processed in exactly the same way as a magnetic tape file, except that it may also be processed for 'update-in-place', as described below.

A feature of disk files is that the file may be updated by over-writing particular occurrences of the existing records; this is called update-in-place. This can be advantageous in terms of processing time and programming convenience, but is disadvantageous in terms of security since the previous version of the record is destroyed. This has to be overcome in practice by making copies of the records before updating.

To perform an update-in-place, it is necessary to issue a REWRITE command following a READ of the record concerned. When a READ command is issued, the COBOL system remembers the location of the record that was read; when a REWRITE command is executed for a sequential file, the record is written back to that same location. The programmer, of course, has arranged for it to be updated in memory between these two operations. The fact that the sequential file is to be processed for update-in-place is signified by opening the file for I-O.

An example will clarify. Suppose a sequential file exists, containing 80-character records. If a record contains nothing but zeros, it is to be replaced by a record containing the characters **ALL ZEROS**.

```
    :
FILE-CONTROL.
    SELECT DISKFILE ASSIGN TO DISK.
    :
FD   DISKFILE.
01   DISKREC       PIC X(80).
    :
PROCEDURE DIVISION.
A1-PROCESS-DISKFILE.
    OPEN I-O DISKFILE
    perform until end of diskfile
        READ DISKFILE RECORD
        AT END
            set end of diskfile true
        not end
            MOVE "**ALL ZEROS** TO DISKREC
            REWRITE DISKREC.
```

To summarise the processing of sequential files on disk:

OPEN OUTPUT   – a WRITE statement places the record in the next sequential location

OPEN INPUT   – a READ gets the record from the next sequential location

OPEN I-O   – a READ gets the record from the next sequential location; a REWRITE replaces the record at the location of the last record read

OPEN EXTEND   – a WRITE statement places the record at the next sequential location beyond the previous end of file.

T3   DIRECT ACCESS BY RELATIVE KEY

This permits access to a record by nominating the number of the record, counting from (relative to) the beginning of the file. This 'relative record number' is put in a RELATIVE KEY data item in working storage. Knowing where the file starts, and the size of the records, the operating system automatically calculates the physical address for retrieval or storage of the record.

When relative keys are used, the relative record number (or some other data which allows the relative record number to be deduced) is normally stored as a data item in the records of the file, but this is not essential.

The File-control paragraph would appear

```
FILE-CONTROL.
    SELECT PERSONNEL-FILE ASSIGN TO DISK
    ORGANIZATION IS RELATIVE
    ACCESS MODE IS RANDOM
    RELATIVE KEY IS RECORD-NUMBER.
```

Note that ORGANIZATION must be spelled with a Z. If ACCESS MODE IS RANDOM is not declared, the compiler will assume that the file is to be read sequentially in relative record number order. The ORGANIZATION of the file is a fixed physical attribute that cannot be changed, after the file is created, by any declaration in the program. The ACCESS MODE can vary from program to program, providing it is compatible with the file's ORGANIZATION (you could not, for example, declare a sequential organisation file for random access). It might be thought that ACCESS MODE, being something local to the program, might better be declared in the File Definition than in File-control, where the ORGANIZATION clause describes the attribute global to all programs; this view is now held by CODASYL but is not yet standard.

An outline of the Data Division for this file could be:

```
FILE SECTION.
FD   PERSONNEL-FILE.
01   PERS-RECORD.
     02   PAYROLL-NO        PIC 9(5).
     :
WORKING-STORAGE SECTION.
     :
     02   RECORD-NUMBER     PIC 9(5) COMP SYNC RIGHT.
```

A relative file in random access mode can be opened for input (READ statements allowed); output (WRITE statements allowed); input-output (READ, REWRITE and DELETE statements allowed, the last logically removing the record from the file so that it cannot be retrieved by later READ statements). The INVALID KEY clause is available with all these verbs, to detect various error conditions that may arise (e.g. an attempt to READ or DELETE records that are not there).

Suppose that there are 1000 records on PERSONNEL-FILE, corresponding to PAYROLL-NOs 10,001 to 11,000. A program is to accept from the operator a payroll number (storing this in W-PAY-NO), retrieve the corresponding personnel record and display this. The Procedure Division entries in outline could be:

```
OPEN INPUT PERSONNEL-FILE
:
ACCEPT W-PAY-NO.
SUBTRACT 10000 FROM PAY-NO GIVING RECORD-NUMBER.
READ PERSONNEL-FILE
INVALID KEY
      display "INVALID PAYROLL NUMBER"
      take other error actions
not invalid
      prepare output from PERS-RECORD
      display output to operator.
```

The possibility of processing a relative file sequentially has already been mentioned. It is also possible to process such a file dynamically (a mixture of relative and sequential access). This facility is the same as that described in the next frame for indexed files.

T4   INDEXED FILES

Probably the most popular form of organisation for direct access is the indexed file (often called indexed-sequential). This is popular because the file can be accessed either sequentially (in the order dictated by a key field data item in the record, which may be a different order from that in which the records were created) or directly (by specifying the key of the desired record).

Briefly, the physical address of a record of known key is traced by the computer through a hierarchy of indexes. The mechanics of this varies slightly from one system to another; the important thing for the programmer is that he can process the whole file in record key order, as if it were a sorted file on magnetic tape. The problem of how the data is stored is handled automatically.

To process an indexed file sequentially in record key order, the File-control statements would appear:

```
SELECT PERSONNEL-FILE ASSIGN TO DISK
ORGANIZATION IS INDEXED
ACCESS MODE IS SEQUENTIAL
RECORD KEY IS EMPLOYEE-NUMBER.
```

EMPLOYEE-NUMBER is the name of a field in the record description entry of PERSONNEL-FILE. In sequential access mode, the indexed file can be created by writing records in record key order (the file must be open for OUTPUT), or updated-in-place by REWRITE or DELETE statements (with the file open for I-O). READ takes the AT END clause under these circumstances; the other verbs take the INVALID KEY clause.

It is also possible to arrange for sequential processing to begin at some place other than at the first record of the file, by using the START verb. For example, if in the above case EMPLOYEE-NUMBER was a group field which contained a two digit department number and a four digit employee serial number, and it was desired to start processing with department 10, we could code:

```
FD   PERSONNEL-FILE.
 :
     02   EMPLOYEE-NUMBER.
          03   DEPARTMENT        PIC 99.
          03   EMP-SERIAL        PIC 9999.
     :
     OPEN INPUT PERSONNEL-FILE.
     MOVE "100000" TO EMPLOYEE-NUMBER.
     START PERSONNEL-FILE
     KEY GREATER THAN EMPLOYEE-NUMBER
     INVALID KEY
          DISPLAY "NO DEPARTMENT HIGHER THAN 09"
          handle error
     not invalid
          repeat until end of personnel file
               READ PERSONNEL-FILE RECORD
               AT END
                    set end of personnel file true
               not end
                    process record.
```

The first execution of the READ statement will retrieve the lowest-keyed record in the file that satisfies the KEY condition specified. Note that the KEY clause must take the data-name that was specified as the RECORD KEY in the File-control paragraph (the reason for this will emerge from frame T5). The INVALID KEY clause in the START statement will be executed if no record on the file satisfies the condition stated.

To process an indexed file randomly, e.g. to read a record from PAYROLL-FILE by specifying the desired record key in EMPLOYEE-NUMBER, the File-control paragraph would contain:

```
SELECT PERSONNEL-FILE ASSIGN TO DISK
ORGANIZATION IS INDEXED
ACCESS MODE IS RANDOM
RECORD KEY IS EMPLOYEE-NUMBER.
```

PERSONNEL-FILE may now be opened for input (for reading an existing record of stated EMPLOYEE-NUMBER), output (for writing a new record of stated EMPLOYEE-NUMBER), or input-output (for reading or writing as before, or for rewriting or deleting an existing record of stated EMPLOYEE-NUMBER).

An indexed file may be processed partly sequentially and partly randomly, by specifying DYNAMIC access mode:

```
SELECT PERSONNEL-FILE ASSIGN TO DISK
ORGANIZATION IS INDEXED
ACCESS MODE IS DYNAMIC
RECORD KEY IS EMPLOYEE-NUMBER.
```

In this case, all the facilities of random access mode apply but in addition the file may be read sequentially from the point of the last record read directly, or from a point specified in a START statement, by a special form of the READ command:

```
READ PERSONNEL-FILE NEXT
AT END
   :
```

It should be appreciated that before any of the random access facilities of indexed organisation can be used, the file must first have been created by WRITEing sorted records to it while open for OUTPUT. This initial creation allows the operating system to create the necessary indexes. After creation, the indexes are maintained automatically.

Exercise

1   An ASSEMBLIES file containing 100-character records has been created with indexed organisation, the record key being ASSEMBLY-NO, which is located in the first 10 digits of the record. ASSEMBLY-NO is in two parts: a five-digit ASSEMBLY-GROUP followed by a five-digit SUB-ASSEMBLY. The records in the file make logical groups, each group comprising one header record for the whole assembly (zeros appear in the SUB-ASSEMBLY field), followed by a variable number of sub-assembly records. The sub-assembly records have the same number for ASSEMBLY-GROUP as appeared in the header record, but of course each sub-assembly record has a unique non-zero number in the SUB-ASSEMBLY field.

A program is to be written to list out the details of all the records for a given assembly. The number of the desired assembly is input in the first five characters of a visual display line; there may be many enquiries to be processed in a given run. The enquiries may appear in any order.

Sketch out the File-control, Record Description and Procedure Division entries necessary for this program.

T5   ALTERNATE INDEXES

A very powerful feature available on larger compilers is the ALTERNATE RECORD KEY facility. This allows the programmer to specify that some other field in the record, in addition to the unique record key primarily chosen to govern the logical sequence of the file, is to be the subject of an index that will allow acces to the records. A record of nominated alternate key may then be accessed directly, or the records may be accessed in alternate key sequence. The alternate record key need not necessarily have unique values in the records, i.e. the same key value may appear in more than one record.

The following example shows how a SALE record may be accessed by SALE-NO, CUSTOMER-NO and SALESMAN-NO.

```
FILE-CONTROL.
      SELECT SALES ASSIGN TO DISK
      ORGANIZATION IS INDEXED
      ACCESS MODE SEQUENTIAL
      RECORD KEY IS SALE-NO
      ALTERNATE RECORD KEY IS CUSTOMER-NO WITH DUPLICATES.
      ALTERNATE RECORD KEY IS SALESMAN-NO WITH DUPLICATES.
      :
FD  SALES
01  SALE.
      02   SALE-NO          PIC 99999.
      02   CUSTOMER-NO      PIC 9999.
      02   SALESMAN-NO      PIC 999.
```

02   SALE–DETAILS etc.

The file is created in the first place by writing records sorted on SALE–NO to it:

```
OPEN OUTPUT SALES
repeat until end of input file
    READ input file
    AT END
        set end of input file true
    not end
        WRITE SALE RECORD FROM input record
        INVALID KEY
            handle error
```

The only way I can think of an invalid key arising under these circumstances, short of hardware error, is if writing the record would cause the file to be extended beyond any maximum file allocation declared by the programmer.

With the file created, subsequent programs may SELECT it in SEQUENTIAL, RANDOM or DYNAMIC mode as desired. Additions to the file, e.g. as a result of a WRITE of a new record to it when the file was open for I–O, will result in all three indexes being updated. The only other change from regular indexed file processing is that the programs, when they are READing the file, must specify which index is to be used. For example, to recover the first sale for customer 27:

```
MOVE 27 TO CUSTOMER–NO
READ SALES RECORD  KEY IS CUSTOMER–NO
INVALID KEY
    PERFORM NO–SUCH–CUSTOMER.
```

The system will continue to consider that CUSTOMER–NO is the key of the record, e.g. in a READ NEXT statement, until a further KEY IS clause is executed. So, to read all the record for customer number 27, continuing from the last example:

```
repeat until CUSTOMER–NO not = 27 or end of sales file
    READ SALES NEXT
    AT END
        set end of sales file true
    not end
        if CUSTOMER–NO = 27
            process sale record
```

ANSWERS – SECTION T

Frame T1

1   200.
2   10 x 8000 = 80,000 characters.
3   400 x 80,000 = 32 million characters.
4   More. There is the same amount of data on each track, the tracks towards the centre are shorter than the outer tracks, therefore the data must be recorded more densely on the inner tracks.

Frame T4

1   FILE-CONTROL.
        SELECT ASSEMBLIES ASSIGN TO DISK
        ORGANIZATION IS INDEXED
        ACCESS MODE DYNAMIC
        RECORD KEY IS ASSEMBLY-NO.
    :
    FD   ASSEMBLIES.
    01   ASSEMBLY-REC.
        02   ASSEMBLY-NO.
            03   ASSEMBLY-GROUP   PIC 9(5).
            03   SUB-ASSEMBLY   PIC 9(5).
        02   OTHER-CONTENTS   PIC X(90).
    :
    FD   ENQUIRIES.
    :
        02   DESIRED-ASSEMBLY-GROUP   PIC 9(5).
    :
    PROCEDURE DIVISION.
        OPEN INPUT ASSEMBLIES
        open other files
        repeat until end of enquiries
            READ ENQUIRIES RECORD
            AT END
                set end of enquiries true
            not end
                MOVE DESIRED-ASSEMBLY-GROUP TO ASSEMBLY-GROUP
                MOVE ZEROS TO SUB-ASSEMBLY
                READ ASSEMBLIES RECORD
                INVALID KEY
                    display message "ASSEMBLY NOT FOUND" etc.
                not invalid
                    repeat until end of ASSEMBLIES file or
                    ASSEMBLY-GROUP not = DESIRED-ASSEMBLY-GROUP
                        edit and display contents of ASSEMBLY-REC
                        READ ASSEMBLIES NEXT
                        AT END
                            set end of ASSEMBLIES file true.

U Inter-program communication

U1 THE OBJECT PROGRAM LIBRARY

We have already met the concept of a program library with the COPY statement (frame Q1). The COPY verb causes the compiler to include code in your program at compilation time by copying statements from the COBOL source statement library.

It is also possible to bring object programs into the machine, at execution time, by copying from the object program library. Just as a utility was used to enter source statements into the source statement library, so a utility, often summoned by the general operating system of the computer, is used to enter object code into the object program library.

This object code may have been produced by COBOL compilations, or it may be the object code resulting from compilation of a program written in some other language.

In practice, the object code that results from any COBOL compilation will usually include calls to many standard subroutines which reside in the object program library. The programmer is not usually made aware of these calls. Typical standard routines would include conversion of a decimal number to an internal binary number; blocking and deblocking records; locating a record on an indexed file given the record key. The COBOL compiler arranges for this sort of subroutine call to be made automatically.

The logic of compilation and execution may now be described as in Figure 48.

This chart suggests that the object program under development is itself added to the object program library. In practice the library is split up into a production library and development libraries. Programs under test may be stored in one of the development libraries; a program is entered into the production library only when it is fully tested and operational.

During development, the object program produced by the compiler may be loaded straight into the machine at step 4, omitting step 3; but the object program may alternatively be saved and loaded directly into the machine, thereby avoiding recompilation every time the program is to be run.

Exercise

1 (a) In Fig. 48, is the object program library used at step 2?
   (b) Do you think the chart is strictly correct at step 2?
   (c) Do you think the chart is strictly correct at steps 1 and 3?

2 Can you write a COBOL program without knowing anything about the object program library?

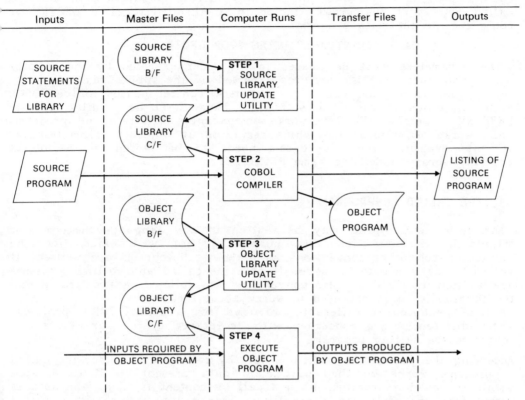

Inputs	Master Files	Computer Runs	Transfer Files	Outputs

Fig. 48: Compilation and execution using the source statement and object program libraries

U2   THE CALL VERB

The COBOL language includes facilities to allow the programmer to call up a subroutine which resides in the object program library. This usually requires passing one or more parameters, i.e. variables or constants which are to be used by the subroutine. A subroutine in the object program library is popularly called a **subprogram**, to distinguish it from a subroutine executed by a PERFORM statement within a program.

In frame K3, we considered the Population Explosion problem (Appendix A) is if it had two distinct components, one to exercise overall control over reading the input and producing the results, the other to print a page of results. The second of these two components could have been implemented as a subprogram. This subprogram would expect two parameters to be passed; the starting population and the growth factor. With these, it can get on with the job of calculating the new populations and printing the lines to make up a page of results.

The general form of the CALL verb is

<u>CALL</u> "subprogram-name" [<u>USING</u> parameter-1 [parameter-2] ...]

If, in the program exercising overall control (the main program, or the calling program), we had placed the starting population in an item called SPOP and the growth factor in another item called GFCTR, we could code in the main program:

CALL "PRINTPAGE" USING SPOP GFCTR.

The parameters must be passed in the order expected by the subprogram, and must have the pictures expected by the subprogram.

After the subprogram has been executed, control passes to the COBOL statement following the CALL statement. Thus, CALL has similar logic to PERFORM; whereas PERFORM works on paragraphs within the program, CALL works on subprograms which reside in an object program library. In this example, the subprogram needs to be stored in the object program library under the name PRINTPAGE.

U3   THE CALLED SUBPROGRAM

The called subprogram may be written in any language the computer manufacturer allows for this purpose. There will exist, for the particular computer, conventions as to how subprograms are written, if successful calls are to be made. If both the called and calling programs are written in COBOL, these conventions are followed automatically and the programmer does not need to worry about them.

A COBOL subprogram differs in two ways from a normal COBOL program. These differences are concerned with acceptance of the parameters and return to the calling program.

Accepting the parameters   When a **call by reference** is made, the called subprogram works on the (parameter) data present in fields located within the calling program. When a **call by content** is made, the data is moved from the fields in the calling program into fields in the called program. The only practical difference is that in the case of call by content, the subprogram can change (or corrupt) the contents of its parameter fields without changing the parameter fields in the calling program.

Standard COBOL programs work on call by reference, although CODASYL has proposed an option of call by content. In either case, the physical location of the data is (originally) outside the subprogram. For this reason, the parameter fields are known as **external** variables to the called subprogram.

These external variables must be declared in some way. COBOL requires that the external variables be grouped together in a special section of the Data Division, the LINKAGE SECTION. Then a special form of Procedure Division declaration is used:

PROCEDURE DIVISION [USING parameter-1 [parameter-2] ...] .

where the parameters are the names of the external variables. The data names used as parameters need not be the same as those used in the calling program, but they must appear in the same order and have the same picture.

Return to the calling program   This is achieved by coding EXIT PROGRAM at the logical end of the subprogram. Control returns to the statement following the CALL statement in the main program.

Continuing the example of frame U2, if the subprogram were written in

COBOL it might appear:

```
:
DATA DIVISION.
:
LINKAGE SECTION.
01   PARAMETERS.
     02   STARTING-POP      PIC 9(10).
     02   GROWTH-FACTOR     PIC 9(6)V9(9).
PROCEDURE DIVISION USING STARTING-POP GROWTH-FACTOR.
:
        MOVE STARTING-POP TO W-POP.
        Repeat for each decade
            COMPUTE W-POP ROUNDED = W-POP*GROWTH-FACTOR
            ON SIZE ERROR
                print size error line
                EXIT PROGRAM
        not size error
            compute density
            on size error
                print size error line
                EXIT PROGRAM
            not size error
                print line of results.
        EXIT PROGRAM.
```

Note how EXIT PROGRAM can be used to obviate the need for a forward GO TO to get out of the iteration. CODASYL have proposed a similar verb, EXIT PERFORM, for use in internal subroutines.

This example glosses over the problem of how input-output operations are achieved in the subprogram when both the called and calling programs are to operate on the same files. This problem is solved differently by different computer manufacturers. Some allow global access to files; others allow a reference to a file to be passed in the list of parameters. Consult your technical manual.

As mentioned in Part 2, the use of a separately compiled subprogram to solve the Population Explosion is something of an overkill. There is rather a large coding overhead when using subprograms in COBOL and this discourages using them frequently for small routines, which are usually better handled by internal subroutines. Nevertheless, a method of working whereby the programmer places well-integrated functions into subprograms of a modest size, each having its own local variables and explicit parameters and each capable of being separately tested, is recommended.

Exercise

1   It was claimed in the text that the variables used as parameters should have the same picture in the calling and called programs. This is not strictly true. Can you propose in what important respects the pictures should be similar?

2   You are designing a subprogram which operates on 100 fields in the calling program. This is probably a mistake (the scope of operations included in the subprogram is too extensive) but assuming you wish to persist, how can you avoid passing 100 names as parameters?

U4   SEGMENTATION AND OVERLAY

We have seen that Procedure Division statements can be split up into sections. This is achieved by declaring:

section-name   SECTION [priority-number] .

The object code produced by the compiler for a section is called a segment. Each segment can be separately filed in the object program library, under its section name.

This segmentation is valuable when the object code produced for the whole program requires more memory than is available in the machine being used, i.e. the program is too large to fit into the computer. On large modern computers this is no longer a worry because the operating system will automatically segment a large program without the programmer needing to intervene, but it may still be a concern on smaller machines without such clever operating systems. Even on a large machine, control over segmentation may be needed to reduce the execution time of a program.

The programmer can arrange for certain segments of the program to be called into the machine only when they are needed, occupying the same memory positions as (**overlaying**) a previously executed segment.

An example will help to make this clear. Suppose a very large program is to be written to produce a report. The program goes through three phases. Firstly, control records are read which are used to to set up tables and flags which dictate the content and format of the report. Secondly, a file is to be read in its entirety and totals accumulated. Thirdly, the report is to be produced using these accumulated totals.

In order to fit the program into the machine, suppose that the code for each phase must be made into a separate segment, producing three segments. The Procedure Division could be coded as follows:

```
        PROCEDURE DIVISION.
        PERMANENT SECTION 0.
            PERFORM CONTROLRECORD.
            PERFORM PROCESSFILE.
            PERFORM GIVEREPORT.
            STOP RUN.
        CONTROLRECORD SECTION 2.
            :
            (read in the control records etc.)
            :
        PROCESSFILE SECTION 1.
            :
            (read the file and accumulate totals)
            :
        GIVEREPORT SECTION 3.
            :
            (produce the report)
            :
```

The priority numbers will be explained in a minute; they are used only to distinguish the overlay sections from the permanently resident sections.

The sequence of events in execution of this progam can be shown diagrammatically as in Fig. 49 opposite.

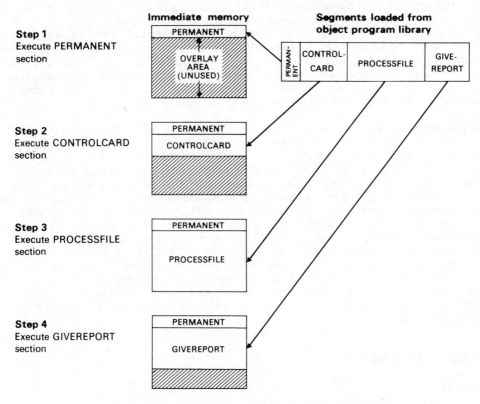

Fig. 49: Steps in an overlayed program

It will be seen that the amount of memory required for this program's procedures is equal to the sum of the permanent section plus the largest overlay section. Loading the segments into memory is done by the operating system as they are required.

Loading a segment, of course, takes some time. If a segment is repeatedly used, e.g. round a loop, the time required for input of the overlays may exceed the time to execute the segment.

You should have a question in your mind at this stage, viz. "How do I know in advance that my program will be too large to fit into the machine? If I assume the worst, and segment it heavily, I may end up paying an unnecessary time penalty through excessive overlay activity."

It is to overcome this problem that the priority numbers exist. A priority number, in the range 0 to 49, is assigned to each section. Sections which are used often are given a low number (meaning high priority) while sections used rarely are given a high number (meaning low priority). Decreasing priority numbers are assigned to sections as their frequency of being used decreases. A section that is used so often that it must be permanently resident (or a section that is too small to bother about, as in our example) is given a priority number of 0. Two or more sections given the same priority number may be joined together to make one segment of code in the object program library.

A 'segment limit number' is defined in the Object-computer paragraph. Sections whose priority number is numerically lower than the segment limit number are permanently resident. Sections whose priority number is equal to or greater than the segment limit are overlayed.

By this device, on the first test of the program, the segment limit number can be set high, say 49. This will make all the sections permanently resident. If the program fits into memory, all well and good. If not, the program can be recompiled with a lower segment limit, such that the least-used segments are overlayed. This process can be repeated until the segmented program is small enough to fit into the machine.

In practice, a similar sort of overlay can also be achieved with called subprograms when the compiler implements these by means of 'co-routines'. When the subprogram is a 'co-routine' this means that instead of being linked up permanently with the main program, it continues to enjoy a separate existence in the object program library and is only brought into memory at execution time, in response to the CALL command. Normally, once called, it will remain in memory and its variables will be unchanged from one call to the next. But if the programmer wishes, he may free up the memory space used by the subprogram by issuing a CANCEL command - CANCEL "subprogram-name". This release the memory for use by other subprograms (or for use by other programs in the case of a multi-programming computer), and will mean that if a further CALL is issued to the same subprogram it will be loaded in again with its variables reset to the values declared at compilation time.

ANSWERS - SECTION U

Frame U1

1   (a) No.
    (b) No. All programs of any complexity are likely to include calls to subroutines which reside on the object program library. The compiler is a very complex program.
    (c) No.
2   Haven't you already?

Frame U3

1   They must have the same length. Numeric items which are to be used in arithmetic should have the same USAGE and decimal point in the same place.
2   Put all 100 variables in a group field. Pass the group field as a parameter. (Incidentally, when considering the number of para-meters which are to be passed in a subroutine call from the point of view of attention span, fields which make a genuine data structure such as a record or table should count as only one parameter.)

Frame U4

1   To ensure that it is selected first to be made into an overlay segment if the segment limit is reduced. Since it is the least used section, overlaying it will give the least time penalty (neglecting differences in the size of the segments - and therefore their loading time; this is not likely to be significant in practice).

Appendix A Example program

THE PROGRAM SPECIFICATION

Overall objectives

The sorted valid transaction records are used to update the customer master file by copying it forward to make a new customer master file. Errors detected in this process are reported on the line printer.

Inputs

The customer master (identification: CUSTMAST) has records as follows:

1–6	Customer number 9(6)
7	Credit code X
8–9	Area code XX
10–169	Customer name and address (4 lines of 40 characters).

The transaction file (identification: TRANS) is the same as CUSTMAST except that there is an additional character at the beginning of the record containing an update code as follows:

I	insert
A	amend
D	delete

Outputs

The output customer master is identical to the input customer master (the files are to be distinguished in the file library by a generation number or version number provided by the operating system).

The error report, after a suitable heading, has detail lines as follows:

1–6	Customer number
10	Credit code
15–16	Area code
19–58	Name and address (continue over 4 lines)
62	Update code
66–	Error message, being one of the following
	1. "INSERTION – RECORD ALREADY ON MASTER"
	2. "NO MASTER RECORD FOR THIS CUSTOMER"

Processing

Both CUSTMAST and TRANS are sequenced in ascending order of customer number. TRANS has already been checked for validity of the fields, and records occur in update code order within customer number.

CUSTMAST is to be written forward as updated by TRANS. If the update code shows an insertion, the TRANS record (without the update code) is to be written forward in the correct place in the master, provided no master record exists already for the customer in question. If the customer is already on file, the TRANS record is to be printed out with message 1. An inserting record is never followed by an amendment or deletion of the same record.

If the update code in TRANS shows an amendment, the master file record is to be written forward after substituting any non-blank fields of TRANS into the master record. An amending transaction may be followed by further amendments or a deletion of the same record.

If the update code shows a deletion, the master record is not to be written forward. A deletion is never followed by another transaction for the same record.

With amendments or deletions, if there is no record on the master file to match the transction, the TRANS record is to be printed out with message 2.

Two blank lines are to be left between each record reported as an error, and between the heading and the first transaction. There are to be 50 lines on each page, although this may be exceeded where necessary to ensure that an error report for a record is not split over a page.

THE PROGRAM LISTING

```
IDENTIFICATION DIVISION.
PROGRAM-ID. CMFU1.
*AUTHOR.        A. PARKIN.
*DATE-WRITTEN.  SEPTEMBER 1982.
*
*UPDATE CUSTOMER MASTER
*======================
*READ TRANS FILE RECORD
*READ OLD MASTER FILE RECORD
*REPEAT UNTIL END OF TRANS FILE
*    REPEAT UNTIL END OF OLD MASTER
*    OR MASTER RECORD KEY NOT LESS THAN TRANS RECORD KEY
*        WRITE NEW MASTER RECORD FROM OLD MASTER RECORD
*        READ OLD MASTER RECORD
*    COMPARE OLD MASTER RECORD KEY WITH TRANS KEY AND EVALUATE
*    TRANS TYPE
*    WHEN = AND AMENDMENT
*        DO 'UPDATE OLD MASTER'
*    WHEN = AND DELETION
*        READ NEXT OLD MASTER RECORD
*    WHEN = AND INSERTION
*        PRINT ERROR - INSERTION OF EXISTING RECORD
*    WHEN (END OF OLD MASTER OR NOT =) AND INSERTION
*        WRITE NEW MASTER RECORD FROM TRANS RECORD
*    WHEN (END OF OLD MASTER OR NOT =) AND (AMENDMNT OR DELETION)
*        PRINT ERROR - NO MASTER
*REPEAT UNTIL END OF OLD MASTER
*    WRITE NEW MASTER RECORD FROM OLD MASTER RECORD
*    READ OLD MASTER FILE RECORD
*
*UPDATE OLD MASTER
*-----------------
*FOR EACH NON-BLANK FIELD IN TRANS RECORD
*    MOVE FIELD TO EQUIVALENT FIELD IN OLD MASTER RECORD
*
*N.B. AMENDMENTS (BUT NOT DELETIONS) MAY BE FOLLOWED BY FURTHER
*AMENDMENTS OR DELETIONS RELATING TO THE SAME CUSTOMER.
*
*PROGRAM ORGANISATION
*====================
*A1-UPDATE-CUSTOMER-MASTER
*    B1-PROCESS-TRANS
*        C1 = B2-WRITE-AND-READ-MASTER
*        C2-UPDATE-OLD-MASTER
*    B2-WRITE-AND-READ-MASTER
/
```

```
ENVIRONMENT DIVISION.
INPUT-OUTPUT SECTION.
FILE-CONTROL.
    SELECT FA-OLD-MASTER      ASSIGN TO DISK.
    SELECT FB-TRANS           ASSIGN TO DISK.
    SELECT FC-NEW-MASTER      ASSIGN TO DISK.
    SELECT FD-PRINTFILE       ASSIGN TO DISK.
/
```

```
DATA DIVISION.
*
*
FILE SECTION.
*
FD  FA-OLD-MASTER.
01  FA-OLD-MASTER-REC.
    02  FA-CUSTOMER-NO         PIC 9(6).
    02  FA-CREDIT-CODE         PIC X.
    02   FA-AREA-CODE          PIC XX.
    02  FA-CUSTOMER-ADDRESS  PIC X(40).
*         FOUR LINES OF 10 CHS DURING PRELIMINARY TESTING
*
FD  FB-TRANS.
01  FB-TRANS-REC.
    02  FB-TRANS-TYPE          PIC X.
        88  INSERTION       VALUE IS "I".
        88  AMENDMENT       VALUE IS "A".
        88  DELETION        VALUE IS "D".
    02  FB-TRANS-DETAIL.
        03  FB-CUSTOMER-NO     PIC 9(6).
        03  FB-CREDIT-CODE     PIC X.
        03  FB-AREA-CODE       PIC XX.
        03  FB-CUSTOMER-ADDRESS.
            04  FB-ADDRESS LINE OCCURS 4 TIMES PIC X(10).
*
FD  FC-NEW-MASTER.
01  FC-NEW-MASTER-REC          PIC X(49).
*
FD  FD-PRINTFILE   REPORT IS R-ERRORS.
/
```

```
WORKING-STORAGE SECTION.
*
 01  WA-ERROR-MESSAGES.
*     ONE OR OTHER OF THESE MESSAGES IS USED IN R-ERROR-GROUP
      02  FILLER                   PIC X(36)
          VALUE "INSERTION - RECORD ALREADY ON MASTER".
      02  FILLER                   PIC X(36)
          VALUE "NO MASTER RECORD FOR THIS CUSTOMER".
 01  WA-MESSAGES REDEFINES WA-ERROR-MESSAGES.
      02  WA-MESSAGE               PIC X(36)
                                   OCCURS 2 TIMES
                                   INDEXED BY WA.
*
 01  WB-GLOBAL-CONDITIONS.
      02  WB-EOF-OLD-MASTER-FLAG PIC X.
          88  EOF-OLD-MASTER      VALUE IS "T".
      02  WB-TRANS-EOF-FLAG        PIC X.
          88  EOF-TRANS           VALUE IS "T".
/
```

```
REPORT SECTION.
RD   R-ERRORS    PAGE LIMIT 2O LINES.
*                 2O LINES DURING PRELIMINARY TESTING
O1   TYPE PAGE HEADING.
     O2   LINE 2.
          O3   COLUMN 14          PIC X(35)
               VALUE "CUSTOMER MASTER FILE UPDATE - ERROR REPORT".
          O3   COLUMN 55          PIC X(4)
               VALUE "PAGE".
          O3   COLUMN 60          PIC Z9
               SOURCE PAGE-COUNTER.
     O2   LINE PLUS 2.
          O3   COLUMN 1           PIC X(11)
               VALUE "CUST # CRDT".
          O3   COLUMN 14          PIC X(12)
               VALUE "AREA ADDRESS".
          O3   COLUMN 30          PIC X(4)
               VALUE "CODE".
*
O1   R-ERROR-GROUP TYPE DETAIL.
     O2   LINE PLUS 2.
          O3   COLUMN 1           PIC 9(6)
               SOURCE FB-CUSTOMER-NO.
          O3   COLUMN 10          PIC X
               SOURCE FB-CREDIT-CODE.
          O3   COLUMN 15          PIC XX
               SOURCE FB-AREA-CODE.
          O3   COLUMN 19          PIC X(10)
               SOURCE FB-ADDRESS-LINE(1).
          O3   COLUMN 32          PIC X
               SOURCE FB-TRANS-TYPE.
          O3   COLUMN 35          PIC X(36)
               SOURCE WA-MESSAGE(WA).
     O2   LINE PLUS 1.
          O3 COLUMN 19            PIC X(10
               SOURCE FB-ADDRESS-LINE(2).
     O2   LINE PLUS 1.
          O3   COLUMN 19          PIC X(10)
               SOURCE FB-ADDRESS-LINE(3).
     O2   LINE PLUS 1.
          O3   COLUMN 19          PIC X(10)
               SOURCE FB-ADDRESS-LINE(4).
*
O1   LINE PLUS 2 TYPE REPORT FOOTING.
     O2   COLUMN 1                PIC X(35)
          VALUE "END OF REPORT".
/
```

```
      PROCEDURE DIVISION.
*
  A1-UPDATE-CUSTOMER-MASTER.
        OPEN INPUT FB-TRANS.
        MOVE "F" TO WB-TRANS-EOF-FLAG.
        READ FB-TRANS RECORD
        AT END
            DISPLAY "PROGRAM ERROR A1 - EMPTY TRANSACTION FILE"
            DISPLAY "CUSTOMER MASTER FILE UPDATE TERMINATING"
            CLOSE FB-TRANS
            STOP RUN.
        OPEN INPUT FA-OLD-MASTER.
        MOVE "F" TO WB-EOF-OLD-MASTER-FLAG.
        READ FA-OLD-MASTER RECORD
        AT END
            MOVE "T" TO WB-EOF-OLD-MASTER RECORD.
        OPEN OUTPUT FD-PRINTFILE.
        INITIATE R-ERRORS.
        OPEN OUTPUT FC-NEW-MASTER.
        PERFORM B1-PROCESS-TRANS             UNTIL EOF-TRANS.
        CLOSE FB-TRANS.
        PERFORM B2-WRITE-AND-READ-MASTER    UNTIL EOF-OLD-MASTER.
        CLOSE FA-OLD-MASTER FC-NEW-MASTER WITH LOCK.
        TERMINATE R-ERRORS.
        CLOSE FD-PRINTFILE.
        STOP RUN.
*
  B1-PROCESS-TRANS.
        PERFORM B2-WRITE-AND-READ-MASTER    UNTIL EOF-OLD-MASTER
        OR FA-CUSTOMER-NO NOT LESS THAN FB-CUSTOMER-NO.
        IF (NOT EOF-OLD-MASTER) AND FA-CUSTOMER-NO = FB-CUSTOMER-NO
            IF AMENDMENT
                PERFORM C2-UPDATE-OLD-MASTER
            ELSE
                IF DELETION
                    READ FA-OLD-MASTER RECORD
                    AT END
                        MOVE "T" TO WB-EOF-OLD-MASTER-FLAG
                ELSE
                    SET WA TO 1
                    GENERATE R-ERROR-GROUP
        ELSE
*       MUST BE EOF-OLD-MASTER OR FA-CUSTOMER-NO > FB-CUSTOMER-NO
            IF INSERTION
                WRITE FC-NEW-MASTER-REC FROM FB-TRANS-DETAIL
            ELSE
*           MUST BE AMENDMENT OR DELETION
                SET WA TO 2
                GENERATE R-ERROR-GROUP.
        READ FB-TRANS RECORD
        AT END
            MOVE "T" TO WB-EOF-TRANS-FLAG.
/
```

```
B2-WRITE-AND-READ-MASTER.
    WRITE FC-NEW-MASTER-REC FROM FA-OLD-MASTER-REC.
    READ FA-OLD-MASTER RECORD
    AT END
        MOVE "T" TO WB-EOF-OLD-MASTER-FLAG.

C2-UPDATE-OLD-MASTER.
    IF FB-CREDIT-CODE NOT = SPACE
        MOVE FB-CREDIT-CODE TO FA-CREDIT-CODE.
    IF FB-AREA-CODE NOT = SPACES
        MOVE FB-AREA-CODE TO FA-AREA-CODE.
    IF FB-CUSTOMER-ADDRESS NOT = SPACES
        MOVE FB-CUSTOMER-ADDRESS TO FA-CUSTOMER-ADDRESS.
```

EXAMPLE TESTS

Test 1

CUSTMAST (1st generation)

```
000001AAAJ. SMITH  5 THE AVE NEWTOWN    LINCS
000002AAZA. JONES  9 NEW ST  OLDHAM     YORKS
000010ZZAD. HOWE   1 OLD RD  MIDBERG    LANCS
999998ZZZE. BROWN  2 DOVE ST TOPTON     NOTTS
```

TRANS

```
                                                  Prediction:
IO00001BBBF. NEWMAN 7 THE AVE OLDTOWN    WARWICKS  error - exists
A000002B                                           ) OK
A000002 XX                                         )multiple
A000002    NEWNAME    NEW ADDR  NEW ADDR  NEW ADDR ) amend
D000010                                            delete 10
IO00500YYYA NEWCUST NEWCUSTAD NEWCUSTAD2NEWCUSTAD3 insert 500
A000600UUUA RONGUN  RONG ADD  RONGADD   RONGADD    error-no master
D000700WWWA NERROR  ERRORADD  ERRORADD2 ERRORADD3  error-no master
I999999CCCC BLACK   4 BLUE RD NIGHTON   LEICS      insert at end
```

Trans file end after old master

ERROR

```
             CUSTOMER FILE UPDATE - ERROR REPORT     PAGE  1

CUST # CRDT  AREA ADDRESS      CODE

000001   B    BB  F. NEWMAN     I  INSERTION - RECORD ALREADY ON MASTER
                  7 THE AVE
                  OLDTOWN
                  WARWICKS

000600   U    UU  A RONGUN      A  NO MASTER RECORD FOR THIS CUSTOMER
                  RONG ADD
                  RONGADD
                  RONGADD

000700   W    WW  A NERROR      D  NO MASTER RECORD FOR THIS CUSTOMER
                  ERRORADD
                  EERRORADD
                  ERRORADD2
                  ERRORADD3
```

(next page)

END OF REPORT

CUSTMAST (2nd generation)

```
000001AAAJ. SMITH   5 THE AVE NEWTOWN    LINCS     correct
000002BXXNEWNAME    NEW ADDR  NEW ADDR   NEW ADDR  amended
000500OYYYA NEWCUST NEWCUSTAD NEWCUSTAD2NEWCUSTAD3 inserted
999998ZZZE. BROWN   2 DOVE ST TOPTON     NOTTS     correct
999999CCCC BLACK    4 BLUE RD NIGHTON    LEICS     inserted
```
(Record for customer 10 correctly deleted).

Test 2

CUSTMAST (2nd generation)

TRANS

```
IOOOOOOIIIAN INSERT INSERT1    INSERT2    INSERT3    insert at front
I999997MMMNEXT INSERINSERT2#1  INSERT2#2  INSERT2#3  insert before end
```

(trans file ends before old master)

CUSTMAST (3rd generation)

```
OOOOOOIIIAN INSERT  INSERT1   INSERT2    INSERT3     inserted
000001AAAJ. SMITH   5 THE AVE NEWTOWN    LINCS       correct
000002BXXNEWNAME    NEW ADDR  NEW ADDR   NEW ADDR    correct
000500OYYYA NEWCUST NEWCUSTAD NEWCUSTAD2NECUSTAD3    correct
999997MMMNEXT INSERINSERT2#1  INSERT2#2  INSERT2#3   inserted
999998ZZZE. BROWN   2 DOVE ST TOPTON     NOTTS       correct
999999CCCC BLACK    4 BLUE RD NIGHTON    LEICS       correct
```

Appendix B
A selection of practical exercises

1 THE POPULATION EXPLOSION

The population of the world in the current year is 4,000 million people. The earth is a sphere of radius 3,984 miles and two-thirds of its surface is water. The surface area of a sphere is 4 x 3.1416 x the square of the radius.

Write a program which will print out the population of the world and the population density (people/square mile of land) at ten year intervals for the next twenty decades (the first detail line starting with the population ten years from now).

The printout is to appear as follows:

First line –	Positions 1–5	Assumed growth rate % p.a. (Z9.99%)
Subsequent lines –	Positions 1–4	The year (9999)
	8–17	The population (99,999,999) in millions
	23–29	The density/square mile (999,999).

The lines are to be double spaced and the results are to be zero suppressed.

The rate of growth per cent is stored on a record in columns 1–4, with an assumed decimal point between the second and third digit. There may be several records in the growth rate file, in which case the results for each growth rate are to be printed on a fresh page (one page for each record read in).

If a size error occurs in the calculations for any record, print SIZE ERROR in positions 1 to 10 and, without printing any further lines on that page, continue to the next record.

2 STUDENT ATTENDANCE

A student file has been maintained in the following format:

Identification: STUDENTS
Data records (blocked in tens)

1–6	Student number
7–25	Student name
	7–21 Surname
	22–25 Initials
26–30	Course code
31–33	Possible hours to date
34–36	Actual hours to date
37–39	Possible coursework mark

40–42   Actual coursework mark

A report is to be produced naming those students who have missed 25% or more class hours, and are thus in danger of failing to qualify to sit the final examination. Students not in danger should not appear on the report.
The report should be printed as follows:

1–6   Student number
10–29   Student name
35–39   Course code
45–47   Possible hours to date
53–55   Actual hours to date
61–62   % attendance (two digits, fractions truncated, followed by percent sign)

The report is to be headed up LOW ATTENDANCE LIST. If there are no low attenders, the message NO LOW ATTENDERS is to follow immediately after the heading line.
The report is to be concluded with a count of the total number of students on the file (each student appears in only one record).

3   POPULATION EXPLOSION PART 2

Amend the report produced in exercise 1 as follows.

(a) A heading POPULATION ESTIMATES: ASSUMED GROWTH RATE = Z9.99% is to be printed at the top of each page, followed by a heading YEAR POPULATION DENS./SQ.M. printed TWICE across the page, i.e. starting in position 1 and again in position 60.

(b) The results are to be listed in the two halves of the page so produced, the first ten decades in positions 1–29 as before, the next ten decades in positions 60–88. The message SIZE ERROR is to appear starting in positions 1 or 60 as appropriate. (Store the results in a table before printing them out.)

4   POEM

A series of English words are held on a magnetic tape labelled POEM. The series of words are divided into variable length lines, of not more than 80 characters each, by the single character "/". Each record on the tape is 800 characters long. The last line of a record continues onto the next record, i.e. lines are broken over record boundaries.
Write a program to read the tape and print the words such that each new line begins in print position 30. The character "*" in the input signifies the end of a line **and** there are no further lines in the record; the next record is to be read in. Any characters beyond the "*" are to be ignored.
The delimiting characters "/" and "*" must not be printed. Empty lines must be printed as blank lines.
At the end of the printout, you must print (with suitable legends) the number of vowels in the file and the number of consonants in the file (special characters, spaces and digits are not to be counted).

5   PURCHASING HABITS

(a) Write a program to create a master file of customers' purchasing habits. Each record has format:

1–40	Name and address
42–45	Four–digit account number
50–55	Number of orders placed over £1,000
60–65	Number of orders placed £1,000 or less
70–80	Average value of orders placed to date.

The records are in account–number order.

(b) Records are available to update the above file. These records have the format:

1–4	Account number
10–20	Value of order placed this week.

Assume the records are in order of account number and that the two fields are numeric.

Perform the update by copying forward, creating a new master, and list on the line printer any transactions for non–existent customers. The value fields have two places of decimals. Not all master records are necessarily updated each week. Design your own report layout.

6   MAGIC SQUARE

A magic square is a two dimension table with the property that the sum of the numbers in each row, each column and each diagonal are all equal.

Write a program, using PERFORM..VARYING, which will establish whether or not a given 4 x 4 table of two–digit numbers is a magic square. Print out the square with a suitable message. Input the squares to be tested from records with a layout of your choice. (Enthusiasts can write the program for tables of any size up to 20 x 20, the table dimension being contained in the record along with the table data.)

7   STUDENT ATTENDANCE PART 2

Amend exercise 2 so that the lines of the report are produced in ascending order of student number within actual hours to date within course code.

8   PURCHASING HABITS PART 2

Amend exercise 5 so that the master file is a relative or indexed file on disk. Update the records in place.

Appendix C
ANS COBOL reserved words

ACCEPT	COMMUNICATION	DUPLICATES	IN
ACCESS	COMP	DYNAMIC	INDEX
ADD	COMPUTATIONAL	EGI	INDEXED
ADDRESS	COMPUTE	ELSE	INDICATE
ADVANCING	CONFIGURATION	EMI	INITIAL
AFTER	CONTAINS	ENABLE	INITIATE
ALL	CONTROL	END	INPUT
ALPHABETIC	CONTROLS	END-OF-PAGE	INPUT-OUTPUT
ALSO	COPY	ENTER	INSPECT
ALTER	CORR	ENVIRONMENT	INSTALLATION
ALTERNATE	CORRESPONDING	EOP	INTO
AND	COUNT	EQUAL	INVALID
ARE	CURRENCY	ERROR	IS
AREA	DATA	ESI	JUST
AREAS	DATE	EVERY	JUSTIFIED
ASCENDING	DATE-COMPILED	EXCEPTION	KEY
ASSIGN	DATE-WRITTEN	EXIT	LABEL
AT	DAY	EXTEND	LAST
AUTHOR	DE	FD	LEADING
BEFORE	DEBUG-CONTENTS	FILE	LEFT
BLANK	DEBUG-ITEM	FILE-CONTROL	LENGTH
BLOCK	DEBUG-LINE	FILLER	LESS
BOTTOM	DEBUG-NAME	FINAL	LIMIT
BY	DEBUG-SUB-1	FIRST	LIMITS
CALL	DEBUG-SUB-2	FOOTING	LINAGE
CANCEL	DEBUG-SUB-3	FOR	LINAGE-COUNTER
CD	DECIMAL-POINT	FROM	LINES
CF	DECLARATIVES	GENERATE	LINKAGE
CH	DELETE	GIVING	LOCK
CHARACTER	DELIMITED	GO	LOW-VALUES
CHARACTERS	DELIMITER	GREATER	MEMORY
CLOCK-UNITS	DEPENDING	GROUP	MERGE
CLOSE	DESCENDING	HEADING	MESSAGE
COBOL	DESTINATION	HIGH-VALUE	MODE
CODE	DETAIL	HIGH-VALUES	MODULES
CODE-SET	DISABLE	I-O	MOVE
COLLATING	DIVIDE	I-O-CONTROL	MULTIPLE
COLUMN	DIVISION	IDENTIFICATION	MULTIPLY
COMMA	DOWN	IF	NATIVE

NEGATIVE	REPORTING	TERMINAL
NEXT	REPORTS	TERMINATE
NO	RERUN	TEXT
NOT	RESERVE	THAN
NUMBER	RESET	THROUGH
NUMERIC	RETURN	THRU
OBJECT-COMPUTER	REVERSED	TIME
OCCURS	REWIND	TIMES
OF	REWRITE	TO
OFF	RF	TOP
OMITTED	RH	TRAILING
ON	RIGHT	TYPE
OPEN	ROUNDED	UNIT
OPTIONAL	RUN	UNSTRING
OR	SAME	UNTIL
ORGANIZATION	SD	UP
OUTPUT	SEARCH	UPON
OVERFLOW	SECTION	USAGE
PAGE	SECURITY	USE
PAGE-COUNTER	SEGMENT-LIMIT	USING
PERFORM	SELECT	VALUE
PF	SEND	VALUES
PH	SENTENCE	VARYING
PIC	SEPARATE	WHEN
PICTURE	SEQUENCE	WITH
PLUS	SEQUENTIAL	WORDS
POINTER	SET	WORKING-STORAGE
POSITION	SIGN	WRITE
POSITIVE	SIZE	ZERO
PRINTING	SORT	ZEROES
PROCEDURE	SORT-MERGE	ZEROS
PROCEDURES	SOURCE	
PROCEED	SOURCE-COMPUTER	
PROGRAM	SPACE	
PROGRAM-ID	SPACES	
QUEUE	SPECIAL-NAMES	
QUOTE	STANDARD	
QUOTES	STANDARD-1	
RANDOM	START	
RD	STATUS	
READ	STOP	
RECEIVE	STRING	
RECORD	SUB-QUEUE-1	
RECORDS	SUB-QUEUE-2	
REDEFINES	SUB-QUEUE-3	
REEL	SUBTRACT	
REFERENCES	SUM	
RELATIVE	SUPPRESS	
RELEASE	SYMBOLIC	
REMAINDER	SYNC	
REMOVAL	SYNCHRONIZED	
RENAMES	TABLE	
REPLACING	TALLYING	
REPORT	TAPE	

Appendix D
ANS COBOL language formats

These formats represent the full 1974 American National Standard for COBOL, excluding the Communications facilities and those facilities which CODASYL now proposes should be dropped from the language. In each case where THRU appears, THROUGH is a legal alternative.

The term 'identifier' means a data-name, or a qualified and/or subscripted data-name.

COMPILER DIRECTIVES

COPY text-name$\left[\left\{\begin{array}{c}\underline{OF}\\\underline{IN}\end{array}\right\}\text{library-name}\right]$

$\left[\underline{REPLACING}\left\{\begin{array}{l}\text{<<pseudo-text-1>>}\\\text{identifier-1}\\\text{literal-1}\\\text{word-1}\end{array}\right\}\underline{BY}\left\{\begin{array}{l}\text{<<pseudo-text-2>>}\\\text{identifier-2}\\\text{literal-2}\\\text{word-2}\end{array}\right\}\right]..$

*

/

IDENTIFICATION DIVISION ENTRIES

IDENTIFICATION DIVISION.

PROGRAM-ID. program-name.

ENVIRONMENT DIVISION ENTRIES

ENVIRONMENT DIVISION.

CONFIGURATION SECTION.

SOURCE-COMPUTER. computer-name $\left[\text{WITH }\underline{DEBUGGING}\ \underline{MODE}\right]$.

OBJECT-COMPUTER. computer-name

$\left[\underline{MEMORY}\text{ SIZE integer}\left\{\begin{array}{l}\underline{WORDS}\\\underline{CHARACTERS}\\\underline{MODULES}\end{array}\right\}\right]$

[PROGRAM COLLATING SEQUENCE is alphabet-name]

[SEGMENT-LIMIT IS segment-number] .

SPECIAL-NAMES.

[implementor-name
$\begin{Bmatrix} \text{IS mnemonic-name-1} & [\text{ON STATUS IS cond-name-1} \\ \text{IS mnemonic-name-2} & [\text{OFF STATUS IS cond-name-2} \\ \text{ON STATUS IS condition-name-5} \\ \text{OFF STATUS IS condition-name-7} \end{Bmatrix}$

$\begin{Bmatrix} [\text{OFF STATUS IS condition-name-2}]] \\ [\text{ON STATUS IS condition-name-4}]] \\ [\text{OFF STATUS IS condition-name-6}] \\ [\text{ON STATUS IS condition-name-8}] \end{Bmatrix}$] ...

[alphabet-name IS
$\begin{Bmatrix} \underline{\text{STANDARD-1}} \\ \underline{\text{NATIVE}} \\ \text{implementor-name} \\ \text{literal-1} \begin{bmatrix} \underline{\text{THRU}} \text{ literal-2} \\ \underline{\text{ALSO}} \text{ literal-2} [\underline{\text{ALSO}} \text{ literal-4}]... \end{bmatrix} \\ [\text{literal-5} \begin{bmatrix} \underline{\text{THRU}} \text{ literal-6} \\ \underline{\text{ALSO}} \text{ literal-7} [\underline{\text{ALSO}} \text{ literal-8}]... \end{bmatrix}] \end{Bmatrix}$

CURRENCY SIGN IS literal-9   DECIMAL-POINT IS COMMA   .

[INPUT-OUTPUT SECTION.

[FILE-CONTROL.

(Format 1: Sequential organisation)

{SELECT [OPTIONAL] file-name ASSIGN TO implementor-name-1

[implementor-name-2] ...

[RESERVE integer $\begin{bmatrix} \text{AREA} \\ \text{AREAS} \end{bmatrix}$ ORGANIZATION IS SEQUENTIAL

[ACCESS MODE IS SEQUENTIAL] [FILE STATUS IS data-name]}...

(Format 2: Relative organisation)

{SELECT file-name ASSIGN TO implementor-name-1 [implementor-name-2]

[RESERVE integer $\begin{bmatrix} \text{AREA} \\ \text{AREAS} \end{bmatrix}$ ORGANIZATION IS RELATIVE

[ACCESS MODE IS $\begin{Bmatrix} \text{SEQUENTIAL} [\text{RELATIVE KEY IS data-name-1}] \\ \begin{Bmatrix} \text{RANDOM} \\ \text{DYNAMIC} \end{Bmatrix} \text{RELATIVE KEY IS data-name-1} \end{Bmatrix}$]

[FILE STATUS IS data-name-2]}...

(Format 3: Indexed organisation)

$\Big\{$ SELECT file-name <u>ASSIGN</u> TO implementor-name-1 [implementor-name-2]...

    [RESERVE integer $\begin{Bmatrix} AREA \\ AREAS \end{Bmatrix}$ <u>ORGANIZATION</u> IS <u>INDEXED</u>

    [<u>ACCESS</u> MODE IS $\begin{Bmatrix} \underline{SEQUENTIAL} \\ \underline{RANDOM} \\ \underline{DYNAMIC} \end{Bmatrix}$] <u>RECORD</u> KEY IS data-name-1

    [<u>ALTERNATE</u> <u>RECORD</u> KEY IS data-name-2 [WITH <u>DUPLICATES</u>]]...

    [FILE <u>STATUS</u> IS data-name-3]$\Big\}$...]

[<u>I-O-CONTROL</u>.

    [<u>RERUN</u> [<u>ON</u> $\begin{Bmatrix} \text{file-name-1} \\ \text{implementor-name} \end{Bmatrix}$]

        <u>EVERY</u> $\left\{ \begin{matrix} \begin{Bmatrix} \underline{END} \text{ OF} \begin{Bmatrix} \underline{UNIT} \\ \underline{REEL} \end{Bmatrix} \\ \text{integer-1 } \underline{RECORDS} \end{Bmatrix} \text{ OF file-name-2} \\ \text{integer-2 } \underline{CLOCK\text{-}UNITS} \\ \text{condition-name} \end{matrix} \right\}$]

    [<u>SAME</u> $\begin{bmatrix} \underline{RECORD} \\ \underline{SORT} \\ \underline{SORT\text{-}MERGE} \end{bmatrix}$ AREA FOR file-name-3 [file-name-4]...]...

    [<u>MULTIPLE</u> <u>FILE</u> TAPE CONTAINS file-name-5 [<u>POSITION</u> integer-3]

        [file-name-6 [<u>POSITION</u> integer-4]]...]...   .]]

DATA DIVISION ENTRIES

[<u>FILE</u> SECTION.

[FD file-name

    [<u>BLOCK</u> CONTAINS [integer-1 <u>TO</u>] integer-2 $\begin{Bmatrix} \underline{RECORDS} \\ \underline{CHARACTERS} \end{Bmatrix}$]

    [<u>RECORD</u> CONTAINS [integer-3 <u>TO</u>] integer-4 CHARACTERS]

    <u>LABEL</u> $\begin{Bmatrix} \underline{RECORDS} \text{ ARE} \\ \underline{RECORD} \text{ IS} \end{Bmatrix}$ $\begin{Bmatrix} \underline{STANDARD} \\ \underline{OMITTED} \end{Bmatrix}$

    [<u>VALUE</u> <u>OF</u> implementor-name-1 IS $\begin{Bmatrix} \text{data-name-1} \\ \text{literal-1} \end{Bmatrix}$ ...]

    [<u>LINAGE</u> IS $\begin{Bmatrix} \text{data-name-5} \\ \text{integer-5} \end{Bmatrix}$ LINES [WITH <u>FOOTING</u> AT $\begin{Bmatrix} \text{data-name-6} \\ \text{literal-6} \end{Bmatrix}$

$$\left[\text{LINES AT } \underline{\text{TOP}} \begin{Bmatrix} \text{data-name-7} \\ \text{integer-7} \end{Bmatrix}\right] \left[\text{LINES AT } \underline{\text{BOTTOM}} \begin{Bmatrix} \text{data-name-8} \\ \text{integer-8} \end{Bmatrix}\right]$$

$$\left[\underline{\text{CODE-SET}} \text{ IS alphabet-name}\right]$$

$$\left[\begin{Bmatrix} \underline{\text{REPORT}} \text{ IS} \\ \underline{\text{REPORTS}} \text{ ARE} \end{Bmatrix} \text{ report-name-1 } \left[\text{report-name-2}\right]\dots\right].$$

$$\left[\text{record-description-entry}\right]\dots\right]\dots$$

$$\left[\underline{\text{WORKING-STORAGE}} \underline{\text{SECTION}}.\right.$$

$$\left[\begin{array}{l} \text{77-level-description-entry} \\ \text{record-description-entry} \end{array}\right]\dots\right]$$

$$\left[\underline{\text{LINKAGE}} \underline{\text{SECTION}}.\right.$$

$$\left[\begin{array}{l} \text{77-level-description-entry} \\ \text{record-description-entry} \end{array}\right]\dots\right]$$

$$\left[\underline{\text{REPORT}} \underline{\text{SECTION}}.\right.$$

$$\left[\underline{\text{RD}} \text{ report-name}\right.$$

$$\left[\underline{\text{CODE}} \text{ literal-1}\right]$$

$$\left[\begin{Bmatrix} \underline{\text{CONTROLS}} \text{ ARE} \\ \underline{\text{CONTROL}} \text{ IS} \end{Bmatrix} \begin{Bmatrix} \text{data-name-1 } \left[\text{data-name-2}\right]\dots \\ \underline{\text{FINAL}} \left[\text{data-name-1 } \left[\text{data-name-2}\right]\dots\right] \end{Bmatrix}\right]$$

$$\left[\underline{\text{PAGE}} \begin{Bmatrix} \underline{\text{LIMIT}} \text{ IS} \\ \underline{\text{LIMITS}} \text{ ARE} \end{Bmatrix} \text{ integer-1 } \begin{Bmatrix} \underline{\text{LINE}} \\ \underline{\text{LINES}} \end{Bmatrix} \underline{\text{HEADING}} \text{ integer-2}\right]$$

$$\left[\underline{\text{FIRST}} \underline{\text{DETAIL}} \text{ integer-3}\right] \left[\underline{\text{LAST}} \underline{\text{DETAIL}} \text{ integer-4}\right]$$

$$\left[\underline{\text{FOOTING}} \text{ integer-5}\right]\right].$$

$$\left\{\text{report-group-description-entry}\right\}\dots\right]\dots\right]$$

DATA DESCRIPTION ENTRIES

(Format 1)

$$\text{level-number} \begin{Bmatrix} \text{data-name-1} \\ \underline{\text{FILLER}} \end{Bmatrix} \left[\underline{\text{REDEFINES}} \text{ data-name-2}\right]$$

$$\left[\begin{Bmatrix} \underline{\text{PICTURE}} \\ \underline{\text{PIC}} \end{Bmatrix} \text{ IS picture-string}\right]$$

$$\left[\underline{\text{USAGE}} \text{ IS} \begin{Bmatrix} \underline{\text{COMPUTATIONAL}} \\ \underline{\text{COMP}} \\ \underline{\text{DISPLAY}} \\ \underline{\text{INDEX}} \end{Bmatrix}\right]$$

$$\left[\left[\underline{SIGN}\ IS\left\{\begin{array}{l}\underline{LEADING}\\\underline{TRAILING}\end{array}\right\}\left[\underline{SEPARATE}\ CHARACTER\right]\right]\right]$$

$$\left[\underline{OCCURS}\left\{\begin{array}{l}integer-1\ \underline{TO}\ integer-2\ TIMES\ \underline{DEPENDING}\ ON\ data-name-3\\integer-2\ \underline{TIMES}\end{array}\right\}\right.$$

$$\left[\left\{\begin{array}{l}\underline{ASENDING}\\\underline{DESCENDING}\end{array}\right\}KEY\ IS\ data-name-4\ \left[data-name-5\right]...\right]...$$

$$\left.\left[\underline{INDEXED}\ BY\ index-name-1\ \left[index-name-2\right]...\right]\right]$$

$$\left[\left\{\begin{array}{l}\underline{SYNCHRONIZED}\\\underline{SYNC}\end{array}\right\}\ \left[\begin{array}{l}\underline{LEFT}\\\underline{RIGHT}\end{array}\right]\right]$$

$$\left[\left\{\begin{array}{l}\underline{JUSTIFIED}\\\underline{JUST}\end{array}\right\}\ \underline{RIGHT}\right]$$

$$\left[\underline{BLANK}\ WHEN\ \underline{ZERO}\right]$$

$$\left[\underline{VALUE}\ IS\ literal\right].$$

(Format 2)

66 data-name-1 <u>RENAMES</u> data-name-2 $\left[\underline{THRU}\ data\text{-}name\text{-}3\right]$

(Format 3)

$$88\ condition\text{-}name\left\{\begin{array}{l}\underline{VALUE}\ IS\\\underline{VALUES}\ ARE\end{array}\right\}\ literal\text{-}1\ \left[\underline{THRU}\ literal\text{-}2\right]$$

$$\left[literal\text{-}3\ \left[\underline{THRU}\ literal\text{-}4\right]\right]...$$

REPORT GROUP DESCRIPTION ENTRIES

(Format 1)

01 $\left[data\text{-}name\text{-}1\right]$

$$\left[\underline{LINE}\ NUMBER\ IS\ \left\{\begin{array}{l}integer\text{-}1\ on\ \underline{NEXT}\ \underline{PAGE}\\\underline{PLUS}\ integer\text{-}2\end{array}\right\}\right]$$

$$\left[\underline{NEXT}\ \underline{GROUP}\ IS\ \left\{\begin{array}{l}integer\text{-}3\\\underline{PLUS}\ integer\text{-}4\\\underline{NEXT}\ \underline{PAGE}\end{array}\right\}\right]$$

$$
\text{TYPE IS} \left\{
\begin{array}{ll}
\underline{\text{REPORT HEADING}} & \\
\underline{\text{RH}} & \\
\underline{\text{PAGE HEADING}} & \\
\underline{\text{PH}} & \\
\underline{\text{CONTROL HEADING}} \ \text{data-name-2} \\
\underline{\text{CH}} \qquad\qquad\quad \underline{\text{FINAL}} \\
\underline{\text{DETAIL}} & \\
\underline{\text{DE}} & \\
\underline{\text{CONTROL FOOTING}} \ \text{data-name-3} \\
\underline{\text{CF}} \qquad\qquad\quad \underline{\text{FINAL}} \\
\underline{\text{PAGE FOOTING}} & \\
\underline{\text{PF}} & \\
\underline{\text{REPORT FOOTING}} & \\
\underline{\text{RF}} & \\
\end{array}
\right\}
$$

[[USAGE IS] DISPLAY].

(Format 2)

level-number [data-name-1]

LINE NUMBER IS $\left\{ \begin{array}{l} \text{integer-1 ON } \underline{\text{NEXT PAGE}} \\ \underline{\text{PLUS}} \text{ integer-2} \end{array} \right\}$

[[USAGE IS] DISPLAY].

(Format 3)

level-number [data-name-1]

[BLANK WHEN ZERO]

[GROUP INDICATE]

[$\left\{ \begin{array}{l} \underline{\text{JUSTIFIED}} \\ \underline{\text{JUST}} \end{array} \right\}$ RIGHT]

[LINE NUMBER IS $\left\{ \begin{array}{l} \text{integer-1 ON } \underline{\text{NEXT PAGE}} \\ \underline{\text{PLUS}} \text{ integer-2} \end{array} \right\}$]

[COLUMN NUMBER IS integer-3]

$\left\{ \begin{array}{l} \underline{\text{PICTURE}} \\ \underline{\text{PIC}} \end{array} \right\}$ IS picture-string

$\left\{
\begin{array}{l}
\underline{\text{SOURCE}} \text{ IS identifier-1} \\
\underline{\text{VALUE}} \text{ IS literal} \\
\underline{\text{SUM}} \text{ identifier-2 [identifier-3]...} \\
\qquad [\underline{\text{UPON}} \text{ data-name-2 [data-name-3]...]} \} ... \\
\qquad [\underline{\text{RESET}} \text{ ON } \left\{ \begin{array}{l} \text{data-name-4} \\ \underline{\text{FINAL}} \end{array} \right\}]
\end{array}
\right\} ...
$

[[USAGE IS] DISPLAY].

PROCEDURE DIVISION ENTRIES

PROCEDURE DIVISION [USING data-name-1 [data-name-2]...]

(Format 1 with sections)

{section-name SECTION [segment-number].

[paragraph-name. [sentence]...]...}...

(Format 2 without sections)

{paragraph-name. [sentence]...}...

(Format 3 with declaratives)

DECLARATIVES.

{declarative-section}...

END DECLARATIVES.

{section-name SECTION [segment-number].

[paragraph-name . [sentence]...]...}...

COBOL VERBS

$$\underline{ACCEPT}\ identifier\ \left[\underline{FROM}\ \left\{ \begin{array}{l} mnemonic\text{-}name \\ \underline{DATE} \\ \underline{DAY} \\ \underline{TIME} \end{array} \right\} \right]$$

$$\underline{ADD}\ \left\{ \begin{array}{l} identifier\text{-}1 \\ literal\text{-}1 \end{array} \right\}\ \left[\begin{array}{l} identifier\text{-}2 \\ literal\text{-}2 \end{array} \right]\ \underline{TO}\ identifier\text{-}m\ \left[\underline{ROUNDED}\right]$$

[identifier-n [ROUNDED]]... [ON SIZE ERROR imperative-statement]

$$\underline{ADD}\ \left\{ \begin{array}{l} identifier\text{-}1 \\ literal\text{-}1 \end{array} \right\}\ \left\{ \begin{array}{l} identifier\text{-}2 \\ literal\text{-}2 \end{array} \right\}\ \left[\begin{array}{l} identifier\text{-}3 \\ literal\text{-}3 \end{array} \right]\ ...\ \underline{GIVING}$$

identifier-m [ROUNDED] [ON SIZE ERROR imperative-statement]

$$\underline{CALL}\ \left\{ \begin{array}{l} identifier\text{-}1 \\ literal\text{-}1 \end{array} \right\}\ \left[\underline{USING}\ data\text{-}name\text{-}1\ [data\text{-}name\text{-}2]...\right]$$

[ON OVERFLOW imperative-statement]

$$\underline{CANCEL}\ \left\{ \begin{array}{l} identifier\text{-}1 \\ literal\text{-}1 \end{array} \right\}\ \left[\begin{array}{l} identifier\text{-}2 \\ literal\text{-}2 \end{array} \right]\ ...$$

CLOSE file-name-1 $\begin{bmatrix} \begin{Bmatrix} \underline{REEL} \\ \underline{UNIT} \end{Bmatrix} \begin{bmatrix} \text{WITH NO} \underline{REWIND} \\ \text{FOR} \underline{REMOVAL} \end{bmatrix} \\ \text{WITH} \begin{Bmatrix} \underline{NO} \text{ REWIND} \\ \underline{LOCK} \end{Bmatrix} \end{bmatrix}$

$\begin{bmatrix} \text{file-name-2} \begin{bmatrix} \begin{Bmatrix} \underline{REEL} \\ \underline{UNIT} \end{Bmatrix} \begin{bmatrix} \text{WITH NO} \underline{REWIND} \\ \text{FOR} \underline{REMOVAL} \end{bmatrix} \\ \text{WITH} \begin{Bmatrix} \underline{NO} \text{ REWIND} \\ \underline{LOCK} \end{Bmatrix} \end{bmatrix} \end{bmatrix}$...

COMPUTE identifier-1 [ROUNDED] [identifier-2 [ROUNDED]]...

= $\begin{Bmatrix} \text{identifier-2} \\ \text{literal} \\ \text{arithmetic-expression} \end{Bmatrix}$ [ON SIZE ERROR imperative-statement]

DELETE file-name RECORD [INVALID KEY imperative-statement]

DISPLAY $\begin{Bmatrix} \text{identifier-1} \\ \text{literal-1} \end{Bmatrix}$ [identifier-2 literal-2] ... [UPON mnemonic-name]

DIVIDE $\begin{Bmatrix} \text{identifier-1} \\ \text{literal-1} \end{Bmatrix}$ INTO identifier-2 [ROUNDED]

[identifier-3 [ROUNDED]]... [ON SIZE ERROR imperative-statement]

DIVIDE $\begin{Bmatrix} \text{identifier-1} \\ \text{literal-1} \end{Bmatrix} \begin{Bmatrix} \underline{BY} \\ \underline{INTO} \end{Bmatrix} \begin{Bmatrix} \text{identifier-2} \\ \text{literal-2} \end{Bmatrix}$ GIVING identifier-3

[ROUNDED] [identifier-4 [ROUNDED]]...

[ON SIZE ERROR imperative-statement]

DIVIDE $\begin{Bmatrix} \text{identifier-1} \\ \text{literal-1} \end{Bmatrix} \begin{Bmatrix} \underline{BY} \\ \underline{INTO} \end{Bmatrix} \begin{Bmatrix} \text{identifier-2} \\ \text{literal-2} \end{Bmatrix}$ GIVING identifier-3

[ROUNDED] REMAINDER identifier-4

[ON SIZE ERROR imperative-statement]

EXIT [PROGRAM].

GENERATE $\begin{Bmatrix} \text{data-name} \\ \text{report-name} \end{Bmatrix}$

GO TO procedure-name

GO TO procedure-name-1 [procedure-name-2]... DEPENDING ON identifier

IF condition $\begin{Bmatrix} \text{statement-1} \\ \underline{NEXT} \text{ } \underline{SENTENCE} \end{Bmatrix}$ $\begin{bmatrix} \underline{ELSE} \text{ statement-2} \\ \underline{ELSE} \text{ } \underline{NEXT} \text{ } \underline{SENTENCE} \end{bmatrix}$

INSPECT identifier-1 TALLYING

$$\left\{ \text{identifier-2 } \underline{\text{FOR}} \left\{ \begin{matrix} \underline{\text{ALL}} \\ \underline{\text{LEADING}} \\ \underline{\text{CHARACTERS}} \end{matrix} \right\} \left\{ \begin{matrix} \text{identifier-3} \\ \text{literal-1} \end{matrix} \right\} \right.$$

$$\left. \left\{ \left\{ \begin{matrix} \underline{\text{BEFORE}} \\ \underline{\text{AFTER}} \end{matrix} \right\} \underline{\text{INITIAL}} \left\{ \begin{matrix} \text{identifier-4} \\ \text{literal-2} \end{matrix} \right\} \right\} \cdots \right\} \cdots$$

INSPECT identifier-1 REPLACING

$$\left\{ \begin{matrix} \underline{\text{CHARACTERS}} \underline{\text{BY}} \left\{ \begin{matrix} \text{identifier-6} \\ \text{literal-4} \end{matrix} \right\} \left[\left\{ \begin{matrix} \underline{\text{BEFORE}} \\ \underline{\text{AFTER}} \end{matrix} \right\} \underline{\text{INITIAL}} \left\{ \begin{matrix} \text{identifier-7} \\ \text{literal-5} \end{matrix} \right\} \right] \\ \left\{ \left\{ \begin{matrix} \underline{\text{ALL}} \\ \underline{\text{LEADING}} \\ \underline{\text{FIRST}} \end{matrix} \right\} \left\{ \begin{matrix} \text{identifier-5} \\ \text{literal-3} \end{matrix} \right\} \underline{\text{BY}} \left\{ \begin{matrix} \text{identifier-6} \\ \text{literal-5} \end{matrix} \right\} \right. \\ \left[\left\{ \begin{matrix} \underline{\text{BEFORE}} \\ \underline{\text{AFTER}} \end{matrix} \right\} \underline{\text{INITIAL}} \left\{ \begin{matrix} \text{identifier-7} \\ \text{literal-5} \end{matrix} \right\} \right] \right\} \cdots \end{matrix} \right\} \cdots$$

INSPECT identifier-1 TALLYING as above REPLACING as above

$$\underline{\text{MERGE}} \text{ file-name-1 ON} \left\{ \begin{matrix} \underline{\text{ASCENDING}} \\ \underline{\text{DESCENDING}} \end{matrix} \right\} \text{KEY data-name-1 } [\text{data-name-2}]\cdots$$

$$\left[\text{ON} \left\{ \begin{matrix} \underline{\text{ASCENDING}} \\ \underline{\text{DESCENDING}} \end{matrix} \right\} \text{KEY data-name-3 } [\text{data-name-4}]\cdots \right] \cdots$$

$$[\underline{\text{COLLATING}} \underline{\text{SEQUENCE}} \text{ IS alphabet-name}]$$

$$\underline{\text{USING}} \text{ file-name-1 file-name-2 } [\text{file-name-3}] \cdots$$

$$\left\{ \begin{matrix} \underline{\text{OUTPUT}} \text{ PROCEDURE IS section-name-1 } [\underline{\text{THRU}} \text{ section-name-2}] \\ \underline{\text{GIVING}} \text{ file-name-5} \end{matrix} \right.$$

$$\underline{\text{MOVE}} \left\{ \begin{matrix} \text{identifier-1} \\ \text{literal-1} \end{matrix} \right\} \underline{\text{TO}} \text{ identifier-2 } [\text{identifier-3}] \cdots$$

$$\underline{\text{MULTIPLY}} \left\{ \begin{matrix} \text{identifier-1} \\ \text{literal-1} \end{matrix} \right\} \underline{\text{BY}} \text{ identifier-2 } [\underline{\text{ROUNDED}}] [\text{identifier-3 } [\underline{\text{ROUNDED}}]] \cdots$$

$$[\text{ON} \underline{\text{SIZE}} \underline{\text{ERROR}} \text{ imperative-statement}]$$

$$\underline{\text{MULTIPLY}} \left\{ \begin{matrix} \text{identifier-1} \\ \text{literal-1} \end{matrix} \right\} \underline{\text{BY}} \left\{ \begin{matrix} \text{identifier-2} \\ \text{literal-2} \end{matrix} \right\} \underline{\text{GIVING}} \text{ identifier-3}$$

$$[\underline{\text{ROUNDED}}] [\text{identifier-4 } [\underline{\text{ROUNDED}}]] \cdots$$

$$[\text{ON} \underline{\text{SIZE}} \underline{\text{ERROR}} \text{ imperative-statement}]$$

$$\underline{\text{OPEN}} \left\{ \begin{matrix} \underline{\text{INPUT}} \text{ file-name-1} [\text{WITH NO REWIND}] \text{file-name-2} [\text{WITH NO REWIND}]] \cdots \\ \underline{\text{OUTPUT}} \text{ file-name-3} [\text{WITH NO REWIND}] \text{file-name-3} [\text{WITH NO REWIND}]] \cdots \\ \underline{\text{I-O}} \text{ file-name-5 file-name-6} \cdots \\ \underline{\text{EXTEND}} \text{ file-name-7 file-name-8} \cdots \end{matrix} \right\}$$

$$\underline{OPEN} \left\{ \begin{array}{l} \underline{INPUT}\ \text{file-name-1}\ [\text{file-name-2}]\ldots \\ \underline{OUTPUT}\ \text{file-name-3}\ [\text{file-name-4}]\ldots \\ \underline{I\text{-}O}\ \text{file-name-5}\ [\text{file-name-6}]\ldots \end{array} \right\}\ldots$$

$$\underline{PERFORM}\ \text{procedure-name-1}\ [\underline{THRU}\ \text{procedure-name-1}] \left[\begin{array}{l} \left\{ \begin{array}{l} \text{identifier-1} \\ \text{integer} \end{array} \right\} \underline{TIMES} \\ \underline{UNTIL}\ \text{condition} \end{array} \right.$$

$$\underline{PERFORM}\ \text{procedure-name-1}\ [\underline{THRU}\ \text{procedure-name-2}]$$

$$\underline{VARYING} \left\{ \begin{array}{l} \text{index-name-1} \\ \text{identifier-1} \end{array} \right\} \underline{FROM} \left\{ \begin{array}{l} \text{index-name-2} \\ \text{literal-1} \\ \text{identifier-2} \end{array} \right\} \underline{BY} \left\{ \begin{array}{l} \text{literal-2} \\ \text{identifier-3} \end{array} \right\}$$

$$\underline{UNTIL}\ \text{condition-1}$$

$$\left[\underline{AFTER} \left\{ \begin{array}{l} \text{index-name-3} \\ \text{identifier-4} \end{array} \right\} \underline{FROM} \left\{ \begin{array}{l} \text{index-name-4} \\ \text{literal-3} \\ \text{identifier-5} \end{array} \right\} \underline{BY} \left\{ \begin{array}{l} \text{literal-4} \\ \text{identifier-6} \end{array} \right\} \right.$$

$$\left[\underline{UNTIL}\ \text{condition-2} \right.$$

$$\left[\underline{AFTER} \left\{ \begin{array}{l} \text{index-name-5} \\ \text{identifier-7} \end{array} \right\} \underline{FROM} \left\{ \begin{array}{l} \text{index-name-6} \\ \text{literal-5} \\ \text{identifier-8} \end{array} \right\} \underline{BY} \left\{ \begin{array}{l} \text{literal-6} \\ \text{identifier-9} \end{array} \right\} \right.$$

$$\left[\underline{UNTIL}\ \text{condition-3} \right]\,]$$

$$\underline{READ}\ \text{file-name}\ [\underline{NEXT}]\ \text{RECORD}\ [\underline{INTO}\ \text{identifier}]$$

$$[\underline{AT}\ \underline{END}\ \text{imperative-statement}]$$

$$\underline{READ}\ \text{file-name}\ \text{RECORD}\ [\underline{INTO}\ \text{identifier}]\ [\underline{KEY}\ \text{IS}\ \text{data-name}]$$

$$[\underline{INVALID}\ \text{KEY}\ \text{imperative-statement}]$$

$$\underline{RELEASE}\ \text{record-name}\ [\underline{FROM}\ \text{identifier}]$$

$$\underline{RETURN}\ \text{file-name}\ \text{RECORD}\ [\underline{INTO}\ \text{identifier}]$$

$$\underline{AT}\ \underline{END}\ \text{imperative-statement}$$

$$\underline{REWRITE}\ \text{record-name}\ [\underline{FROM}\ \text{identifier}]$$

$$[\underline{INVALID}\ \text{KEY}\ \text{imperative-statement}]$$

$$\underline{SEARCH}\ \text{identifier-1}\ \left[\underline{VARYING} \left\{ \begin{array}{l} \text{index-name} \\ \text{identifier-2} \end{array} \right\} \right]$$

$$[\underline{AT}\ \underline{END}\ \text{imperative-statement}]$$

$$\underline{WHEN}\ \text{condition-1} \left\{ \begin{array}{l} \text{imperative-statement-2} \\ \underline{NEXT}\ \underline{SENTENCE} \end{array} \right\}$$

$$\left[\text{WHEN condition-2} \begin{Bmatrix} \text{imperative-statement-3} \\ \underline{\text{NEXT}} \text{ SENTENCE} \end{Bmatrix} \right] \ldots$$

<u>SEARCH</u> <u>ALL</u> identifier-1

$\quad$ [<u>AT</u> <u>END</u> imperative-statement]

$\quad\quad$ <u>WHEN</u> special-condition-1 [<u>AND</u> special-condition-2] ...

$$\begin{Bmatrix} \text{imperative-statement-2} \\ \underline{\text{NEXT}} \text{ SENTENCE} \end{Bmatrix}$$

(special-condition)

$$\begin{Bmatrix} \text{data-name-1} \begin{Bmatrix} \text{IS} \underline{\text{EQUAL}} \text{ TO} \\ \text{IS} = \end{Bmatrix} \begin{Bmatrix} \text{identifier-3} \\ \text{literal-1} \\ \text{arithmetic-expression} \end{Bmatrix} \\ \text{condition-name-1} \end{Bmatrix}$$

$$\underline{\text{SET}} \begin{Bmatrix} \text{index-name-1} \\ \text{identifier-1} \end{Bmatrix} \begin{Bmatrix} \text{index-name-2} \text{]} \ldots \\ \text{identifier-2} \text{]} \ldots \end{Bmatrix} \underline{\text{TO}} \begin{Bmatrix} \text{index-name-3} \\ \text{literal-1} \\ \text{integer} \end{Bmatrix}$$

$$\underline{\text{SET}} \text{ index-name-1 [index-name-2]} \ldots \begin{Bmatrix} \underline{\text{UP}} \text{ BY} \\ \underline{\text{DOWN}} \text{ BY} \end{Bmatrix} \begin{Bmatrix} \text{identifier} \\ \text{integer} \end{Bmatrix}$$

$$\underline{\text{SORT}} \text{ file-name-1 ON} \begin{Bmatrix} \underline{\text{ASCENDING}} \\ \underline{\text{DESCENDING}} \end{Bmatrix} \text{KEY} \{\text{identifier-1}\} \ldots$$

$$\quad \left[\text{ON} \begin{Bmatrix} \underline{\text{DESCENDING}} \\ \underline{\text{ASCENDING}} \end{Bmatrix} \text{KEY} \{\text{identifier-2}\} \ldots \right] \ldots$$

$\quad$ [<u>COLLATING</u> <u>SEQUENCE</u> IS alphabet-name]

$$\quad \begin{Bmatrix} \underline{\text{INPUT}} \underline{\text{PROCEDURE}} \text{ IS section-name } [\underline{\text{THRU}} \text{ section-name-2}] \\ \underline{\text{USING}} \text{ file-name-2 file-name-3} \ldots \end{Bmatrix}$$

$$\quad \begin{Bmatrix} \underline{\text{OUTPUT}} \underline{\text{PROCEDURE}} \text{ IS section-name-3 } [\underline{\text{THRU}} \text{ section-name-4}] \\ \underline{\text{GIVING}} \text{ file-name-3} \end{Bmatrix}$$

$$\underline{\text{START}} \text{ file-name } \left[\underline{\text{KEY}} \text{ IS} \begin{Bmatrix} \underline{\text{EQUAL}} \text{ TO} \\ = \\ \underline{\text{GREATER}} \text{ THAN} \\ > \\ \underline{\text{NOT}} \underline{\text{LESS}} \text{ THAN} \\ \underline{\text{NOT}} < \end{Bmatrix} \text{data-name} \right]$$

$\quad$ [<u>INVALID</u> KEY imperative-statement]

$$\underline{\text{STOP}} \begin{Bmatrix} \text{literal} \\ \underline{\text{RUN}} \end{Bmatrix}$$

STRING $\begin{Bmatrix} \text{identifier-1} \\ \text{literal-1} \end{Bmatrix}$ $\begin{bmatrix} \text{identifier-2} \\ \text{literal-2} \end{bmatrix}$ ... DELIMITED BY $\begin{Bmatrix} \text{identifier-3} \\ \text{literal-3} \\ \underline{\text{SIZE}} \end{Bmatrix}$

$\begin{bmatrix} \begin{Bmatrix} \text{identifier-4} \\ \text{literal-4} \end{Bmatrix} \begin{bmatrix} \text{identifier-5} \\ \text{literal-5} \end{bmatrix} ... \underline{\text{DELIMITED}} \text{ BY} \begin{Bmatrix} \text{identifier-6} \\ \text{literal-6} \\ \underline{\text{SIZE}} \end{Bmatrix} \end{bmatrix}$ ...

INTO identifier-7 [WITH POINTER identifier-8]

[ON OVERFLOW imperative-statement]

SUBTRACT $\begin{Bmatrix} \text{literal-1} \\ \text{identifier-1} \end{Bmatrix}$ $\begin{bmatrix} \text{literal-2} \\ \text{identifier-2} \end{bmatrix}$ ... FROM identifier-m [ROUNDED]

[identifier-n [ROUNDED]]... [ON SIZE ERROR imperative-statement]

SUBTRACT $\begin{Bmatrix} \text{literal-1} \\ \text{identifier-1} \end{Bmatrix}$ $\begin{bmatrix} \text{literal-2} \\ \text{identifier-2} \end{bmatrix}$ ... FROM $\begin{Bmatrix} \text{literal-m} \\ \text{identifier-m} \end{Bmatrix}$

GIVING identifier-n [ROUNDED]...[identifier-o [ROUNDED]]...

[ON SIZE ERROR imperative-statement]

SUPPRESS PRINTING

UNSTRING identifier-1 [DELIMITED BY [ALL] $\begin{Bmatrix} \text{identifier-2} \\ \text{literal-1} \end{Bmatrix}$

[OR [ALL] $\begin{Bmatrix} \text{identifier-3} \\ \text{literal-2} \end{Bmatrix}$]...]

INTO identifier-4 [DELIMITER IN identifier-5] [COUNT IN identifier-6]

[identifier-7 [DELIMITER IN identifier-8] [COUNT IN identifier-9]]...

[WITH POINTER identifier-10] [TALLYING IN identifier-11]

[ON OVERFLOW imperative-statement]

USE AFTER STANDARD $\begin{Bmatrix} \underline{\text{EXCEPTION}} \\ \underline{\text{ERROR}} \end{Bmatrix}$ PROCEDURE ON $\begin{Bmatrix} \text{file-name-1 file-name-2} \\ \underline{\text{INPUT}} \\ \underline{\text{OUTPUT}} \\ \underline{\text{I-O}} \\ \underline{\text{EXTEND}} \end{Bmatrix}$

USE BEFORE REPORTING identifier

WRITE record-name [FROM identifier]

[INVALID KEY imperative-statement]

WRITE record-name $\left[\underline{\text{FROM}}\text{ identifier-1}\right]$

$\left\{\begin{array}{l}\underline{\text{BEFORE}}\\\underline{\text{AFTER}}\end{array}\right\}$ ADVANCING $\left\{\begin{array}{l}\text{identifier LINES}\\\text{integer LINES}\\\text{mnemonic-name}\\\underline{\text{PAGE}}\end{array}\right\}$

$\left[\underline{\text{AT}}\left\{\begin{array}{l}\underline{\text{END-OF-PAGE}}\\\underline{\text{EOP}}\end{array}\right\}\text{ imperative-statement}\right]$

CONDITIONS

$\left\{\begin{array}{l}\text{identifier-1}\\\text{literal-1}\\\text{arithmetic-expression-1}\\\text{index-name-1}\end{array}\right\}$ IS $\left[\underline{\text{NOT}}\right]$ $\left\{\begin{array}{l}\underline{\text{GREATER THAN}}\\\underline{\text{LESS THAN}}\\\underline{\text{EQUAL}}\text{ TO}\\>\\<\\=\end{array}\right\}$ $\left\{\begin{array}{l}\text{identifier-2}\\\text{literal-2}\\\text{arith-expression-2}\\\text{index-name-2}\end{array}\right\}$

identifier IS $\left[\underline{\text{NOT}}\right]\left\{\begin{array}{l}\underline{\text{NUMERIC}}\\\underline{\text{ALPHABETIC}}\end{array}\right\}$

arithmetic-expression IS $\left[\underline{\text{NOT}}\right]$ $\left\{\begin{array}{l}\underline{\text{POSITIVE}}\\\underline{\text{NEGATIVE}}\\\underline{\text{ZERO}}\end{array}\right\}$

Index